What Lacan
Said about Women

CONTEMPORARY THEORY SERIES

Series Editor: Frances Restuccia,
Professor of English, Boston College

Gender in Psychoanalytic Space:
Between Clinic and Culture
Muriel Dimen and Virginia Goldner, eds.

Topologies of Trauma:
Essays on the Limit of Knowledge and Memory
Linda Belau and Petar Ramadanovic, eds.

Re-inventing the Symptom:
Essays on the Final Lacan
Luke Thurston, ed.

Art: Sublimation or Symptom
Parveen Adams, ed.

Lacan and Contemporary Film
Todd McGowan and Sheila Kunkle, eds.

What Lacan Said about Women:
A Psychoanalytic Study
Colette Soler

What Lacan Said about Women

A Psychoanalytic Study

Colette Soler

Translated by
John Holland

OTHER

Other Press
New York

This work originally appeared in French as *Ce que lacan disait des femmes: Etude de psychanalyse*. Copyright © 2003 Editions du Champ Lacanien.

Translation © 2006 John Holland

Production Editor: Mira S. Park

This book was set in 11 pt Goudy by Alpha Graphics of Pittsfield, NH.

10 9 8 7 6 5 4 3 2 1

Library of Congress Cataloging-in-Publication Data

Soler, Colette.
    [Ce que Lacan disait des femmes. English]
    What Lacan said about women : a psychoanalytic study / by Colette
Soler ; translated by John Holland.
        p. cm.
    Includes index.
    ISBN 1-59051-170-0 (978-1-59051-170-1) (pbk. : alk. paper)
1. Lacan, Jacques, 1901- 2. Women. 3. Women and psychoanalysis. I. Title.
    BF109.L28S6513 2005
    155.3'33—dc22
                                                                    2005007146

Contents

III
DIFFERENTIAL CLINIC

IV
THE MOTHER

x / Contents

VIII
CONCLUSION

IX
APPENDIX

Preface

We are honored and thrilled to include the work of such a daz-
zling, erudite Lacanian as Colette Soler in Other Press's Contemporary
Theory Series. Soler's *What Lacan Said about Women* takes refreshing
risks in broadening the field of psychoanalysis, especially by entering
the cultural studies arena. With the exquisite prose and penetrating
insights that she is famous for, Colette Soler, in this candid new text,
shares her psychoanalytic, theoretical, and clinical expertise as well as
her astute perceptions about social issues now throwing our world into
turmoil.

Winner of the *Prix Psyché* for the best work published in the fields
of psychology and psychoanalysis in 2003, *What Lacan Said about Women*
addresses cultural critics, especially those in gender and women's studies, along with anyone involved in clinical practice and/or contemporary theory. This study has the ability to transform neophytes within
the field of Lacanian theory into informed thinkers; and it can substan-
tially supplement and refine the knowledge of those who think of themselves as Lacanian veterans.

Soler spins out a seductive explication of Lacan's thought on the controversial question—which never fails to intrigue—of sexual difference. She takes up other steamy Lacanian topics as well, again with the subtlety that these topics deserve: Lacan's conception of Woman and her relation to masochism, femininity and hysteria, love and death, and the impossible sexual relation. Pushing beyond what has already been established, *What Lacan Said about Women* also addresses more down-to-earth topics such as depression in Lacan, why depressives are un-loved, and the mother in the unconscious after the empire of the father has fallen. Soler's analysis teases out the implications of the texts that Lacan produced from the 1950s to the 1970s, linking them to pertinent cultural preoccupations such as the effects of science on contemporary conceptions of the feminine and transformations of the institutions of the family and marriage.

Soler's genius lurks in the details, however. It is due to its delicacy and precision that *What Lacan Said about Women* opens up psychical space—at a time when such fragile space is critically threatened by multiple forces of robotic banalization operating within our increasingly virtual society. As a result Soler's writing, like great art and literature, can have the crucial impact of enabling its readers to rediscover interiority as constitutive of the world.

With this new study, elegantly translated by John Holland, Other Press's Contemporary Theory Series once again presents rich Lacanian work. We reiterate that our interest is in smart theoretical writing of all stripes and that we put a premium on studies with vital practical consequences that expose the overlap of theory with the mundane. This series welcomes all theory being done currently in, for example, film studies, aesthetics, and feminist, queer, and other political contexts.

Frances L. Restuccia
Series Editor

Translator's Note

Colette Soler's book *What Lacan Says about Women*, was, as the author notes, originally conceived of as a series of lectures delivered to members of psychoanalytic schools. It can be read, however, by anyone interested in the topic announced by the title, and can be approached by those who have only begun to read Lacan as well as by those who have been studying his work for years. Soler's study covers a wide range of material and raises questions that involve a number of intellectual fields. In terms of Lacan's own thought, it extends from the work of the 1950s, devoted to a reading of Freud's concepts of femininity and masculinity, to the path-breaking texts of the 1970s on the logic of sexuation and the identification with the symptom. Clinicians seeking an understanding of Lacanian clinical practice will find discussions of topics such as depression as well as an innovative treatment of the end of analysis. Those interested in cultural critique will find examinations of the limits of the ideology of contract and human rights and discussions of the implications of the "capitalist discourse."[1]

In my handling of Lacan's terminology in this translation, I have usually followed the precedents set by Bruce Fink in his excellent translations of *Encore* and *Ecrits: A Selection*.[2] My rendering of *pas tout* has depended on the context in which the term appears. I have usually rendered it as "not-whole," but have translated it as "not all" whenever what is in question is the impossible attempt to assemble a closed set of women. In cases in which there is an adverbial use of the term, I have usually translated it as "not completely": women are not located completely in the phallic function. I have chosen to retain the French terms, *signifiance* and *lalangue*.

The distinction between *le dire* and *les dits*, to which the author refers throughout much of the work, received its classical treatment in Lacan's text "L'étourdit," to which the author refers any readers who are interested in examining these concepts.[3] I have translated *le dire* as the "saying," while for *le dit* I have used locutions such as "what is said."

Parlêtre, a term that Colette Soler examines in some detail in this book, has been translated in one word, as "speakingbeing." I have reserved "speaking being" as the translation of the more commonly used term *être parlant*. "Speakingbeing" is, of course, considerably weaker than *parlêtre*, which creates a sense of unity and continuity between two terms that had sometimes been considered to be opposed.

"The process of translating is an experiment," as David Lynch has said in another context. "There is a lot of experimentation involved

---

1. Colette Soler has been much concerned with drawing out the implications of Lacan's scattered remarks on the capitalist discourse, a fifth discourse that is to be added to the classical four: those of the master, the hysteric, the university, and the analyst. Her most recent formulations on the subject, which postdate the texts found in this volume, can be found in her essay, "Le saint et le capitalisme," in *Champ Lacanien: Revue de psychanalyse* 1 (2004): 91–106.

2. Jacques Lacan, *The Seminar, Book XX, Encore, On Feminine Sexuality: The Limits of Love and Knowledge*, trans. Bruce Fink. (New York: W. W. Norton & Co., 1998); *Ecrits: A Selection*, trans. Bruce Fink, in collaboration with Héloïse Fink and Russell Grigg. (New York: W. W. Norton & Co., 2002).

3. "L'étourdit" first appeared in the journal of the Ecole freudienne de Paris, *Scilicet* 4, 1973, pp. 5–52. It has been reprinted in *Autres Ecrits* (Paris: Editions du Seuil, 2001), pp. 449–495.

and a lot of serendipity and a taking advantage of accidents." The translator's task is to render what cannot be transmitted fully from one language to another; much must necessarily be lost in this movement. This is the case not only in the attempt to discover approximations of Lacan's terminology, but also for my endeavor to find something like an English equivalent of Colette Soler's style. *Ce que Lacan disait des femmes* is written in a complex and individual style, in which the chain of the author's argumentation follows very closely the syntext of the French language. My rendering of her text in the very different syntax of English has involved a constant give and take between the requirements of our language and those of her thought. In reviewing the result, I am left with the sense that something has been lost, but I hope also that the text has benefited occasionally from the serendipity of the fortunate accident.

I would like to thank Judith Feher-Gurewich and Frances Restuccia of Other Press for their valuable comments and suggestions. I owe a special debt of gratitude to Karen Harper for her patient and painstaking responses to the numerous questions that arose during the translation of this book.

John Holland
Grenoble
January 18, 2005

Introductory Note

This volume is an arrangement and recasting of a series of texts dating, for the most part, from the 1990s. All of them have the goal of explaining and bringing up to date the significance of Jacques Lacan's contributions to the controversial question of the difference between the sexes in the unconscious and civilization.

The Prologue is an article that appeared in 1989 in the *Magazine littéraire* 271, on one of the inaugural cases of psychoanalysis: that of Anna O. The Appendix is the unpublished text of a lecture concerning the logic of sexuation, which was given in May 1977 at the École freudienne de Paris. These two texts deal with the question that underlies the entire volume: that of the difference between femininity and hysteria and the impact of both of them on society.

I

PROLOGUE

1

Anna O., the First

Freud would not have invented psychoanalysis without the gracious cooperation of hysterics. Among these patient teachers, one stands apart: Anna O., the first one. As the first case related in the *Studies on Hysteria*, which Sigmund Freud and Joseph Breuer published in 1895, she demonstrated for the first time that the hysterical symptom reacts to speech. This was the "talking cure," as she called it to her marveling physician. This physician was not Freud himself, but his friend, Joseph Breuer, who took care of her from December 1880 to June 1882, after she had fallen sick from her father's mortal illness.

What is most striking about Anna O. is not her symptoms, which were the classical ones of the hysterics of her age. It is, instead, that there were at least two Annas. There was Anna the sick woman, unhappy and anguished but normal, and then there was the Other, who sleepwalked, in a state of self-hypnotic absence, and who was mad, mean-spirited, and subject to hallucinations. The split was spectacular. One did not know the other, and each had her time on stage. One had the day, the other the night; the first followed calendar time, the second the moment of the traumatism from the preceding winter, when she saw her father's decline. Sometimes they did not even speak a common language, since the second had forgotten German in favor of English. It is easy to understand how this enacted division, in a young person who was seductive, cultivated, and intelligent, succeeded in holding spellbound that adept of Helmholtz's school, Joseph Breuer. If he did not give up, it was because Anna O. revealed something astonishing to him: when Anna the sleepwalker spoke, in the course of her hypnotic absences, the other Anna was cured of her symptoms. This major discovery allowed Breuer to invent the cathartic method of remembering under hypnosis. This was not yet the idea of the unconscious, nor yet the psychoanalytic method, and it would take ten more years for Freud, in the autumn of 1892, to abandon hypnosis and reach the threshold of free association, but the path had already been marked out.

Thus Anna O. contributed to the progress of science. Such a contribution could not be made without paying a price. The *Studies on Hysteria* suggest that she was cured, but we know that this was fallacious and that Breuer's text conceals the secret of the end of her treatment. This secret was deposited in some of Freud's letters, and was made known by Jones, his biographer. It is half-said [*mi-dire*], for those who already know it, at the end of *Studies on Hysteria*, when Freud insists on emphasizing the major role of the bond with the physician in treating hysteria.

Breuer had always wanted to believe, contrary to Freud's idea, that in Anna O. the erotic component was remarkably absent. The light dawned on him from the outside through the voice of his wife, Mathilde; she was too much a part of the matter not to grasp that the epistemophilic desire was not the only one to animate the treatment that Breuer administered so generously to his patient. The treatment that was supposed to be asexual suddenly led Breuer into a marital crisis. Passing suddenly without any warning from misunderstanding to panic, he abruptly ended the treatment. The next day, Anna O., a prey to fantasies of childbirth, greeted him with these words: "This is Breuer's child who's coming." QED, but the putative father had already fled, resolved to know nothing more about it. A year later, he confided to Freud that he wished that death would deliver the unfortunate Anna O. from her persistent ills, and more than ten years later, it took all of Freud's insistence and friendly rhetoric for him to consent to publish the case, without its true ending; it can easily be guessed that he regarded Anna O.'s very existence as a witness for the prosecution.

Breuer discovered transference without succeeding in taking it into account. What was missing in this man with the long, gentle, melancholy face was not intelligence, knowledge, or perseverance, but moral courage. This was one of the great reproaches that Freud made about him. For us, between Breuer, who wanted to know nothing about what he *did*, however, know, and Freud, who noted and concluded—between the panic of the one and the tranquillity of the other's gaze—what comes through clearly is the ethical component that cannot be eliminated whenever a new knowledge appears.

As for Anna O., she was very much left to her own devices. We know nothing of the young abandoned woman's fantasies. They doubtless placed her in the position of a third party between Mathilde and Joseph Breuer, and also between Martha, her friend, and Freud himself. In reality, she was the injured third party: Breuer refused her his symbolic child, whereas Mathilde obtained the real child, and she was also not Freud's patient. Whatever the case may have been, over ten years later, during precisely the period of *Studies on Hysteria*, we find her again in a completely different context: devoted to social work, under her real name, Bertha Pappenheim.

Neither wife nor mother, she knew how to sublimate her sacrificed femininity: she became the mother of the orphans whom she took in, the advocate and defender of women's rights. She did not defend, it is true, those of all women. Her vocation, instead, was for the whore and the orphan. Having passed joyously from privation, which she had taken upon herself, to activism and protest, she visited, with both resolution and humor, Middle-Eastern brothels, to which she felt called by the degradation of women, and in a pioneering way, negotiated as an equal with men of power. Here, then, both Annas were brought back together and pacified in a single reparative vocation. We know from her letters that during these voyages, she wrote to her "daughters," the first faithful, whom she had saved and trained to follow the profession with dedication. The only marks of her past aspirations were a curious passion for lace—doubtless a metonymy of the feminine finery that she had renounced—and a hatred for psychoanalysis, which she always proscribed in her establishments.

Bertha Pappenheim, the first social worker of her time, remains in what she called the "chain of daughters," a virgin among virgins, identified with her fidelity to her position as daughter of her father, Sigmund Pappenheim, since this was his name. She illustrated this name by the works of her self-sacrifice, at the very moment when the other Sigmund immortalized her as Anna O., in publishing the *Studies on Hysteria*. Thus Anna was a divided woman who was caught between two periods, between the time before and after psychoanalysis, between two methods, between two therapists, and was brought back together by her vocation. She remains for us, when all is said and done, torn between the two names that she received from the two Sigmunds in her life: her father and Freud.

II

CHE VUOI?

2

A Woman

Thirty years ago now, for the first time since Freud, Lacan introduced something new concerning sex in relation to the analytic experience, "sex" being taken here in the old sense of the term—"the sex"—which designated not the two sexes, but only the one that was first called the weaker, and then more recently, the second. These innovative elaborations were accompanied by a denunciation, one that was discreet and decent, but also explicit and vigorous. Lacan stigmatized the "scandal" of analytic discourse. What is scandalous is the inability to think what is specific to femininity, and still more, the Freudian "forcing," which measured women by the standard applied to men. This scandal, epistemic in itself in both of its aspects, has been intensified, Lacan said, by being "smothered" in the analytic community. In any case, it is clear that this is not unrelated to sexed prejudices, since no saying (*dire*) escapes from the partiality of sexed identity.

Obviously, Lacan's theses did not go unnoticed; they quickly went around the world, especially in the context of the feminist movements of the period. There is nothing astonishing in this: Freud's phallocentrism was being held so much against him, and his clear reduction of women was being questioned and rethought. Perhaps it should be concluded that the supposed resistance of the English language to the theses of psychoanalysis could itself be a function of the psychoanalysts' own discourse.

I will therefore take up again a question I have been asking myself for a long time. I formulated it as early as 1992 at the conference of the École de la cause freudienne,[1] when I asked our Lacanian movement how far we had pushed the consequences of the theses that Lacan formulated in "L'étourdit," and the seminar *Encore*.

Once launched, the theme of women made the rounds of this community, and besides, our age itself has sped up our interest in the question. Where have we gotten today with the scandal of analytic discourse? Has this scandal been reduced or has its face merely changed?

RESPONDING BY MEANS OF THE OEDIPUS COMPLEX

Freud resorted to the Oedipus complex as both a response and a solution, but we must ask to which question and which problem.

Sex is a matter of differentiations that are not only subjective but also biological, and that are supposed to be natural: those of living sexed organisms. These differentiations had been visible in anatomical differences, long before science showed us the genetic and hormonal determinants that give rise to the sexed body. Life, God knows why—which means that no one knows why—maintains the sex ratio among living beings: there are more or less as many males as females. We can see that humans, who are all speakingbeings (*parlêtres*), never become too muddled in their "coïterations," as Lacan said, and that they are not reluctant to reproduce themselves by the paths of "nature." It is true that the new techniques conditioned by science could change this fact, but we have not reached that point yet, although the birth rate—whether too high or too low—has begun to be a problem.

It has been impossible, since the Freudian discovery, to call upon instinct to explain this fundamental given of human experience: the

---

1. It was devoted to "Beyond the Oedipus Complex."

reproduction of bodies. The unconscious knows nothing of biology and, as far as life is concerned, accommodates nothing other than what Freud discovered in it: the divisions (*morcellement*) of the drives, which are called partial—oral, anal, scopic, and invocatory. What is missing is what would be the genital drive, which would designate a sexed partner for each person. Thus we reach the question that Freud formulates in one of the notes added over the course of the years to the *Three Essays on the Theory of Sexuality*: If there are only partial drives, and if, when it is a matter of love and the "object relation," the narcissistic choice of the counterpart is primary, how can we account for the attraction between the sexes? If maleness is not enough to make the man, nor femaleness the woman, how, then, was what appears as the heterosexual norm established? The question can be reformulated by means of Lacan: How does language, which produces the subject as a lack in being (*manque à être*), set him/her up to accomplish the purposes of life? How does it do so in spite of its denaturing of the instincts?

The Freudian Oedipus complex responds to this question. Freud discovers that in the unconscious—and it should be added, in discourse in general, as our legal status of being either a man or a woman shows—anatomical difference is made to pass through the signifier and is reduced to the problematic of having the phallus; this occurs despite the fact that the partial drives, in themselves, know nothing of sexual difference. Thus it is the orientation of sexed desire that needs to be explained. We can already see that for Freud, in terms of this fundamental lack of knowledge, homo- and heterosexuality are equal.

The Freudian unconscious responds to the following question: How can a man love a woman sexually? The Freudian answer, reduced to its essentials, is that this cannot be done without renouncing the primordial object, the mother, and the jouissance to which this object refers. In other words, there must be a castration of jouissance. We know that Freud tried to apply this explanation to the feminine side, but encountered a number of surprises and disavowals. I will note, however, that in the end he recognizes the failure of his attempt. His famous question, "What does a woman want?," confesses this in the end and can be translated as follows: the Oedipus complex makes the man, but not the woman.

Thus there was a movement beyond the Oedipus complex, a movement that Lacan formalized by referring to logic. The unconscious, if it adheres to language, also adheres to the latter's logic. Thus we have the formula that the unconscious is pure logic. Pure logic regulates what is completely different from it: the living jouissance of the body. It is therefore not astonishing that Lacan reformulates the differences between the sexes both by the opposition between two kinds of logic, that of the phallic whole for men and of the phallic not-whole for women, and two types of jouissance, one of which is phallic and the other that is called supplementary.

Does this mean that he refuted the Freudian Oedipus complex? He put it in question, interrogated and criticized it, and, in the end, in "L'étourdit," reduced it to its logic: the logic of set theory, of the whole. In doing so, he does not, however, properly speaking, refute it, and he himself considers that he maintains it. All of it can be preserved, he says, on the condition of recognizing the logic to which I have referred. It is this logic that *makes* man, every man, by means of the great law of castration, and which leaves him, in matters of castration, only the jouissance that is called phallic, the jouissance that is as limited and discontinuous as the signifier itself.

As a result, in logicizing the Oedipus complex, Lacan also reduces its range, and this reduction is the decisive step: for whoever is called a woman, something else is in question. Rather than remaining within the phallic whole, this other goes far beyond it, for this other thing is no less connected to "the being of *signifiance*." The other, supplementary jouissance, which, far from excluding the reference to the phallus, is added to it, can be situated in another logic, one that is not that of sets, but of the not-whole. On this point, therefore, Lacan diverges explicitly and precisely from Freud, concerning the sexes' relation to castration. I will quote him:

> Unlike him, let me say it again, I do not oblige women to gauge by the shoehorn of castration that charming corset that they do not raise into the signifier.[2]

Although castration is recommended, for what is called "the foot," it must be foreseen that one can do without it.

---

2. Jacques Lacan, "L'étourdit," *Scilicet* 4 (Paris: Editions du Seuil, 1973), p. 21.

Shouldn't this entail some consequences at the level of what is required in analysis? The reference to castration is so necessary to analysis—and particularly to a definition of its end—that one can at least deduce from it a question for what Lacan names the "not-whole" (*pas-tout*), a new noun by which he designates what is not in the phallic whole. And if the clinic of the end of analysis also involves the not-whole, why not ask how the two intersect?

THE MANIFESTATIONS OF THE NOT-WHOLE

Logical construction dispenses neither with collecting the facts nor with constructing a clinic of the not-whole. Lacan himself mentions what he calls its "manifestations." He qualifies them as sporadic, which contrasts them with the phallic function for every man. *Encore* begins an inventory of such manifestations. The ecstasies of the mystics—although not all of them—are placed side by side with the specifically feminine jouissance of the genital relation, and with access to the existence of Kierkegaard. We have done little to enrich this series since Lacan formulated it.

However, we cannot be content here, any more than elsewhere in psychoanalysis, with remaining silent about what is impossible to say, in order to place ourselves back within a single logic. First of all, because if Woman, written with a capital letter, is impossible to identify as such, since she "does not exist," this does not prevent the feminine condition from existing. By this, I am not designating the various miseries that society, according to the period, has inflicted on women, nor, indeed, those that they themselves have inflicted on some of their objects; I am thinking, instead, of the fate of the subjects called upon to bear the weight of the bar placed over women, a bar that Lacan writes for us in its difference from the barred subject, $. Next, because Lacan's application of Russell's logic to the problematic of woman must be stated from a specific position, just as the law of the master is, his saying (*dire*) of it can be questioned. As Lacan suggests, the memory of half of a chicken, in the book that he read as a child, may have fixed for him the primal intuition that preceded his elaboration of the division of the subject; here, I am concerned with his first idea of the other sex. For this reason, I am interested in all the formulas that, well before his invention of the not-whole, Lacan gave of women. There are many of them, and I have chosen one.

I am intrigued by a remark in the seminar on transference, which came to me as a stroke of good fortune. Coming back to Claudel while reexamining the Oedipus complex, Lacan notes in passing that with his feminine characters, Claudel was clumsy and missed woman! Lacan credits him, however, with one exception, in *Break at Noon* (*Partage de Midi*), where, with Ysé, he succeeded in creating a true woman. This gives us the occasion to look for the mark by which Lacan thinks that she can be recognized!

This play, like the rest of Claudel's work, is very much neglected today. Is he too much of a poet, too fervent a Christian, or too subtle? I don't know. Concerning this play, *Break at Noon*, we know that for Claudel, not everything was fiction, and that he rewrote it three times. It deals with what is impossible in love, which is not an impossible love. Its construction is both very pure and very symbolic: three acts, three settings, three kinds of light, three men, and one woman. Ysé is a wife, the mother of two boys, but she announces, "I am the impossible one."[3] De Ciz is the husband. Let's say that he is occupied: he is leaving to seek his fortune. Amalric, the man of the first missed encounter, is the realist and atheist, the one who takes, rather than being taken. When Ysé, in Act I, bantering seriously, asks, "She gives herself to you, and what does she receive in exchange?," he answers:

> All of this is too fine for me. Hell, if a man has to spend all his time
> Worrying preciously about his wife, to know whether he has really measured
> The affection that Germaine or Pétronille deserves, checking the state
> of his heart, things get tricky! [p. 1008]

In short, he says it: "I am Man" (p. 995). Then there is Mesa, who has already retired from the world of men, who seeks God and encounters woman. As for herself, the beautiful Ysé—for, of course, she is beautiful—will allow us to answer a question: What does she want, if she is truly a woman?

---

3. Paul Claudel, *Partage de Midi*. Paris: Bibliothèque de la Pléiade, 1967, p. 1000. Unless otherwise indicated, I am citing the first version, from 1906. References for all further quotations will appear in the text.

WHAT DOES THIS WOMAN WANT?

We already know what she has—a husband and children—and she says enough about them to show us that they make her happy, and that from the moment she comes on stage, she is inscribed in the dialectic of phallic exchange. We also learn very quickly that this kind of happiness is not what she wants:

Ah? Well, if I hold to this happiness, whatever you may call it,
How other I would be! May a blame fall upon me if I am not ready to shake it from my head
Like an arrangement of my hair that can be undone! [p. 998]

And then we hear her very pressing demand, which she addresses to her husband at the beginning of Act II. Having just landed in China, he is getting ready to leave again for some unspecified location, on uncertain and shady business; this, he believes, is the price of fortune.

Ysé—Don't leave.
De Ciz—But I am telling you that it is absolutely necessary! . . .
Ysé—Friend, don't leave. . . .

I am abridging the situation a bit, but she insists, then begs, and pretends to be afraid:

A second time, I beg you not to go away and leave me alone.
You reproach me with being proud, with never wanting to say and ask anything. Then be satisfied. You see me humiliated.
Never leave me. Never leave me alone.

Nicely stupid, he understands nothing and believes that she is confessing his triumph:

It must be confessed in the end that a woman needs her husband.

Then she expresses a doubt: "Don't be too sure of me." He does not believe this, and she has to say more clearly what she means:

I don't know; I feel a temptation in myself. . . .
And I pray that this temptation does not come to me, for it must not.
[pp. 1017–1018]

Here is the fatal word. It is not because of the dangers of China that she is appealing to him, but because of the thing that is closest to her. What she asks him to do is to protect her from herself. A passage that was suppressed in the stage version and put back in the new version of 1948 says, in an even rawer way, what a husband is for, at least for Ysé:

After all, I am a woman, and it is not so complicated.
What does a woman need
Other than security, like the honey bee active in a hive
That is clean and enclosed?
And not this horrible freedom! Haven't I given myself?
And I wanted to think that now I would be quite calm,
That I was guaranteed, that there would always be someone with me
A man to lead me. . . . [p. 1184, new version]

This does not say what Ysé's temptation is. What the evidence shows is that she is tempted by another love, and perhaps by a love that is other. This is what we could believe if we questioned not her demand but her conduct. Ysé betrays three times: she betrays each of the three men. In Act II, she betrays De Ciz, the obtuse husband who understands nothing, for Mesa, the man of the absolute, whom she tears away from God. In Act II, she is with Amalric, who has swept her away from Mesa, and whom she will betray in turn: leaving him to sleep through his life, she returns, in an ultimate epithalamium, to Mesa and death. The latter, which is always present, as a counterpoint to love—whether betrayed or chosen—forbids us from reading Claudel, as people have been tempted to do, as a Marivaux—who, for that matter, is misread—in terms of feminine cunning, terms that are always very convenient.

Was Ysé's temptation that of mad love: a love so total that, annihilating everything, it is akin to death? Perhaps. Ysé explains this to De Ciz so that he will keep her from it, to Amalric, in order for him to measure what is missing in him, and to Mesa, so that he will know.

Ysé to Mesa:

You know that I am a poor woman and that if you call me in a certain way . . . by my name,
By your name, by a name that you know and that I, listening, don't
There is a woman in me who will not be able to stop herself from answering you." [p. 1005]

And again in the admirable duet in Act II:

> . . . Everything, everything and me!
> It is true, Mesa, that I exist alone and here is the world
> Repudiated, and what use is our love to others?
> And here are the past and the future renounced
> At the same time. I no longer have family and children and husband and friends,
> And the whole universe around us
> Emptied of us . . .
> But what we desire is not at all to create but to destroy, and ah!
> There is nothing left except you and me, and in you only me,
> And in me only your possession and rage and tenderness both of destroying you and of no longer being hampered. . . . [p. 1026]

Here it is, people will say: the all too well-known wish to be unique—a wish that must be distinguished from the claims of privilege, which belong to the register of distributive justice—and the exaltation of love into death. This theme is not only not new but is quite classical (see, for example, Denis de Rougemont's *Love in the Western World*). Claudel/Ysé only elevates it to the absolute dimension: not to mystical love, but rather to the mystique of love, which appears in the place from which God has stolen away. It is the temptation of a total love, one that is as absolute as it is oppressive, which sweeps away not only the muddlings of compromise, but which also voids even the dearest objects of their substance. It puts all difference to death and affirms itself only in the form of the annihilation—which is to be distinguished, of course, from negation—of all the objects that are correlated to the phallic function, that is, to lack. Ysé evokes this deleterious side when she speaks of her temptation:

> Understand what race I come from! Because a thing is bad,
> Because it is mad, because it is ruin and death and perdition for me and everything,
> Isn't it a temptation to which I can hardly resist? [p. 1018]

Isn't this more than a simple appeal for love? Through this appeal, isn't it the call for something more radical: the temptation par excellence of annihilation?

THE MARK OF WOMAN

What, finally, does Ysé want? It would be a bit too simple to conclude, from her fluctuations, that she does not know what she wants, as is said so often of women. Instead, these fluctuations translate what she does not dare to want—in the sense of a will that she can assume as her own—what she desires in the sense of the unconscious, as the Other. She may not know what it is, except that it is manifested in the form of a temptation against which she appeals to her husband and to more temperate loves. She cannot evoke it except as the power that bars everything that the Other has brought into existence; it is a fascination with the abyss, which is "inhuman and akin to death."[4] Thus, what reigns over the splendid Ysé, with her beautiful laugh and all her childish mischievousness, is the mortal aspiration that breaks every human bond, an aspiration that effaces the men she loves and also the sons who are left offstage, but about whom she says, at several points, how precious they have been to her. They are effaced in the name of a wish for the abyss, a vertigo for the absolute, for which love and death are only the most common names, and for which "jouissance" would not be inappropriate. It is not betrayal that, in Ysé, makes the mark that is specific to woman. She certainly does betray, but not one object for another, one man for another; instead, she betrays all the objects that respond to the lack inscribed by the phallic function, and she does so to the profit of the abyss. This quasi-sacrificial trait of annihilation is the specific mark that designates the threshold, the border, of the portion that is not at all phallic, of the not-all; it is the absolute Other.

I find confirmation for this hypothesis in the fact that Lacan, after having mentioned Ysé on p. 352 of the seminar on transference, refers also to Léon Bloy's forgotten book, *La femme pauvre* (*The Poor Woman*), about which he affirms that it contains numerous touches that should interest psychoanalysts. For example, near the very end of the novel, there is a sentence—which is stupefying for those who have read Lacan—concerning the heroine: "She even understood, and this is not very far from sublime, that Woman really exists only on the condition

---

4. These are the terms that Lacan applies to truth itself.

of having no bread, no shelter, no friends, no husbands, and no children. It is only in this way that she can force her lord to come down." If we are to believe this author, to assume this renunciation in this way still leaves two paths open: those of the saint and the whore, according to the two modalities that he always supposes, those of beatitude and sensual delight. Such formulations show us that women's fate owes much to the period and what takes refuge, in our time, in the poor tragedies of the love life—infinity within the grasp of poodles, as Céline said—could have found another field in the ages of ardent faith. In any case, this same trait of renunciation, or more precisely of detachment from the place of objects, can be recognized in Kierkegaard, in his approach to ex-sistence. Perhaps this other jouissance could be shown off to advantage by the opaque prestige of lyricism or the mysteries of poetic writing; I want to emphasize, instead, that this mark of what I have called annihilation indicates a structure at work. Indeed, if the not-whole is related to "a good at one remove (*au second degré*) that is not caused by a little *a*,"[5] its difference could only be noticed through a procedure that has a subtractive quality; this procedure is properly that of a separation, where an annulling—in the libidinal sense of the term—emancipation is affirmed in regard to any object. This is neither the hysterical evasion nor a negating ambivalence, for in both of these, we discover only the empty parenthesis where all the subject's objects come; this other aim, on the contrary, also effaces the void from which the object takes its sustenance. The result, as we can glean from Freud's text "On Narcissism: An Introduction," is sometimes the appearance—as it is believed to be—of sovereign freedom!

CLINICAL PROGRAM

This perspective allows us to examine and throw new light on many affirmations made by analytic theory concerning those who are called women. While canvassing the field, I will give a few samples.

---

5. Jacques Lacan, *The Seminar: On Feminine Sexuality; The Limits of Love and Knowledge; Book XX, Encore 1972–1973*, trans. Bruce Fink (New York: W.W. Norton & Company, 1998), p. 77.

The first is that of the poor woman. In Léon Bloy's approach, she allows us to say something new about the famous couple of the rich and the poor woman, which haunted the Rat Man, and which, thanks to Freud, was immortalized in analytic theory. It is not the same to show, as Freud did, that the trait of having or not having the phallus adapts a woman to man's fantasy, and to realize, on the other hand, that the one who is poor—poor in terms of all the objects in the phallic series—can nevertheless be rich in another good, as Lacan says, one that demands nothing from man's fantasy. It could turn out, without any excess of subtlety, that the poor woman is rich in another sensual delight or beatitude. This would go along with the fact that Lacan, in the pages in which he mentions Bloy's poor woman, notes that the saint, who renounces everything, is rich, of course, in jouissance.

Second, there is the abstinent woman. I could take up again Freud's text of 1931 on feminine sexuality. Of the three orientations prescribed to the little girl by the fate of the notorious penis envy, special attention has been paid to the last two: the masculinity complex and what he calls the normal feminine attitude. The first of these involves the phallicism of having and its metonymy. The second, which leads to her heterosexual choice of the man as a substitute for the father, is deployed, instead, as a phallicism of being—"being the phallus"—which appropriates woman to respond as object to the man's phallic lack. The first orientation on Freud's list consists, in his terms, of a complete renunciation of all sexuality. Freud, of course, gives us no examples of this choice, but the fate of privation that is mentioned here, the ascetic renunciation as a supposed effect of the first vexation is ambiguous; it clearly indicates that sexual desire has been elided, not only in act but in fantasy as well, but it leaves the relation to the other jouissance perfectly indeterminate.

This leads me to reexamine the place of fantasy for the subject who is located on the feminine side, and who, let us not forget, if we stay with Lacan's thesis, can be anatomically male or female. If the fantasy uses an object of surplus jouissance in order to absorb castration, the subject can have a fantasy only inasmuch as he is inscribed in the phallic function, in the logic of castration. In this sense, the not-whole, as such, cannot be thought as subject to a fantasy. Isn't this what Lacan is saying when he emphasizes, in *Encore*, that it is only on the man's side that the object a is the partner that makes up for the failure of the sexual relation? (That the fantasy, like the partial drives, was discovered by Freud through the words of hysterical women is not an objection, for the hysteric as such is not in the register of the not-whole. She identifies, rather, with what is subject to castration: that which, as Lacan says, is "*hommosexual* or *beyondsex*."[6]) The question of the child as object and of its place in the barred Woman's division in her relation between the phallus and the silence of the S(Ⱥ) could be introduced in this context.

From another angle, its full weight must be given to Lacan's affirmation that a woman has an unconscious only "from the place from which man sees her"[7]; this situation leaves her own unconscious in a strange suspense, if no knowledge responds to it and if it ex-sists to an Other that "works in such a way that she knows nothing."[8]

Yet more essentially, can we ask such a subject to want what she desires, to consent to what the thing in her wants: to an unknown that is barren of any object, whereas the consent to the final destitution of analysis is conditioned by the glimpse of the object? I believe that, in reality—I mean in practice—analysts tend, instead, to take the recourse of suggesting that she hook up to the phallic whole, under its various forms—there are several of them. This, at least, is how I explain their too obvious and benevolent partiality for the *conjugo* and maternity. I even have some reasons for thinking that Lacan operated in the same way. This does not, however, exclude the question of the differential traits that mark the end of analysis. The disidentification and dephallization of the end of analysis do not ordinarily leave the subject unsecured: whatever her vacillation in the moments of the pass, she quickly finds her equilibrium, for she remains ballasted by the object—the object in its consistency as jouissance. The same thing could be formulated in terms of the fundamental symptom, but it is not necessarily so for the barred Woman, beyond the purchase that she has in the phallic function. We must come back to this question later.

---

6. Jacques Lacan, *Encore*, p. 85. (Lacan's pun combines the word "*homme*" [man] with "homosexual." [Translator's note.])

7. *Encore*, p. 99. It is amusing, as Lacan notes on p. 87 of *Encore*, that Freud had first attributed the object *a* as cause of desire to woman. "That is truly a confirmation that, when one is a man, one sees in one's partner what one props oneself up on."

8. *Ibid.*, p. 90.

3

What Does the Unconscious Say about Women?

This question is justified to the extent that the unconscious is a knowledge, and this is the case as long as it is deciphered in what the analysand says (*les dits*).

Freud's discovery concerning sexuality was badly received within the culture. When we wonder why, we habitually mention the mores of the period, but it is not certain that they alone were responsible. In any case, it is common knowledge that Freud was accused of pansexualism. It is, however, a curious pansexualism, for sex (*le sexe*), which is said to be everywhere, isn't, and in truth, is nowhere. I am speaking of the Sex, written with a capital letter in order to designate, as it does in French, that half of speaking beings who are called women. In the unconscious that he deciphers, Freud discovers that there is no opposite Sex that would inscribe the feminine difference. This is striking, and we can follow the procedure by which he tries to make up for this absence in his attempt to give an account of heterosexuality.

THE FREUDIAN WOMAN

As early as 1905, he discovers the drives—as partial drives. Thus he speaks of the primal "polymorphous perversion," which means that there is no genital drive in the unconscious. The child constructs many theories concerning the relation between the sexes, but like a Cantor, he has to invent them.[1] He constructs them on the basis of the metaphor of the partial drives, which he has experienced. Now the latter say nothing about the difference between men and women; they are to be found in the little boy as well as in the little girl, and they do not touch the question of what distinguishes woman's essence as woman.

Next, Freud suddenly becomes aware of the prevalence of a single signifier, the phallus, which he calls the penis. He formulates the difference in anatomical terms, which he maintains constantly: having the penis or not. Thus he constructs his thesis—the scandalous point for feminists—which makes lacking the phallus the principal dynamic of the whole libido and which affirms that the subject's sexed identity is forged on the basis of the fear in the one who has it, of losing it, and the envy, in the one who is deprived of it, of having it. Making the castration complex the linchpin of becoming a man or a woman, Freud, implicitly at least, introduces the idea of a denaturing of sex in the human being. The sexed being of the organism, which, moreover, is not reduced to anatomy, is not sufficient to give rise to the sexed being of the subject. As proof of this distinction, there are the constant and easily perceptible worries of subjects concerning the degree to which they conform to the standards of their sex. There is almost no woman who is not preoccupied, at least periodically, with her femininity, and no man who does not worry about his manliness. This is not to speak of the transsexual, who is certain that there has been an error concerning her/his anatomy, and that s/he really belongs to the other sex.

Finally, concerning "object choice," everything begins with narcissism. This is what Freud perceived in 1914, in his text "On Narcis-

---

1. Colette Soler, "L'enfant avec Cantor," July 9, 1990. Sixth International Encounter of the ECF.

sism: An Introduction," which Lacan would take up again with his mirror stage. The first object is one's own ego, which the homosexual choice of the counterpart would next take over.

Here Freud calls upon the Oedipus complex to explain how we become a man or a woman. The myth aims at founding the sexual couple, through prohibitions and ideals for each sex.

What then, on these bases, is a woman for Freud? We know that he distinguishes three possible ways in which penis envy can develop, only one of which seems to him to lead to true femininity. This is as much as to say that, for him, not all women are women. When we say, "all women," we are using the definition given on the birth certificate or the driver's license. This definition is itself determined by anatomy, at the moment of birth; if there is a phallic appendage, they say, "It's a boy," and if there is not one, they say, "It's a girl." The phallocentrism of the birth certificate obviously precedes Freud's own! Yet when we say that "Not all of them are women," we refer implicitly to an essence of femininity that escapes anatomy and the birth certificate, an essence whose origin can be questioned. Its Freudian definition is clear and simple. Woman's femininity derives from her "being castrated": she is a woman only because the lack of a phallus incites her to turn toward a man's love. This is, first of all, that of the father—who himself has inherited a love transference that was first addressed to the mother—and later that of the husband. To sum up: in discovering that she is deprived of the penis, the girl becomes a woman if she expects the phallus—which is the symbolized penis—from the one who has it.

A woman is thus defined here only by the paths of her partnership with a man, and the question is that of the unconscious conditions that allow a subject to consent or not. It is here that feminists protest, rejecting what they perceive as a hierarchical arrangement of the sexes. The feminist objection did not have to wait for contemporary women's movements. It arose in Freud's very entourage, and was conveyed by Ernest Jones. It is made in the name of the principle of equality and denounces the injustice of making the lack of the phallus the kernel of feminine being, thus situating it as a minus value. For Freud, this objection is evidently homogeneous with what he calls phallic protest, but this fact does not decide whether or not it is valid.

IS LACAN FREUDIAN?

When Lacan reexamines the question, some years after the aborting of the quarrel over the phallus, he takes a path that is not Freud's.

In appearance, however, he follows Freud's thesis completely. The first page of the text "The Signification of the Phallus," for example, vigorously reaffirms the prevalence of the castration complex in the unconscious and in our becoming either a man or a woman. We know, he says,

> that the unconscious castration complex functions as a knot:
> (1) in the dynamic structuring of symptoms . . .
> (2) in regulating . . . development . . . namely, the instating in the subject of an unconscious position without which he could not identify himself with the ideal type of his sex or even answer the needs of his partner in sexual relations without grave risk, much less appropriately meet the needs of the child who may be produced thereby.[2]

This is very categorically Freudian: the possibility of the heterosexual couple and a happy maternity is regulated by an ideal identification conditioned by the castration complex. Not only does Lacan take up Freud's thesis, but he also justifies it. It is like a wager that Freud's orientation is correct. These theses are so surprising and paradoxical that one must suppose that they were imposed on Freud, the one individual who was able to discover the unconscious, and who, therefore, had a unique access to it. Lacan takes up Freud's thesis again and condenses and clarifies it, while trying to grasp what makes it intelligible: what is in question is not the penis but the phallus, a signifier that, like any signifier, has its place in the discourse of an Other that is always transindividual. Apart from this conversion, which, in some respects, changes everything in what Lacan himself calls "the quarrel of the phallus," Freud and Lacan apparently go hand in hand in affirming the "phallocentrism" of the unconscious.

There are, in fact, two stages in Lacan's developments on these questions. The first and more Freudian is located in the period around 1958, the period during which he produced "The Signification of the

2. Jacques Lacan, "The Signification of the Phallus," trans. Bruce Fink, in collaboration with Héloise Fink and Russell Grigg. *Ecrits: A Selection* (New York: W.W. Norton & Company, 2002), p. 271.

Phallus" and his "Guiding Remarks for a Congress on Feminine Sexuality." Then there are the more manifestly innovative theses of the period of 1972–1973, with "L'étourdit" and *Encore*.

Yet the logical formulas of "sexuation," produced in 1972, do not object at all to the phallocentrism of the unconscious. Lacan refutes the Oedipus complex as a myth and as the comedy of the "Father-Orang, the declaiming Utan,"[3] in order to reduce it to the logic of castration alone; he adds that this logic does not regulate the whole field of jouissance, a part of which does not pass to the phallic One and remains real outside the symbolic. To say that Woman does not exist is to say that woman is one of the names of this—real—jouissance. As for women, who themselves exist, those whose anatomy gives them this status on their birth certificates or driver's licenses, they are no less in the grip of the primacy of the phallus. To say that they are not completely (*pastoutes*) within the phallic function and to recognize an other jouissance than the one that is organized by castration is not to credit them with some "anti-phallic nature." Lacan clarified this in order to avoid any misunderstanding. In the controversy over the phallus, he thus places himself quite explicitly on Freud's side, in order to affirm, "on the basis of clinical facts,"[4] that the phallic semblance is the master signifier of the relation to sex and that it organizes, at the symbolic level, the difference between men and women as well as their relations.

It will therefore be necessary to examine women at three levels: in terms not only of the dialectic in play in sexed desire, but also of the modes of their phallic jouissance in common reality as well as in the sexual relation, and finally with respect to the subjective effects of supplementary jouissance, which femininity conceals and which makes woman not the other sex, but the absolute Other. This can be approached only through the paths of their saying (*dire*).

THE LAW OF DESIRE

In fact, from the beginning, although he claims that he is merely following Freud, Lacan starts to reshape Freud's terms. First, when the penis is recognized in its value as signifier, its function changes. The

---

3. Jacques Lacan, "L'étourdit" *op. cit.*, p. 13.
4. Jacques Lacan, "The Signification of the Phallus," p. 272.

phallus, signifier of lack, lends itself to representing, besides sexual difference, the lack in being that language generates for any subject, and
a parity in lack is thereby reestablished.

Next, Lacan introduces a new distinction. The relations between
the sexes "revolve around . . . being and . . . having . . . the phallus."[5]
The expression "being the phallus" does not occur in Freud. It must
obviously be a transformation of the binary opposition, "having it or
not," which Freud did use. This is not to say, however, that it contra-
dicts his formulations. Lacan's argumentation highlights, instead, that
in the relation between the sexes, having or not having the penis makes
one a man or a woman only by means of a conversion. Freud accentuated the demand for love as specifically feminine. Lacan, by a slight
shift, emphasizes that, in the relation of sexed desires, woman's lack of
the phallus is converted into the benefit of being the phallus, which is
what is missing from the Other. This "being the phallus" designates
woman inasmuch as, in the sexed relation, she is called to the place of
the object. In love, by the grace of the partner's desire, lack is converted
into an almost compensatory being-effect: she becomes what she does
not have. In other words, as early as this period, feminine lack had already been made positive.

In these texts, there is an implicit, undeveloped response to egalitarian objections. Indeed, even more than responding to them, it situates their logic. Yet would such a protester, whoever s/he may be, be
satisfied to see a woman gratified with a phallic being? This is not certain. For she is the phallus only at the level of her relation to the man.
It is always for another, never in herself, that a woman can be the phallus, which brings us back to her partnership with man, which Freud had
already emphasized. Lacan's formulation doubtless accentuates both the
desire and the demand made to the man, but it maintains a definition
of feminine being that must be mediated by the other sex. Hence the
series of successive formulas that specify "woman's" place. All of them
make her the masculine subject's partner: being the phallus, which is
the representative of what the man lacks, then being the object-cause
of his desire, and finally being the symptom in which his jouissance is
fixed. All of these formulas define woman in relation to man and say
nothing of her possible being in herself, but only of her being for the

---

5. Ibid., p. 279.

Other. This gap implicitly underlies all the developments on feminine sexuality.

If we question what condemns her to this relative being, without contenting ourselves with vague allusions—so dear to structuralists—to the differential definition of signifiers, which, here, are those of sex, an answer comes easily: in sexual body-to-body contact, man's desire, indexed by his erection, is a necessary condition—sometimes even more than necessary, since the act of rape makes it a sufficient condition. This is so much the case that, if this desire falters, there can be all sorts of erotic play, but nothing of what is called making love. In this sense, the "sexual" relation [rapport] places the erect organ of masculine desire in the master position, and as a result, a woman can be inscribed in this relation only in the place of the correlate of desire. It is thus not astonishing that everything that is said of women is stated from the point of view of the Other, and concerns more her semblance than her own being; the latter remains what is "foreclosed" from discourse.

CLINICAL ELEMENTS

Many very precise clinical facts, at the level of women's saying (dire), could be mentioned here. Especially important among these is the girl's great complaint about her mother, whom she reproaches for not having transmitted to her any savoir-faire concerning femininity.

This complaint, of course, is not always direct. It can take the form of a denunciation either of the mother's non-femininity or of her hyper-femininity; in the most frequent cases, it can also borrow the detours of metonymy, which substitutes one reproach for another. For such a subject, to deplore that she did not learn the secrets of being a good cook would mean, for example, that something about sexuality was not transmitted to her. One could also mention the hysteric's very frequent protest against her submission to the Other, since her dream of autonomy is only the counterpart, in the ego, of the alienation that results from her demand.

It is also at the level of the phallic metaphor of woman that what is most admissible in the feminist objection is founded. When women denounce the original constraint that a culture's "images and symbols" exercise on them, they are not wrong—and it was Lacan's merit to admit it, unlike Freud. Woman is an invention of culture, an "hystoric" who changes faces according to the period.

Yet it must not be forgotten that this subjection is a function of the demand internal to the social relation. A logic is at work there, which comes to the surface in some of the most extreme current positions of American feminists. The September issue of *TLS*[6] presented a fiercely ironic review of a book by Marianne Hexter. Her thesis goes to extremes, since concerning questions of rape and sexual harassment, she wants to get rid of the border that most other women recognize as the threshold of abuse, that of non-consent. She sees this as a vain subtlety, and whether there is consent or not, denounces the heterosexual relation in itself as the fundamental cause of feminine alienation. Although such excesses can seem laughable, this position is not illogical, since this alienation is a function of being inscribed in the sexual demand.

Freud never came into contact with the truly hard-line feminists of the past century. I am sorry about this, for it is quite diverting to imagine how he would have commented on them. What is certain is that when he produces his "masculinity complex," he does not do so without a certain contempt, and lets a clear note of disapproval come through. In his eyes, the only acceptable fate for a woman—which could be called the "taking upon herself of castration"—is to be a woman for a man.

Lacan, who always tried to distinguish the psychoanalyst from the master, approached these questions without having any recourse to the latter's norms, and confined himself only to the constraints of structure. This orientation prevails, for example, when he affirms that women are not "oblig[ed]" to have the relation to castration that conditions the sexual bond with man. In the psychoanalyst's eyes, the only thing that is obligatory is what is impossible to avoid, and the relation between the sexes, on the contrary, is only possible. The result is the excessive character of Freud's position, which is so normative and thus also dated.

What is the origin of this divergence between Freud and Lacan? Is it a simple question of taste, even of prejudices, of Lacan's greater

---

6. The reference is from 1992.
7. Lacan, "L'étourdit," p. 29.

liberalism as made possible by the evolution of thinking in our culture? It is probable that the period counts for something, but it does not explain everything. I think, rather, that by going further than Freud in terms of structure, Lacan succeeded more than his predecessor in isolating logical constraints, as opposed to social norms. I have just used the term "liberalism," but to be guided by the real is not liberalism, even if the real gives us the norm. In any case, the feminist argument, which is itself highly normative, will certainly not deliver women from their phallic cross. They are certainly free to distrust men, and it is possible, and is always becoming easier, for women to avoid men. The development of science gives them new means of doing so; allowing them to disjoin procreation from the act of the flesh, it opens the way to motherhood without men. Lacan notes this—it is a question of taste, and here we can be liberal—but on the other hand, the weight of the phallic is not thereby lightened for them. Avoiding it is impossible for anyone who speaks as such; as soon as the signifier is in the Other of discourse, the phallus is in play once the slightest demand is made to any other—male or female—beginning especially with the mother, who is determinant here, as Freud saw.

"APPEARANCES OF THE SEX"

The phallic dialectic includes constraints for those who take part in it. It is in charge, especially, of what can be called the comedy of the sexes, which obliges each of the partners to "play the part of the man" or to "play the part of the woman," and to take the path of a seeming (paraître), which has the contrasting function, on one side, of protecting possession and of "mask[ing]" the lack thereof, in the other."[8] At the Other's ball, feminine masquerade and virile parade respond step by step to each other, and although they may give rise to laughter, they are not simulated. The repression of the phallus, which orders the relation between man and woman, hollows out the place where the "seeming" (paraître) is master. Yet let us not be mistaken about appearance: being is its Siamese twin.

---

8. "The Signification of the Phallus," p. 279.

The masquerade is, to take up Karen Horney's expression, an effect of the veil, but it does not hide; instead, it betrays the desire that orients it.[9] This means that interpretation does not go behind the veil, but concludes with what is sketched out of the demands of the Other, with what haunts these demands. Every use of finery, inasmuch as it maneuvers the appearance, reveals the object's affinity with its envelope. Even at the level of the cause of desire, the clothing thus makes the woman. The object can always advance only as masked, for it is only an object inasmuch as the Other recognizes its own marks in it. This is why Don Juan is a myth. "I cannot say what you are for me," the subject says. To this, let us add the statement, addressed to the object: "but you show me what I am . . . Happiness!"

People, in general, like masked balls. In this way, they are like the small child who plays at reproducing the *fort-da* that he is experiencing. Yet as Lacan was quite pleased to repeat, at the end of the ball, it wasn't he and it wasn't she.[10] Does the ball, however, ever end? It wasn't he and it wasn't she; the gap between the semblance and the real is evoked in this assertion only by negation, and the "fortunate" imagination itself would have trouble representing what would happen "if it *were* he, and if it *were* she." Therefore, long live comedy, which alone is reciprocal. It wasn't he and it wasn't she, but it nevertheless was it (*ça*).

To the question of knowing how far the rule of the semblance goes in the relation between the sexes, Lacan said, in 1958, that it goes up to the act of copulation. Thus, there is nothing beyond it. The touch of the Other, by which the alterity of the sex is denatured, does not spare the intimacy of the bedroom, and the masquerade is not a piece of clothing that can be taken off once we are past the door, because there is no door beyond which any supposed nature will reassert its rights. How could jouissance-effects be spared by this? As proof, there is feminine frigidity, which is the result, for the Lacan of 1958, of a defense that is

---

9. I am following Jacques-Alain Miller's development of a remark of Lacan's on the function of the mask in Gide.

10. The reference is to Alphonse Allais's story, "A Very Parisian Drama" ("Un drame bien Parisien"). Raoul and Marguerite are looking for each other at a masked ball. When they finally find each other and remove each other's masks, "Both, at the same time, cried out in shock, for neither recognized the other. He was not Raoul. She was not Marguerite." (Translator's note.)

conceived "in the dimension of masquerade which the presence of the Other releases in its sexual role."[11] There is also the option of homosexuality, which is conceived of as a response to the disappointment of the demand.[12] This means that identifications, the effects of a desire, are also the cause, if not of sexual jouissance, at least of the paths that lead to it.

The divergence between the sexes concerning the phallic semblance is reflected in the male and female ways of taking trouble, as we say: one parades as desiring and the other as desirable. On one side, there is ostentation; a man wraps himself in peacock's plumes, with a nuance of defensive intimidation. On the other side, a woman makes herself into a chameleon and gives the process a scent of derision. This is the price of making someone consent and someone desire. There are various ways of doing so, but what remains is structure, which always envelops the point of the subject's lack, leaving no place for a new treatise on seduction.

It is understandable that masquerade is most visible in women, and goes to the point of an abnegation: it is a *Verwerfung*, as Lacan says, of her being. "Let us not forget that images and symbols *for* woman cannot be isolated from images and symbols *of* women."[13] The expression "images and symbols" anticipated the term "semblance," which was introduced much later, and the sentence itself inscribed in feminine subjectivity what had been lodged originally in the Other.

Why, however, is this said about woman rather than about man? Don't the verdicts of the Other have their own weight for him, and couldn't it be objected that the images and symbols of woman cannot be isolated from those of man? There are, in fact also semblances of manliness, which are imposed from childhood on, especially by mothers, who in their worry about the future of their son, measure him, by anticipation, by their ideal of man, and push him to incarnate the masculine standard. There are, of course, exceptions, not to speak of anomalies. We sometimes see mothers who push their sons to play the

---

11. Lacan, "Guiding Remarks for a Congress on Feminine Sexuality," ed. Juliet Mitchell and Jacqueline Rose, trans. Jacqueline Rose. *Feminine Sexuality*. (New York: W.W. Norton & Company, 1982), pp. 93–94.

12. Lacan, "The Signification of the Phallus," p. 280.

13. Lacan, "Guiding Remarks for a Congress on Feminine Sexuality," p. 90.

"girl," but this is not the most frequent case, and the mother's own pathology is evident here.

Essentially, however, virile parade and feminine masquerade are not homologous. Virile parade itself "femini[zes]"[14] by unveiling the rule of the desire of the Other. The dissymmetry between the two lies in the fact that woman, in order to include herself in the sexual couple, must not so much desire as make someone else desire by conforming to the conditions of the man's desire. The reciprocal is not true. For women, the agency of semblance is accentuated, even intensified by their place in the sexual couple, which obliges them structurally to dress themselves in the colors displayed by the desire of the Other. In other words, since the phallus is a term that is always veiled—repressed—the conditions of desire remain unconscious for each of us. In this gap of repression, the imaginary proliferates, the ideals of sex take on their vigor, and the demand for love, which can itself be formulated, is brought out.

An entire industry is trying, in order to maintain the sexual market, to standardize the imaginary conditions of the fantasy in masculine desire. It is succeeding in part, but what psychoanalysis teaches us is that this does not prevent there from being specific imaginary conditions for each person. The result is that seduction, rather than being a simple technique, may be an art, and is not always only a matter of the automatisms programmed by the collective imaginary. Women, in "making someone desire," do not escape from the interferences of the unconscious, which is always singular, and when confronted with its mystery, they resort to the masquerade, which plays on the imaginary in order to adjust itself to the Other and to captivate what is unknown—desire. Man, himself, is led into this only to the extent that he enters into this demand: by not only desiring sexually, but also by wanting the consent, and even more than consent, the response of the other desire.

FEMININE DESIRE INTERPRETED

If a woman is inscribed in the sexual couple only in terms of "allowing herself to be desired," this position as the partner of masculine

---

14. Lacan, "The Signification of the Phallus," p. 280.

desire leaves in the shadows the question of her own desire, the desire that conditions this consent. Here is what Freud came up against, which did not lead him to give up his affirmation about the little girl, "She has seen it and she knows that she is without it and wants to have it"[15] but which nevertheless leads him, in the end, to his famous question: "What does woman want?"

The expression of feminine desire is, in fact, problematic. Freud's doctrine at least had the merit of highlighting the distinction between all the desires that are possible for women and what would be a feminine desire, properly speaking. He says that there is a single libido, since desire as such is a phenomenon of the subject, and is linked to castration. Thus it is correlated essentially with the lack on the level of having (*manque à avoir*), which has nothing specifically feminine about it. This, indeed, is why the notion of "masculinity complex" is not only tainted by prejudices but also conceptually confused. Everything belonging to the desire to acquire, to appropriate, serves for man as the metonymy of his having the phallus. In the name of what would the desire for having be forbidden to women, whether it takes the form of wealth, power, influence, success—in short, all the "phallic" quests of everyday life? On this point, the difference between Freud and Lacan is quite perceptible. Lacan was not bad-tempered with women, either in his texts or his analyses, and was little inclined, it seems, to discourage them from acquiring whatever appealed to them, if it was possible. Yet this wish, which is inherent in the subject, has nothing specifically feminine about it, and woman's desire as such, if there is any sense in speaking of it, would be something else.

Freud sees only one variant of the desire to have—in the form of having the love of a man or a phallic child. Beyond that, he gives up. In his previously mentioned solutions to penis envy—renunciation, masculinity, femininity—it must be emphasized that in the third case of "normal" evolution, the subject does not renounce phallic possession, as in the first case. What distinguishes the womanly woman, according to Freud, is that unlike the second case, she does not intend to

---

15. Sigmund Freud, "Some Psychical Consequences of the Anatomical Distinction between the Sexes," trans. James Strachey. *Standard Edition of the Complete Psychological Works of Sigmund Freud.* Vol. XIX (London: Hogarth Press and the Institute of Psycho-analysis, 1961), p. 251.

procure the phallic substitute for herself; she expects it from a man, especially in the form of the child. She does not renounce it, but she consents to reach it by the mediation of the partner. Thus the Freudian woman is, fundamentally, the one who is willing to say "thank you."

This obviously implies, although Freud does not formulate it thus, a subjectivation of the lack that supposes that she acquiesces in, rather than protests against, the unjust distribution of the semblance and that she also admits that she is at the mercy of the encounter with man's desire.

Lacan's formulas do not disagree with this—quite to the contrary, since he says that it is the absence of the penis that makes the phallus. This means that she is an object only on the condition of incarnating for the partner the signification of castration and of presenting herself as a minus—this is why Lacan attached such great importance to Léon Bloy's *La femme pauvre*, which I spoke of above. The formula can be generalized: it is the lack—penis or not—that makes the object be. Thus we have the example of a man, Socrates himself, who by exhibiting the lack of his desire, becomes the object of Alcibiades's transference.[17] It is thus possible for anyone, male or female, to be homologous to a woman: namely, what is coupled with the One on the mode of the object.

Nevertheless, for a woman, as for anyone who offers herself/himself in the place of the object, including the analyst, being an object does not yet say anything about the objects that she has—those that cause her own desire—or about what appropriates her to the place of the object in the relation. On these points, Lacan is far from Freud, and where the latter had given up, he takes up the challenge.

WOMAN IS NOT THE MOTHER

He does so, first of all, by refusing to confirm the Freudian reduction of woman that is based on interpreting her in terms of the mother. As we know only too well, for Freud the love of a man culminates in

16. Jacques Lacan, "The Subversion of the Subject and the Dialectic of Desire," *Ecrits: A Selection*, p. 308.

17. *Ibid.*, pp. 309–310.

the child who is expected on the margins of the sexual relation, and who is the only object that "causes" a woman's desire. Yet it is paradoxical to say that her children are the answers to a woman's sexed desire. The child is certainly a possible object *a* for a woman, but this possibility offers itself in the context of the phallic dialectic of having, which is not specific to her, and only rarely saturates sexual desire; properly feminine being, if it exists, is situated elsewhere.

Between the mother and woman, there is a gap, which is easily perceptible in experience. The phallic child can sometimes fill it up and silence the feminine requirement, as we see in cases in which such a maternity radically modifies the mother's erotic position. Yet fundamentally, the gift of a child only rarely allows the question of desire to be closed. The child as the remainder of the sexual relation can work quite well to obstruct a part of a woman's phallic lack; the child is not, however, the cause of the feminine desire that is in play in sexual physical contact.

It is not enough to say that she lends herself to the desire of the Other; the desire that sustains this consent must also be examined. Inasmuch as it is not reduced to the demand to be the lack of the Other, its sexed cause would be situated, rather, on the side of the "attributes she cherishes" in her partner,[18] in Lacan's graceful words. In other words, it is placed on the side of the male organ, which the phallic signifier transforms into a "fetish," and promotes to the rank of surplus jouissance.[19] In summary, thus, if the jouissance of copulation is "articulated to a surplus jouissance," the cause of desire, and if the object *a* of the fantasy plays this role for a man, what takes this position for a woman is the fetishized semblance excised from the partner. From this first dissymmetry, a second results: for man, the partner remains the absolute Other, while for woman, he becomes the castrated lover.

Beyond this new articulation of feminine phallicism, Lacan proceeded to a sort of deduction of a specific feminine desire to which the masquerade forbids any direct access. This desire can, indeed, only be deduced, since the masquerade veils it, making it impossible to reach directly.

---

18. Lacan, "The Signification of the Phallus," p. 280.

19. *Ibid.*, p. 279 and "Radiophonie," *Scilicet* 2/3, Paris: Editions du Seuil, 1970, p. 90.

Paradoxically, and I am astonished that this has not been emphasized more, it is in the context of considerations on feminine homosexuality that Lacan introduced this desire. His demonstration takes
place in several stages. Far from accentuating any supposed renunciation of femininity in lesbians, he emphasizes, on the contrary, that such
femininity is their supreme interest; he mentions a fact brought to light
by Jones, who, he says, has "clearly detected here the link between the
fantasy of the man as invisible witness and the care which the subject
shows for the jouissance of her partner."[20]

This says, as a first thesis, that if the homosexual woman sets herself up as a rival as subject with man, it is in order to exalt femininity,
which she locates on the side of her partner and thus participates in
only by proxy. Next comes a remark on the "naturalness with which
such women appeal to their quality of being men."[21] Third, and finally,
"Perhaps what this reveals is the path leading from feminine sexuality
to desire itself."[22] This is a remarkable sentence, which could obviously
not apply to a man, since for him the path goes from desire to the act,
and not the reverse. Thus, from women's "playing the man," in sexual
activity or elsewhere, Lacan makes the induction concerning the desire that underlies such activities: in "playing the man," they revealed
what a woman as such aspires to.

This desire is manifested, he says, as "the effort of a jouissance
wrapped in its own contiguity . . . to be *realised in competition with* (*à l'envi
de*) desire, which castration releases in the male."[23] Here, then, is the
answer to the famous question, "What does woman want?" This desire
is foreign to any quest for having, and unlike the demand for love, is not
the aspiration to being. It is defined as the equivalent, if not of a will to

---

20. Lacan, "Guiding Remarks for a Congress on Feminine Sexuality," p. 97.
Translation altered.

21. *Ibid.*

22. *Ibid.*

23. *Ibid.* Jacqueline Rose translated "*à l'envi de*"as "in the envy of." In preferring
the expression "in competition with," I am following the first translation of Colette
Soler's article done by François Raffoul and David Pettigrew and revised and edited
by Bruce Fink. See Colette Soler, "What Does the Unconscious Know about Women?"
Reading Seminar XX: Lacan's Major Work on Love, Knowledge, and Feminine Sexuality,
ed. Suzanne Bernard and Bruce Fink (Albany: State University of New York Press,
2002), p. 106.

jouissance, at least of an aiming at jouissance. Yet it is a question of a particular jouissance, which is excepted from the "discrete" and therefore limited character of specifically phallic jouissance. More, indeed, than a simple wish, it is an applying of herself, an "effort" that competes with the man's; to describe this competition, I would gladly risk the formula, "to get off just as much as he desires." I will note, moreover, that the expression "in competition with," which connotes emulation, is intensified on the following page when Lacan observes that, in the sexual relation, the "claimants of sex" and the "holders of desire," namely, women and men respectively, "work against each other as rivals."[24]

THE ABSOLUTE OTHER

As we see, Lacan's response to the question of feminine desire already involved a consideration of an other jouissance, a jouissance that is other than "phallic" enjoyment, with which the unconscious maintains us.

Phallic jouissance, as the jouissance of the One, is located, limited, and outside the body. It is a jouissance that is syntonic to the signifier, as discrete and parceled out as it is; it therefore lends itself to thinking in terms of pluses and minuses, and becomes thereby the partner to the subject as such. It is thus the correlative of the lack in jouissance (*manque à jouir*), and founds the imperative of the jouissance of the superego, where guilt is maintained. The masturbatory jouissance of the organ creates the paradigm in the field of eroticism, which, for man, is displaced to the heart of the sexual relation, while for woman, its equivalent was believed to be found in clitoral jouissance. It has other forms, however, which can be surveyed: from the takeover of territory that had once belonged exclusively to men up to the establishment of a series of anonymous organs by our modern female collectors. Phallic jouissance is not limited, however, to the register of eroticism. It also underlies the whole of the subject's accomplishments in the field of reality, and makes up the substance of all the satisfactions that can be capitalized.

---

24. *Ibid.*

Thus we must ask the question: What place does the quest for phallic jouissance leave to the "closed field" of the sexual relation, and what displacements of the border between love and copulation does it preside over in current discourse?

How does the map of tenderness get along with modern man and woman's busy schedule?[25] The evolution of our ways of thinking, mores, and social groups is placing this field of reality more and more under the sign of unisexuality.[26] Women, whose jouissance was for a long time confined by the dominant discourse to the home—including husband and child—are now finding themselves in a new situation: they have seen the opening of all the doors of competition, which is always phallic. These changes, specific to our age, have had indirect consequences on conduct and sexed ideals—to which I will return—and have especially had new subjective effects. Most often, these are effects of discordance: the division of the subject is intensified in women by an accentuated division between her jouissances.

A jouissance "enveloped in its own contiguity" is something else. This jouissance does not fall under the bar of the signifier, knows nothing about the phallus, and is therefore not caused by an object *a*. This jouissance is foreclosed from the symbolic and is "outside the unconscious." Can we conceive of a clinic of this jouissance, which leads us to believe that women do not say everything (*ne disent pas tout*) because they do not say anything at all about it (*n'en disent rien du tout*)?

This is the jouissance "that femininity hides [*dérobe*]," as Lacan says, and this final term, which can also be translated as "steals," introduces a double nuance, both of appropriation and dissimulation.[27] It must not be imagined, indeed, that supplementary jouissance is illustrated only by mystics, with whom analysis deals very little. We must distinguish it as well from the jouissances that theory has situated as pregenital, and with which the child, independently of his/her sex, is initiated in the relation with the mother, the primordial object. The little polymorphous pervert's partial drives certainly bring the body into

---

25. The "map of tenderness" (*carte du tendre*), an allegorical map of the landscape of love, is to be found in *Clélie*, a novel by Madeleine du Scudèry (1607–1701). (*Translator's note.*)

26. See the chapter "Hysteria in the Time of Science."

27. Lacan "L'étourdit," p. 23.

play, but they obey the fragmented structure of the signifier and are just as much outside the body as phallic jouissance is. In this sense, the pregenital is not the other jouissance, and the relation with the mother's body is not the key to this jouissance.

The question is that of the sexual relation [rapport], or rather of the nonrelation between the two jouissances.[28] This is why Lacan refers to Teiresias, and does not content himself with distinguishing between clitoral and vaginal jouissance, to which analytic theory had given an approximate formulation in order to approach the ecstatic character of this jouissance—the only trait that brings it close to that of the mystics. The idiot gets off in solitude on the One, especially on the one of the organ; someone who is ecstatic, on the contrary, gets off—in a way and on the basis of what we do not comprehend—on an unlocated jouissance, the cause of which escapes us. Of this ecstatic jouissance, the unconscious, where signifiers and images proliferate, knows nothing. It can be felt and manifested in experience. It is a real jouissance that is concealed by definition. Hence its evocation in a structure that is necessarily beyond, as I said earlier: beyond the phallus, beyond the object, beyond the consistency of the saying (dire), and which negatives everything that does not also go beyond. It is without measure and the subject finds herself "outstripped" by it. Phallic jouissance, on the other hand, does not go beyond the subject. I am not going to claim that it is homeostatic, for it can be disturbing, can give rise to pathos, as we know, but it remains suited to the subject's measurements; in this, it is like the object a, which certainly divides the subject, but which is also adjusted to the gap in the latter. The other jouissance makes woman Other—the absolute Other. This is why Lacan can say ironically, in "L'étourdit," that everyone who loves women, whether s/he is a man or woman, is heterosexual. Yet how can what has always frightened us so much be loved?

What use can the analyst make of these indications? The unconscious knows a lot, but by definition, it knows nothing of the other jouissance.

---

28. One of the senses of the French word "rapport," translated here as "relation," is of a mathematical ratio. It is thus to be distinguished from "relation sexuelle," a formulation that the author also utilizes. In order to indicate which term is being used, the French word has often been added in brackets (Translator's note).

It is not by chance that analysis has put the accent on phallic jouissance, for only the jouissance that has passed into the signifier concerns analytic practice. The unconscious does not cease to articulate lack, the captivating images, and the letters in which jouissance becomes fixed. It is also from within phallic jouissance that it makes a remainder appear, and shows that jouissance does not always say everything. Yet this is not an objection to analysis, for what *can* be studied are the subjective consequences of this other jouissance, what I have called the "commandments"[29] of an encounter with a jouissance that abolishes the subject, that "goes beyond" the latter,[30] leaving it between "a pure absence and a pure sensitivity,"[31] and which can only be "brought back to life and aroused again"[32] without being made into a signifier. This encounter divides the feminine being and thus generates defenses, appeals (*recours*), and specific requirements.

I will conclude, therefore, that it is not necessary for the unconscious to know more about women, since this "more"—a quantitative expression—only makes what is Other more insistent, an Other that neither knows nor imagines, but that becomes an edge for everything that is said. As far as jouissance is concerned, "Nothing more can be said of this than what the 'not enough' (*pas assez*) responds."[33]

---

29. See the chapter "Because of Jouissances."

30. "L'étourdit," p. 23.

31. "Guiding Remarks for a Congress on Feminine Sexuality," p. 95.

32. "L'étourdit," p. 23. The word that Lacan uses is "*re-suscitée*," which combines "*ressuscitée*" (resuscitated) with "*suscitée*" (aroused). (Translator's note.)

33. Jacques Lacan, "Ou pire," *Scilicet* 5, 1975, p. 9.

III

DIFFERENTIAL CLINIC

Introduction

To say that woman is the absolute Other is to say that she will not be at all like what could be said about her, that she remains outside the symbolic, and is real in the double sense of what cannot be said, and of what derives jouissance from the non-phallic. By definition, the absolute Other challenges any possible attribution of qualities to her.

Is the analytic movement, in its effort at constructing a clinic of woman, condemned either to speak of someone else, particularly the mother, or to enumerate everything that *woman isn't?* I can also say that "everything can be said about her," but in the sense that *anything* whatever can: there will always be a possible example of it, and a host of counterexamples. Women, by definition, are originals. They are a race of jouissance.

What does not exist can, nevertheless, be spoken of. As Lacan says, "She is called woman (*on la dit-femme*) and defamed (*diffâme*)."* The

---

*Jacques Lacan, *Encore*, p. 85.

centuries have witnessed this, which may be a history of warding off terror. There is a racism of jouissances but there is no clinic of Woman, other than one that would be imaginary and projective.

A clinic of women affected by being not-whole, whether in the hysterical, obsessional, phobic, or psychotic mode, is not, however, to be excluded.

4

Hysteria and Femininity

In the eyes of what is left of psychiatry, the hysteric is misunderstood. The psychoanalyst, on the other hand, must not, on the pretext
of not missing her, recognize her everywhere and confuse hysteria with
femininity. We are suffering from a frequent clinical confusion concerning hysteria; every neurotic woman who presents herself to an analyst
is supposed, almost *a priori*, to be hysterical, at least if she is not sus-
pected of being mad. This is a clinical error, and Lacan always insisted
on taking the opposite direction, since hysteria is something very precise. He gave us its paradigm in a fabulous analysis of Freud's account
of the dream of the "beautiful butcher's wife."

As an introduction, and to indicate the horizon of my developments, I
will mention two of Lacan's theses.

> The hysteric . . . is the unconscious in action [*en exercice*], who pushes
> the master to get on with things [*met le maître au pied du mur*] by produc-
> ing a knowledge.[1]

---

1. Jacques Lacan, "Radiophonie," p. 89.

Let us note that this definition does not specify that the hysteric is a woman. Its implication that there is some hysteria in every subject could give a renewed vigor to the somewhat forgotten notion of the hysterical kernel of neurosis.

The second thesis, which is much later and more surprising, claims that in hysteria, a man is superior to a woman.[2] This is astonishing, for we can recognize that this is not the common prejudice. Yet why do we have this prejudice, and why do we confuse hysteria with femininity?

The commentary on the dream of the "beautiful butcher's wife," which Lacan places in the fifth chapter of "The Direction of the Treatment," entitled "Desire Must Be Taken Literally," is very instructive. In this short passage, a true masterpiece of precision and density, he does not enter into a polemic with his contemporaries, as he does in the rest of the text, but puts forth his own thesis. With this single example, he makes a triple demonstration: first, of the linguistic structure of the unconscious, which he commented on for ten years; next, what the properly Freudian unconscious is—a desire signified by the linguistic structure of the dream; finally, what the unconscious hysterical wish is.

THE STRUCTURE OF LANGUAGE (LANGAGE)

Freud discusses this dream to show that the dream is the expression of a desire, although its statement (énoncé) describes the failure of a desire, or rather the failure of a wish. Here is the dream.

> I wanted to give a supper-party, but I had nothing in the house but a little smoked salmon. I thought I would go out and buy something, but remembered then that it was Sunday afternoon and all the shops would be shut. Next I tried to ring up some caterers but the telephone was out of order. So I had to abandon my wish to give a supper-party.[3]

---

2. Jacques Lacan, "Joyce le symptôme," Joyce avec Lacan (Paris: Navarin, 1987), p. 35.

3. Sigmund Freud, The Interpretation of Dreams, trans. James Strachey. Standard Edition of the Complete Psychological Works of Sigmund Freud, Vol. IV (London: Hogarth Press and the Institute of Psycho-analysis, 1953), p. 52.

We know that Lacan extracts from Ferdinand de Saussure's texts a matheme that is not found there, but that condenses his analyses. He writes the capital S of the signifier over the small s of the signified, in order to indicate that the signified is produced by the signifier, that it is its effect.

$$\frac{S}{s}$$

This already says that the signified is radically distinguished from the referent, the things themselves, the real that we aim at when we speak. Next, Lacan, rereading Freud with Jakobson, recognizes in metaphor and metonymy[4] the two operations by which something of the signified is engendered. Metaphor substitutes one signifier for another, S' for S; it represses the first signifier, making it pass to the rank of the signified. The result is what Lacan calls a positive meaning-effect (*effet de sens*), which he writes with a plus at the level of the signified,

$$\frac{S'}{S} \rightarrow S \,(+)\, s$$

Metonymy combines two signifiers—and combination is not substitution—without engendering a supplement of meaning, which Lacan writes with a minus at the level of the signified:

$$(S \rightarrow S') \rightarrow S \,(-)\, s$$

THE DREAM IS A METAPHOR

Lacan reads the dream of the beautiful butcher's wife by means of this linguistic structure, which it illustrates marvelously. For his demonstration, he uses, of course, Freud's commentary, which analyzes not only the dream text, but also the associations called up by the dream.

The slice of smoked salmon that appears in the dream is, Freud says, an allusion to the dreamer's friend, who claims to desire salmon,

---

4. See the formulas of metaphor and metonymy developed in the text "The Instance of the Letter in the Unconscious," in *Ecrits: A Selection*, p. 155.

but forbids herself from eating it. It happens that the beautiful butcher's wife does the same with caviar; she claims to want caviar and persuades her husband of this, but insists that he not buy it for her. That a woman dreams of caviar, a food that is not sold at the butcher's shop, already opens onto something that is elsewhere—at least in terms of food. From this, Freud boldly deduces that the behavior of these two coupled hysterics has the signification of a desire for an unsatisfied desire. All of this precedes the dream and is not yet a part of the unconscious.

Lacan does not discuss this thesis of Freud's. He makes it into a matheme and writes it in terms of the structure of signifier and signified: "the desire for caviar" is the signifier, the signified of which is "the desire for an unsatisfied desire":

$$\frac{S}{s} \quad ; \quad \frac{\text{``desire for caviar''}}{\text{``desire for an unsatisfied desire''}}$$

We see that Lacan does not reduce the signifier to the elements of language (*la langue*), since he makes the "desire for caviar" into a signifier. Any discrete element, which can be isolated and combined with other discrete elements, which can also be isolated, and can take on meaning, can be called a signifier. Here, it is "the desire for caviar," but it can also be an image and even a gesture. Lacan mentions, for example, that a slap can be a signifier as soon as it enters into a combinatory structure of representations; this can also be the case of a somatic element, a kind of physical pain, as can be seen in the hysterical conversions that Freud brought to light.

The caviar that Freud speaks about does not, however, appear in the dream. What appears is the salmon, which is substituted for caviar by a metaphoric effect; the latter makes one signifier (caviar) disappear in favor of another: salmon. The dream's metaphorical structure can already be written:

$$\frac{S'}{S} \to S' \, (+) \, s \quad ; \quad \frac{\text{Salmon}}{\text{caviar}} \to \text{Salmon} \, (+) \, s$$

As Lacan says, "But what is metaphor if not a positive meaning effect, that is, a certain access gained by the subject to the meaning of her desire?"[5] We can see that the positive meaning effect, which is the plus of positive meaning produced by metaphor, is nothing other than what Freud names the desire of the dream, which is very much unconscious.

$$(+) \; s = desire$$

Meaning is thus desire itself. The sentence can be clarified if we develop the two levels of the matheme of the signifier and the signified. Just as the combinatory of signifiers is developed in a chain, which can be symbolized by the binary of S_1 and S_2, so also the signified itself is present in two guises. First, there is the signification, which is grammatical. This is what is used in textual explications, when a sentence is examined according to its grammar, its words, and their semantic definition. Yet this does not exhaust the signified, since for every signification that is produced, we can ask, and we generally do not fail to do so, what it "means" (*veut dire*). This question concerns what the enunciation aims at. There is thus always some meaning that is in excess of the signification:

$$\frac{S_1 \to S_2}{s} \begin{array}{l} \nearrow \; \text{signification} \\ \searrow \; \text{meaning (sens)} \end{array}$$

"What does this mean (*veut dire*)?" leads us back, in the last analysis, to "What does it want?" The problem is not so much to know what the subject wants to say to you as what this subject wants in speaking. These are the ABCs of deciphering, which lead to the interpretation of desire, and from such concerns, Lacan disengages the structure of language, without which interpretation would have no rules. The dream is a metaphor that makes the dimension of desire present. Yet this does not yet say what this unconscious desire is.

To reach unconscious desire, we cannot simply stay with the unsatisfied desire of the two friends: one with her salmon and the other with her caviar. The latter, indeed, is not an unconscious but a

---

5. Lacan. "The Direction of the Treatment," *Ecrits: A Selection*, p. 247.

preconscious desire, since it has been deduced simply from the patient's explicit speech. Unconscious desire is not deduced from explicit speech but is approached, through metaphor, as the signified. It is therefore necessary to "go further in order to know what such a desire means in the unconscious."

METONYMY IN THE DREAM

Before coming to the interpretation of unconscious desire, I will first examine metonymy. We must first distinguish unsatisfied desire from the desire for unsatisfied desire. There are two difficult paragraphs concerning this subject. Unsatisfied desire is signified by the signifier caviar, inasmuch as it "symbolizes this desire as inaccessible. . . ." Here we are at the level of the elementary matheme:

$$\frac{S}{s} \quad ; \quad \frac{\text{Caviar}}{\text{unsatisfied desire}}$$

Yet, Lacan continues, as soon as desire "slips . . . into the caviar, the desire for caviar becomes this desire's metonymy—rendered necessary by the want-to-be in which this desire sustains itself."[6] Let us write this operation with the matheme of signifier over signified:

$$\frac{\text{Caviar}}{\text{unsatisfied d.}} \longrightarrow \frac{\text{d. for caviar}}{\text{d. for unsatisfied d.}} \cdot \text{caviar} \longrightarrow \text{d. caviar} : (\text{-}) \text{ s}$$

Why is the desire for caviar a metonymy of unsatisfied desire and not a metaphor for it? Lacan comments on the same page on what he calls the scant meaning of metonymy, the "minus" written at the level of the signified in the general formula. "Metonymy," he says, "is, as I have been teaching you, an effect which is rendered possible by the fact that there is no signification that does not refer to another significa-

---

6. *Ibid.*

tion; the most common denominator of those significations is produced in it—namely the scant meaning (commonly confused with what is meaningless), I repeat, the scant meaning that turns out to be at the root of this desire, conferring upon it the hint of perversion one is tempted to point to in the present case of hysteria."[7]

I will leave to the side for the moment his accent on perversion.

I want to emphasize first that there has been no substitution of signifiers: unlike the metaphor of the dream, in which the salmon has repressed the caviar, which reappears only through association, none of the terms—caviar and desire for caviar—has disappeared from the chain. On the level of the signified, when we pass from unsatisfied desire to the desire for unsatisfied desire, is there a plus? There would seem to be: it is not the same to mention the lack of caviar (the unsatisfied desire) and to make it understood that this lack is desired (the desire for unsatisfied desire). Why does Lacan say then that there is no positive meaning effect?

This can be understood only through the distinction between meaning (*sens*) and signification. The significations of "unsatisfied desire" and "desire for unsatisfied desire" are different. Yet on the level of meaning, which is to be placed in the denominator of these significations, what has been transferred? (It is worth noting that Freud uses the term "transference," for the first time, in relation to the work of signifiers in the dream.) What is transferred is nothing other than the indication of a lack, which is inherent in all desire, and which insists. "Unsatisfied desire" and the "desire for unsatisfied desire" do not have the same signification, but they have the same meaning of a lack in the subject:

S	caviar	d. for caviar
s ↗ signification ↘ meaning	unsatisfied d.	d. for unsatisfied d.
	meaning of lack	meaning of lack

The single meaning that insists in both unsatisfied desire and the desire for unsatisfied desire is only a "scant meaning," that of the same

---

7. *Ibid.*

lack, which cannot tell us what the specific unconscious desire of the dream is. This is what resolves the question of the possible perverse accent. To whoever would be tempted to ascribe our two friends' strategy of privation to a penchant for masochism, Lacan responds that this is only an appearance, and "The truth of this appearance is that the desire is the metonymy of the want-to-be."[8] What then can be said of the subject of the unconscious, inasmuch as it wants something determinate?

THE SUBJECT OF THE UNCONSCIOUS

The subject of the unconscious is not the nice hysteric who recounts her dream to Freud, in the dimension of the transferential call: "Well, my dear professor, what do you have to say about that?" You'd better get to work! The subject of the unconscious, if we could incarnate it—but, of course, we cannot, and so I am using the modal "could"—would be the agent of the metaphorical substitution.

This subject is not the person, who goes through all her pantomimes, but what is determined by this metaphor. It is thus equivalent to the desire that it signifies. We find this subject "In a signifying flow whose mystery lies in the fact that the subject doesn't even know where to pretend to be its organizer."[9]

We must thus distinguish, on the one hand, the unconscious as a linguistic structure that is deciphered—the signifying formations of metaphor and metonymy—and on the other, the unconscious meaning that is transferred in this combinatory of the chain, and that can only be interpreted. This is the unconscious as desire, as unconscious subject.

THREE IDENTIFICATIONS

The rather simple interpretation of the beautiful butcher's wife's dream proceeds by means of the distinction among three identifications.

---

8. *Ibid.*
9. *Ibid.*, p. 248.

It has been known for a long time—from before the invention of psychoanalysis—that the hysterical subject tends to make identifications, but hysterical identification is complex and stratified.

The First Identification

This is with the friend, and we can mark its coordinates on Lacan's schema L, in which the imaginary axis is crossed by the axis of the symbolic relation of subject to subject:

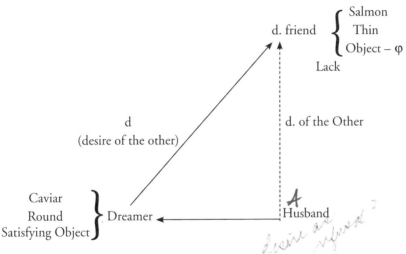

More than being an identification with a single signifier, it is an identification with a kind of conduct (refusing what one says one wants) that already indicates desire. It is to be situated on the imaginary axis, as an identification, via an index of the signifier, with the desire of the other—without a capital "o"—the counterpart.

The index of this identification with the friend is the patient's desire for caviar, which reproduces the friend's desire for salmon. As inaccessible or refused objects, caviar and salmon are the signifiers of their unsatisfied desire.

This identification with the friend's desire can only be apprehended, however, in relation to a third term, which can be written as A, a place that happens to be filled here by the husband, the one who is to be made to desire. He must be located at the place of the Other, with a capital letter, since, in order to seduce him, she must orient herself in relation to his desire; this desire is itself located only by means of his demand, as the meaning of his demand.

This structure can be read easily, for the husband's demand is very explicit. He is a man who claims to know what he wants: he likes curvaceous women. It happens that the patient, who is curvaceous, has everything to satisfy his demand. The friend, on the other hand, is very thin, and does not have the prerequisites for the husband's sexual satisfaction; for this reason, the husband's discreet interest in her raises a question. A desire has been indicated, but in a negative mode: he has another interest, for something that cannot satisfy him, although his drives are already being satisfied. The line of dehiscence between desire and a demand for satisfaction is obvious here.

We can find this again in the two friends in the conjuncture of the dream. The friend has made a request: she wants to come for dinner. She conveys this signification through her compliment to the butcher's wife: "You eat so well at your home." Its meaning is completely different, and our witty butcher's wife understands this: it pleases her friend to awaken a desire in the husband, the man who likes "the piece of ass," although nothing suggests that she would like to offer herself as a delicacy for the butcher. The opposite is the case.

The patient's dream is presented as a wish that is conveyed by a demand, and even by a call, which responds to the friend's request and is symbolized by the telephone. The signification is clear; she would like to please her friend, but the supposed intention of the dream fails, thus revealing another: "If you think that I'm going to help you captivate my husband's lack. . . ."

The friend intervenes here as what sustains the desire—a desire that is to be understood simply as a lack—whereas the butcher's wife is the object of satisfaction. In this case, we have a minimal, very precise illustration, of a paradigmatic division in the hysteric: the split between the object of satisfaction and that of desire, between the jouissance-object and the lacking object. The notion of object-cause, which Lacan uses at certain periods of his teaching, condenses these two aspects of the object: it is, on the one hand, the object that is lacking and sustains desire, and on the other, the object as surplus jouissance. It thus has a double function: to cause the lack and to fill it up. The hysteric dissociates these two aspects:

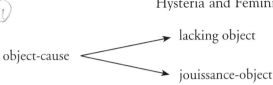

object-cause → lacking object

object-cause → jouissance-object

The Second Identification

The imaginary identification with the friend was thus not just any identification. Its motive force is on the symbolic axis of the subject's relation with the Other, who, in this case, is the husband. More precisely, what underlies this identification is a question about the desire of the Other: "Couldn't it be that he too has a desire that remains awry when all in him is satisfied?"[10] Does the butcher's wife look at her friend from the butcher's point of view? She interrogates the *agalma*, the friend's charm, the mystery of her seductive thinness from the man's point of view. The subject, signified by the metaphor of the dream, is therefore the question of the Other—here, the man—with whom, as subject, she has identified.

"The subject becomes this question here. In this respect, the woman identifies with the man, and the slice (*tranche*) of smoked salmon comes to occupy the place of the Other's desire."[11]

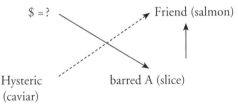

$ = ?

Friend (salmon)

Hysteric
(caviar)

barred A (slice)

Where does this slice of smoked salmon come from? This is the first time that Lacan introduces this signifier, whereas the translation of the dream-text mentioned "a little salmon." It is, in fact, a condensation: the salmon comes from the friend and the slice comes from the husband. Playing the *bon vivant*, he had spoken of a "nice piece of ass."[12]

---

10. *Ibid.*, p. 250.
11. *Ibid.*, p. 251.
12. *Ibid.*, p. 249. Lacan's original expression is "*une tranche* [a slice] *du train de derrière d'une belle garce.*" *Ecrits* (Paris: Editions du Seuil), p. 625. (Translator's note).

Thus the slice, like the "scant" meaning, is not the whole; it becomes the signifier of the desire of the Other. When Lacan says, "the woman identifies herself with the man," this is neither a rabbit that he pulls out of his hat nor a study of behavior and imaginary posturing; it is the result of the deciphering of signifiers. This has nothing to do with any psychological intuition.

There are thus two identifications. The first, with the friend, is on the imaginary axis, and the second is on the symbolic: it is the identification with the man's desire. We can immediately see that the hysterical woman's identification with the man does not at all exclude a pantomime of femininity; the patient's game with the caviar is a part of the feminine masquerade. Her playing the man's part [*faire l'homme*]"[13] is at the unconscious level of desire and has nothing to do with any boyish appearance.

The Third Identification

If we remained only with this second identification, we would be led to think of the hysterical subject as an eternal question. She would be someone whose being could be defined with a formula: that of the question of the Other. Yet the question of the Other is not ineffable. It has a signifier: the phallus, which is defined here as the signifier of the lack, and in relation to which there is a third identification. "To be the phallus, even a somewhat skinny one—isn't that the ultimate identification with the signifier of desire?"[14]

$$\frac{\Phi}{\$} = ?$$

This expression of a final identification looks forward to Lacan's developments, in "Position of the Unconscious," concerning what he calls the axis of separation, in which the subject separates him/herself from the signifiers of the Other by identifying with the signifier or the objects of his/her desire. The three identifications in play in the dream

---

13. Depending upon the context, "*faire l'homme*" can be translated as "playing the man's part" or "making the man."

14. *Ibid.*, p. 251.

are thus quite distinct: the first is an identification with the object that sustains desire; the second is with the subject of desire; the third is with the signifier of desire. The subject, if she said "I," could say, "I am certainly a lack in being (*manque à être*), but at least I can be what is lacking in the Other. "Being the phallus" is the formula of desire in the witty butcher's wife's dream, and it is a wish to make herself be through the Other's lack.

HYSTERIA AND THE FEMININE POSITION

Lacan also uses the same expression, "being the phallus," to designate women's position in the sexed relation (*relation*). Should we conclude from this that hysteria is one with femininity, as etymology, which derives "hysteria" from the uterus, would apparently have it?

Let us distinguish the wish to be the phallus from the position in the sexual relation (*relation*) that makes a woman into the phallus. The latter indicates not an identification but a place, that of the complement of masculine desire. The formula of the fantasy, $S \diamond a$, visualizes the dissymmetry between the desiring subject and the partner as the object that is complementary to his desire. This object can be approached as the image of a, but also as a signifier, since there are symbolic conditions for the choice of object—and as the jouissance of a. In all cases, it takes on its value by being what responds to the subject's phallic lack. What translates this dissymmetry is that, in the sexual relation (*relation*), it is necessary that the man desire, while it is sufficient for the woman to allow herself to desire—it is sufficient for her to consent. Thus we must examine the question of what, beyond this consent, is a specifically feminine desire.[15]

The question cannot be decided by the sexual act, for there are various ways of locating oneself in such a desire. On this point, Lacan distinguishes very categorically between the woman's and the hysteric's ways, although they can be combined. To identify with desire, as in the case of the hysteric, excludes identifying with the object of jouissance.

---

15. See the chapters, "A Woman" and "What Does the Unconcious Say about Women?"

This thesis can be found throughout Lacan's teaching, although his way of formulating it varied according to the period.[16]

Thus we have the idea, which can always be verified, that in the relation with the partner, the hysterical subject conducts a strategy of subtraction. An "eluding," as Lacan says, and Freud had already brought to light the double movement of seduction and refusal, the hand that lifts the skirt and the one that pulls it back down. The beautiful butcher's wife shows this in a charming and inoffensive form: she does not refuse herself to her husband's jouissance, and we know exactly what jouissance she herself gets from this, but we know that the only thing that interests her is what is unsatisfied in her husband. If she identifies with her friend, it is to try, at least imaginarily, to make her satisfied husband dissatisfied. There is nothing malign about this; there is only the wish to make herself into what is lacking in the Other.

The case of Dora is no less exemplary. For her, it is true, the Other is divided. There are two men: Herr K., the man who has the organ and would like to get off, and the father, who is said explicitly to be impotent. He is certainly interested in Frau K., and he obtains some benefit from this, but in any case, he is not interested in her, in terms of the specifically phallic jouissance of the organ. For the beautiful butcher's wife, these two men—the man of sexual jouissance and the man with an impotent sexual desire—have been united into a single man: the butcher of jouissance and the butcher of desire. Yet what fascinates both of these men is the *agalmatic* object, which makes them desire. From Frau K. to the Madonna, this is all that interests Dora.

It should not be concluded from this that the hysterical subject refuses any jouissance to herself. She is a subject who consumes the lack,

---

16. I will give only a few markers of these developments: "Intervention on Transference," in 1951, already imputed to Dora a difficulty in identifying with her sex; in 1958, the case of the beautiful butcher's wife gives the paradigm of the choice of the lack of desire over jouissance. Lacan reaffirms this in 1973, in his "Introduction to the German Edition of the *Ecrits*": "the hysteric identifies with the lack taken as object, and not with the cause of lack." Finally, in 1979, in a lecture on Joyce (*Joyce avec Lacan*, p. 35), he distinguishes explicitly between a woman as symptom and the symptom-hysteric.

and this is very much a jouissance, but it is not a living jouissance. In other words, to get off on the lack and to get off on the flesh are very different things. What defines the hysterical position very precisely is the will to leave jouissance unsatisfied. What certainly helps mislead clinicians is that hysterics, especially today, do not refuse to sleep with men, and may even collect lovers. Yet to conclude from this that they are devoted to jouissance. . . . The psychoanalytic clinic is not guided by an observation of conduct, even if it often allows us to account for the anomalies and mysteries of such conduct.

A woman's position is different, and Lacan defines it in the opposite way. I have already mentioned his interpretation of feminine desire in his 1958 text, in which he responded to Freud's famous question, "What does woman want?" The response can be summarized as "She wants to obtain jouissance." Not only does it [ça] get off more, which was the message of Teiresias, but it also wants to get off.[17]

It could not be said that the hysterical subject wants to have jouissance, nor could we say the contrary. What, then, does she want? We can disengage a formula from what has already been said. The hysteric, in introducing a lack of satisfaction into the jouissance of the Other, aims at extra being (un plus d'être). A woman wants to get off; the hysteric wants to be. She even requires that she be—be something for the Other, not an object of jouissance, but the precious object that nourishes desire and love. A table of the differential traits that Lacan proposes for the two structures can be drawn up. On woman's side, on the left, the reference is to jouissance, and thus there is a plus; on the hysteric's side, on the right, there is a reference to desire, a minus. On the left side, there is a wanting to get off; on the right side, there is a wanting to be. To complete the table, we must characterize of the truth of this actual jouissance and clarify a woman's wanting to obtain it. It is matched by wanting to give jouissance to someone else. The jouissance that a man gets from a woman divides her, as Lacan says in "L'étourdit." This means that the partner's jouissance comes in the place of the cause of her own desire. Let us distinguish clearly between the woman's bid

---

17. Lacan often translates Freud's term "es," which the Standard Editiion renders as the "id," as "ça." (Translator's note).

for jouissance (*offre à jouir*) for the Other—that differs from the hysteric's bid for desire (*offre à désirer*)—and on the other hand, the jouissance that is specific to woman. Indeed, it often happens that there are women who want neither to make the man get off—this is the hysteric's primary perversion, which Freud had no difficulty in perceiving—nor to get off, for jouissance is not necessarily desirable.

Woman	Hysteric
ref. Jouissance + wanting to get off or make a man get off $S(\cancel{A})$	ref. Desire − wanting to be $\$ \longrightarrow S_1$ $\overline{}$ $a \qquad S_2$

$$S(\cancel{A})$$
$$\uparrow$$
$$\Phi \longleftarrow \text{---} \quad \cancel{\text{Woman}}$$

MAKING (SOMEONE) DESIRE

In writing the discourse of the hysteric, Lacan wants to show, first, what is most valuable about her: she obtains from the master the production of a knowledge, as the relation of Socrates to Plato and of the hysterics to Freud shows:

$$\frac{\$}{a} \quad \frac{S_1}{S_2}$$

Yet her truth is different from this, and there is a gap between this truth and what her discourse obtains, for the hysterical subject would like—I am using the modal "would" to mark its impossibility—there to be *a knowledge of the object.* She wants the Other to be able to say what the precious object, woman as *agalma*, is; what is a question, indeed, is not only for the hysteric to make the Other desire sexually, but to make him say what the cause is. Thus there is the lack of satisfaction that hits up against what is impossible to say and which is maintained by all the kinds of knowledge that are produced. "Tell me what your desire is aiming at, in me or the other!" This question, which certainly keeps lovers talking, also has a function connected with the superego. This is not, however, the superego of a push-to-jouissance, but rather that of a push-to-knowledge. This is where Charcot fell short. The hysterical subject is certainly seeking a man, but a man who is animated by the desire to know; she is seeking a man to know the object.

The result, in the history of psychoanalysis, is that the series of partial objects was established thanks to the hysterics whom Freud listened to. They were all animated with desire as the desire of the Other—the man—and they instructed Freud not about woman, but about the cause of masculine desire. For a woman, divided (écartelée) as she is between the signifier of the phallus (Φ) and that of the lack in the Other, S(A̶), the partner is not the object a.

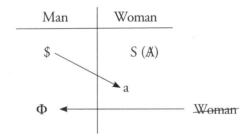

Hysterics were necessary for this; the a priori of the sexual prejudice that judges the partner by its own standards led people to believe that they were talking about women, whereas, as in the butcher's wife's dream, they were speaking the language of the male partner.

On these questions, it is true, Lacan varied his formulations. In the place where he distinguished the sexes by "having or being the phallus," he came to say, "having or being a symptom." The two formulas are not equivalent; instead, they are the opposite of each other. The phallus is a negative function of lack; the symptom is a positive function of jouissance. Thus wanting "to be the phallus," by which Lacan stigmatized the hysteric at one time, means precisely not wanting to be the symptom. This is what he makes explicit in the second lecture on Joyce, in 1979, in which he accentuates again the difference between the hysteric's and the woman's position. A woman, he says, is specified by *being* a symptom. This is not the case with the hysteric, who is characterized by "being interested in the other's symptom," and who is therefore not the last symptom, but only the "next-to-last."

To be a unique symptom, at least for One, is not, properly speaking, the hysteric's requirement, as we have known since Dora. This is translated in experience by the fact that, even one to one, the hysterical subject does not make up a couple, but at least a triangle and sometimes more. The clinical difficulty is that the reciprocal is not true. A woman, whether she is obsessional, phobic, or even psychotic, can also have something to do with what I could call her rivals in the symptom, without the latter taking on the role that the other woman plays in hysteria. Moreover, the obsessional man has his own triangle, for he nourishes his desire with that of an alter ego. For the hysteric, in any case, to be interested in the other's symptom means not to consent to *being* the symptom. Yet this is also not to have a symptom that is identical with a man's. Contrary to what one may imagine too hastily, whoever is not *one* woman is not necessarily a man. Lacan, indeed, notes that Socrates is not a man. There is a third position: that of having a symptom by the proxy. This does not imply the body-to-body relation, as Lacan makes clear. We could follow in Lacan's teaching all the formulas by which he progressively approaches this affirmation. It is certain that Dora is interested in Frau K. as a symptom, but she does not want to be Frau K. and she slaps Herr K. when he offers her his wife's place. Since the beautiful butcher's wife bears, in reality, her husband's assiduous attentions, she shows even more clearly that she only dreams of leaving the place of the symptom and, as Lacan says in *L'envers de la psychanalyse*, of leaving her dear butcher to someone else. As for Socrates, it is quite clear that he does not want to be Alcibiades's symptom, but that he is interested in Agathon, the one who holds that place.

We can understand, nevertheless, why hysteria lends itself to confusion with the feminine position and why it is more frequent in women. Femininity implies the relation with the Other, man, in order to make oneself into a symptom. A woman's accent on the "making him get off" does not exclude "making him desire," which is its condition. Thus, it seems to me, the hysterical kernel in women is accentuated. The hysteric is also mediated by the Other, but for different ends, and not in order to make herself into his symptom. As a discourse, hysteria determines a subject who is never alone, even if she is isolated, a subject who is always coupled in reality with another who is defined by the master signifier, and whom the subject interrogates concerning his desire to know about the sex. Her desire is nourished by the symptom of the Other, to the point that it could almost be said that she makes herself its cause, but the cause, in this case, is that of knowledge. It is not that the desire for knowledge animates her, but that she would like to inspire it in the other.

How can the hysteric's "making the man" (*faire l'homme*) be situated? The expression has several meanings. First of all, it designates the hysteric's challenge, her "show us if you are a man," in the sense of "Will the brave men stand up?" but also her identification with a man. This identification, however, is not just any identification, and it is here that we often make mistakes. It can be an identification with his possession of the phallus, or on the contrary, with his lack of it. Both, indeed, can be found together in the same subject, but the specifically hysterical identification—which we find in Dora and the beautiful butcher's wife—as Lacan reformulates it in his text of 1973, "Introduction to the German Edition of the *Ecrits*," is to identify with the man inasmuch as he is not fulfilled, as he is also unsatisfied, and as his jouissance is castrated. The clinician can easily get lost here, for the consequences of this identification can be present in experience in the form of the semblances of extreme femininity. Take a look at the beautiful butcher's wife: on the imaginary, visible level, she acts as a woman, in competition with her friend. Yet the result of this masquerade is that on the symbolic level, as subject, she identifies with the man as lacking.

We can also grasp why Lacan can argue that in hysteria, man is superior to woman. The desire to make someone desire knowledge is not limited, in him, by jouissance. If we follow Lacan, Socrates, in this respect, is the paradigm. He calls to Alcibiades, wants to involve him in his dialectic, in the elaboration of philosophical knowledge, but seeks to worm out of him the effect neither of love nor of jouissance. So little does he seek it that when Alcibiades offers it to him, he refuses it and remains completely unruffled in the face of the younger man's passion.

In this relation to the Other, let us not, however, forget God, the barred Other par excellence. When Lacan affirms, in *Encore*, that what a woman is concerned with is God, the statement seems enigmatic, especially if we apply it to contemporary women. Yet there is always, beyond man, an Other who is more Other than man, precisely because of the latter's phallic quality. The conviction that the phallic key tells us what is essential about man animates what women say when they talk to each other. Lacan touched on the same aspiration when he said in 1958 that regardless of whom a woman embraces, what she really wishes for herself is a castrated man[18]: an Other whose enigma would not be limited by the phallic key.

FEMININE LOVE

In order to mark out the border between femininity and hysteria, I am going to come back now to women's love, which is often said to be jealous and exclusive. It is jealous because it demands being. Indeed, it does more than demand it: in its moments of reciprocal plenitude, it succeeds in producing, as a temporary effacement of the effect of lack in being, a transitory corrective to castration. This rather obvious side of the common experience is accentuated in hysteria, but is not peculiar to it. It is more or less present in all subjects, despite some differences between men and women.

On the other hand, feminine love is jealous because it is connected—and this is what is most interesting—with the characteristics of her jouissance. Unlike phallic jouissance, the other, supplementary jouissance "goes beyond" the subject. It does so, first of all, by being heterogeneous to the discontinuous structure of the phenomena regulated by language, with the consequence that this jouissance does not provide an identification.

We can see how this is different from a man's situation, since phallic jouissance, which has the same discontinuous structure as the phenomena of the subject, has a value as identification. Men boast of their performances, which are always phallic, and the more they accumulate phallic jouissance, the more they see themselves as men. This begins in elementary school when boys show each other their organs, compare

---

18. Lacan, "Guiding Remarks for a Congress on Feminine Sexuality," p. 95.

them, and exercise them by seeing who can pee the furthest. The organ does not yet function on the strictly sexual plane, but discourse has already let the boy know that he is going to be measured by it. Later, there will be sexual conquests, which will be counted when one is a man. It even happens sometimes, and this is an amusing phenomenon, that celebrities, on the advice of their publicists, will claim to have a mistress whom they have never been involved with, because this shows that they are real men. Indeed, where we come from, all the well-known men of politics, show business, or sports deck themselves out with a woman. This is a fact. Perhaps nothing less is necessary if a man is to touch the imaginary that is specific to a community. It is as if we knew that in showing his woman, a man is showing himself. We can see, furthermore, that the decomposed families of our day have not yet become the norm. At all levels—in politics, the professions, money—a man assures himself of being a man through a phallic appropriation.

It is not the same situation for a woman. Phallic jouissance—that of power—in love or elsewhere, is certainly not forbidden to her. It is obvious that what has been called women's liberation gives them more and more access to all of its forms. The problem is that to do as well as men does not make you a woman. Thus there arise the subjective conflicts that psychoanalysis has been able to locate for a long time, and the forms of which vary with the period; they go from phallic appropriation to a sense of being troubled about being a woman, as is sometimes said.

The other, specifically feminine jouissance does not provide women with any more reassurance. Except in exceptional cases, a woman does not make herself recognized as a woman by the number of her orgasms or the intensity of her ecstasies. Far from publicizing this jouissance, she may happen to hide it. In other words, since she cannot become Woman (La femme), what remains is to be one woman, chosen by a man. She borrows the "one" from the Other, in order to assure herself that she is not just any subject. This is precisely what she is as a speaking being, who is subject to phallicism, but she would like, in addition, to be identified as a chosen woman. We can thus understand why women, whether or not they are hysterics, love love more than men do.

5

Are Women Masochistic?

*[E]verything gets ascribed to woman in so
far as she represents, in the phallo-centric
dialectic, the absolute Other.[1]*

The question that was a stumbling block for Freud, "What does
woman want?," continues to haunt discourses, and an answer has been
circulating: she wants to suffer. Psychoanalysts, hard pressed to grasp
the essence of femininity, forged the thesis of feminine masochism. It
seemed inconceivable to them that a subject could offer herself as an
object—the case of woman in her relation to man's desire—without
being a masochist! The masochist, playing out his scenario, strives to
show himself "ironically" as an object: "do with me what you will."
Women, on their side, deplore, at the top of their voices, what the alienation specific to their position leads them to bear. They deplore it to
the point that one wonders what can push them to take this position,
since nothing obliges them to do so if they do not want to. Lacan notes
this. Thus there is also the cry of the feminists I have mentioned, those

---

1. Jacques Lacan, "Guiding Remarks for a Congress on Feminine Sexuality,"
p. 94.

who, pushing their extreme position to the point of wanting to proscribe every sexual relation, interrogate their female colleagues by asking, "Women, are you masochists?" Yet it is not the crossing of the limits of the pleasure principle that constitutes masochism; that, rather, would be the universal masochism of the speaking being, which has nothing specifically feminine about it.

The guilty statements of this conception come from Freud, especially in his two texts of 1919 and 1924, "A Child Is Being Beaten" and "The Economic Problem of Masochism." The thesis does not maintain that there are masochistic women—there are some, and there are also masochistic men. It is also not contented simply to affirm that women suffer—they suffer, indeed, from the lack of the phallus, but no more than men suffer from the threat of castration. Freud's thesis affirms that feminine desire is masochistic in essence, that it aims to attain jouissance through pain, even to make itself the martyr of the other. This is a prejudice, Lacan says, and even a "monstrous" one. Post-Freudian analysts, especially women, were more than willing to maintain this prejudice, and the thesis has "remain[ed] unchallenged in face of the accumulation" of clinical facts that go in the opposite direction.[2] Yet beyond Freud's specific statements, is this really his thesis?

THE METAPHOR OF MASOCHISM

Freud's formulas, at least if we isolate them, seem to leave no place for doubt. There are many of them, and I will quote the two most striking. Mentioning the scenarios of masochistic men, he says and repeats that "their masochistic attitude coincides with a feminine one."[3] More radically still, he introduces the notion of "feminine masochism," by distinguishing it from erotogenic or moral masochism, and defines it as the "expression of the feminine nature."[4]

---

2. *Ibid.*, p. 92.

3. Sigmund Freud, "A Child Is Being Beaten: A Contribution to the Study of the Origin of Sexual Perversions," trans. Alix and James Strachey. *Standard Edition of the Complete Psychological Works*, Vol. XVII (London: Hogarth Press, 1955), p. 197.

4. Sigmund Freud, "The Economic Problem of Masochism," trans. Joan Riviere. SE XIX, p. 161.

Freud comments enough on these formulas for there to be no doubt about what they mean in context. They do not aim at throwing light on the problem of femininity, but rather on perverse fantasies and practices, especially in men.[5] They inscribe the imaginary equivalence that Freud discovers between the masochist's tendency to "get himself beaten" and what he calls the feminine "role" in the sexual relation. In order to get himself treated as the father's object—an expression that Freud makes equivalent to getting himself treated as a woman—the masochist has no other recourse than to get himself beaten. We see that here, the term "feminine position" should be clarified. It does not designate directly what we call a subjective position. It refers, first of all, to a place in the sexual couple, where it is the other, man, who is the subject of desire. Freud's insistence on emphasizing the link between the masochistic fantasy and oedipal desire, the strongly affirmed identification of the other who does the beating with the father—even when in the subject's conscious imagination, it is the mother—indicates clearly that he is exploring one of the versions of the sexual couple.

He enumerates, first of all, the metonymies of representations of jouissance: "being gagged, bound, painfully beaten, whipped, in some way maltreated, forced into unconditional obedience, dirtied and debased"[6]; then the order and varieties of drives implied: oral, anal, sadistic, whether one offers oneself to be "eaten up, beaten, possessed sexually"[7]; finally, the series of incarnations of the object: the dependent child, the bad child, the woman as castrated and undergoing coitus. As we see, Freud is exploring methodically one of the versions of the object that complements masculine desire. And he discovers, to his surprise, without quite stating it, what Lacan will formulate some years later: this object is asexual. This is what he says in qualifying it as "pregenital." Masochism is thus invoked here, in fact, as what makes up for the nonexistent sexual relation, according to Lacan's later formula. It is a metaphor.

Freud's definition of what is "unmistakeably masochistic in character"[8] confirms this. Masochism, according to him, substitutes one

---

5. *Ibid.*, p. 162.
6. *Ibid.*, p. 165.
7. *Ibid.*
8. Freud, "A Child Is Being Beaten," p. 185.

formula of jouissance for another: "being beaten" is substituted for "being loved" in the genital sense. Freud qualifies this substitution as "regressive," which is usually repeated without our thinking any more about it. With this qualification, he really introduces something very precise, which, most often, remains unnoticed. For Freud, regression means a real change in the unconscious. Repression effaces a desire from the stage, but maintains it unchanged, similar to itself in the unconscious. Regression, on the contrary, as Freud says, changes the state of things in the unconscious. What is he saying, if not that the desire and the jouissance that he calls regressive are really different? We can deduce that for Freud, being an object in a masochistic way and being an object in the sexual relation are two different modes of desire and jouissance. Freud certainly qualifies the masochism that he discovers in men as "feminine." He does so to mark that, in the genesis of this masochism, if the subject ends up aspiring to be beaten, it is to be like the woman possessed by the father. Yet since he adds that a regressive substitution produces a real change in the unconscious, he indicates, precisely, the heterogeneity of the masochistic and feminine aspirations; he shows that being beaten and being in the place of woman are not the same.

It is noteworthy, incidentally, that when Freud tries to approach the question of feminine desire, in his later texts of 1925, 1931, and 1932,[9] he does not have recourse to masochism. The sequence of his elaborations should be noted. He answers, first, for the little girl: she wants the penis. If one were to ask, "What does man want"—it is striking that no one dreams of asking this question without already having the answer—it would have to be said that he wants an object whose value as surplus jouissance (*plus-de-jouir*) compensates for the minus jouissance (*moins de jouir*) of castration. In spite of their differences, the two sexes are equal here in their common reference to the phallus. Freud uses only one compass to distinguish man from woman: the avatars of castration, a single reference, the only one that can be verified. He therefore approaches the specificity of women only by the subjectiva-

---

9. See respectively the papers "Some Psychical Consequences of the Anatomical Distinction between the Sexes: Moral Masochism, *SE* XIX; "Female Sexuality," *SE* XXI; and the chapter "Femininity," in the *New Introductory Lectures on Psychoanalysis, SE* XXII.

tion of the lack of the phallus. Let us note parenthetically that this lack is precisely what opens up for woman the possibility of being an object, without being the beaten object—although it sometimes happens that she gets herself beaten, whether she wants to or not. The sequence of Freud's developments thus begins by reducing the Other to the One. Has he been reproached enough for this?

This reproach is not completely justified. Freud, reaching the end of his elaborations on the question of "What does woman want?," indicates unquestionably that he perceives the "partiality" of the phallic solution, in the sense of incompleteness, rather than of bias and preference. The first pages of the text "Femininity" set down very explicitly that "psycho-analysis does not try to describe what a woman is"; that, Freud says, is a "task it could scarcely perform." This remark follows two precise observations. In the first, Freud asks himself anew about the possibility of assimilating passiveness and femininity. He concludes categorically that this conception "serve[s] no useful purpose and adds nothing to our knowledge."[10] In the second, he returns to the hypothesis of masochism. He reaffirms that masochism is feminine, for the "suppression of women's aggressiveness . . . is prescribed for them constitutionally and imposed on them socially,"[11] but he recoils from affirming that women are masochistic as such. He notes that there are masochistic men as well, and draws the consequence of this: we "are already prepared to hear that psychology too is unable to solve the riddle of femininity."

My conclusion is that Freud perceived that the reference to the phallus did not exhaust the question of femininity, and that he did not confuse what is beyond the phallus with the masochistic drive. In this sense, the thesis of the "masochistic woman" is not Freud's: he introduced and explored it, but knew how to recognize that it was not the answer.

I note moreover that at the end of his article on feminine sexuality, Freud passes in review—and it is a rare case in his work—the various contributions brought to the question by his contemporary students. He mentions Helene Deutsch's article on women's

---

10. Freud, "Femininity," p. 102.
11. Ibid.

masochism.[12] One would therefore expect him to take a position on this thesis, but he does not do so at all. It is rather piquant to see that he congratulates her for something very different: her recognition of the primary, preoedipal relation to the mother. He thus remains, in his sound prudence, one step ahead of some of the post-Freudians. Exploring the masochistic fantasy, he discovers, in reality, something else. First of all, he finds the function of fantasy itself, inasmuch as it transcends clinical structures for both sexes and remains, in part, isolated from the symptomatic content of the neurosis. Then, he discovers the affinity between suffering and what, since Lacan, we have called jouissance. In fact, the texts that Freud devotes to masochism, which are precious in many respects, teach us nothing about women in themselves, but a lot about the sexual nonrelation and the paradoxical jouissance of the speaking being.

The post-Freudian confusions may not be worth so much interest. Lacan, in taking up the question again, rejects them as falling short of Freud's work. Most of them have placed very heterogeneous phenomena under the heading of masochism. Under this category, they have confused, first of all, masochistic perversion properly speaking, and second, what the activity of the drive implies about what is beyond the pleasure principle, and third, more generally, what each subject pays for his desire, as the price of the surplus of jouissance that his fantasy ensures for him. Fantasy certainly rests on a limit to jouissance, but one can also notice, in every case, that the logic of a life is reduced to an elementary arithmetic that founds what is *a priori* in the fantasy; the entire question about this concerns the surplus jouissance that is to pass by losses and profits. To consent to paying this price, however, does not make one a masochist. If so, what is in question would be the universal masochism of the subject, and we would have to say that we are all masochists; this is all the more true if there is a decisive desire.

These confusions are certainly not innocent, especially when women are in question. We sometimes perceive strange prejudices, where the idealizing function of the imputation of masochism comes to the surface. I will extract from Helene Deutsch's book *A Psychology of Women*[13] an

---

12. Freud, "Female Sexuality," p. 227.
13. Helene Deutsch, *A Psychology of Women: A Psychoanalytic Interpretation*, Vol. I (New York: Grune & Stratton, 1944), p. 288.

example that is both paradigmatic and amusing: her commentary on the character of Carmen. With a touching freshness, she explains why this character moves every woman profoundly. It is because Carmen's behavior with men is like that of a child who pulls the wings off a fly. Such actions have shaken every woman to the depths of her being. Very well, then, but why? Is it because she is going to spirit away the precious organ, which has been turned into a signifier? Not at all! Here is Helene Deutsch's priceless commentary: each woman recognizes Carmen's tragic and unconscious "archfeminine masochism."[14] For, let us not be mistaken, in destroying a man, she is destroying her own heart, and ensuring her own loss. This is certainly surprising. Let us imagine for a moment this argument applied to all the tormenters in the world, to the torturers of every kind who have made up human history. . . .

IMPRESSIONS OF MASOCHISM

A differential clinic of the masochistic and the feminine positions thus remains to be made. I will begin to do so with this observation: there must be something that lends itself to a confusion, in order for the thesis to be argued, and I will mention some clinical facts. Among others, there is the following: women themselves deplore their own masochism. What, then, do a masochist and a woman have in common? The answer is simple: both of them, in the couple that they form with the partner who is supposed to be desiring, put themselves in the place of the object. This place obviously evokes a third term: the analyst. The masochist, the woman, and the analyst form a series in that all three of them play the role of a "semblance of the object"—by modes that are, of course, very different; nothing allows us to suppose that whenever someone makes him/herself a semblance of the object, the same desire is always in question. Thus we must raise the question of masochistic desire, feminine desire, and the desire of the analyst.

When we speak of woman's being, let us not forget that this being is divided between what she is for the other and what she is as subject of desire, between, on the one hand, a being that complements masculine

---

14. *Ibid.*, p. 38.

castration, and on the other, her being as subject of the unconscious. Lacan sometimes noted that the direct cause of her place in the sexual couple is not her own desire but the desire of the other. For her, it is enough to allow herself to desire, in the sense of giving her consent. The phenomenon of rape indicates sufficiently that this consent is not even a necessary condition. Lacan, in the course of the years, as his teaching progressed, designated this being for the Other with various formulas. We can isolate three of them: "being the phallus," which no one can be in herself, "being the object" and finally, in 1975, "being the symptom," but all of them leave unanswered the question of the desire of whoever comes at the place of this object. This is why the desires of the masochist, woman, and the analyst are problematic to us.

It remains then for a woman, as I have indicated above, to deduce her desire from her position in the sexual couple, since one can obviously suppose that the consent mentioned a moment ago is the index of a desire. Freud himself understands it in this way when he slides from the erotic role—being possessed genitally—to the subjective "disposition" that is supposed to correspond to it, and which he formulates with a wish: to be loved . . . by the father.

I have said "to play the role of the object [faire l'objet]," not to signify a pretense but because the expression has the merit of permitting us a nuance of artifice that emphasizes that being for the Other cannot be realized without the mediation of the semblance. The imaginary is therefore also in play. It is true of the analyst who lends him/herself to the transference, like the woman whose masquerade was recognized even before Joan Riviere named it. Contrary to what could be believed, this is also true of the masochist, who passes to the act only on a stage. Freud rightly emphasized the game-like quality of this scenario, whereas Lacan, on various occasions, pointed out that masochism should not be taken to be true; the masochist, whom he qualifies as a "delicate humorist," exalts " a demonstrative figure through his simulation."[15]

We can try to give a first approximation of the guises of the object in these three cases: the masochist wants himself to be a disparaged object; he cultivates the appearance of something that has been cast off and makes himself into a piece of trash. A woman, on the con-

15. Jacques Lacan, "La psychanalyse dans ses rapports avec la réalité," *Scilicet* I, Paris: Editions du Seuil, 1958, p. 58.

trary, dresses herself up in phallic brilliance in order to be the *agalmatic* object. The analyst, depending on the metamorphoses imposed on him by transference, passes from the status of the *agalma* of the subject-supposed-to-know, which he is at the beginning, to the state of a scrap, which he becomes in the end. Thus the question is to know what can push him to reproduce this "arrangement."

These differentiations are merely a first approximation, for the *agalmatic* object becomes powerful only through the lack that it includes. This structural fact is the foundation of what could very well be called a "masochistic masquerade." Without it, the thesis of feminine masochism would have been less plausible. Masquerade, doubtless, has several facets. Most often, it hides lack, playing with the beautiful or with having in order to cover it over. Yet there is also a masochistic masquerade, which, conversely, makes a display of the lack, or pain, or even the pain of lack. The masochistic masquerade sometimes goes to the point of creating rivalries on the basis of insufficiencies, and even of fomenting false weaknesses.

An example from my practice has remained memorable for me in this respect. It is that of a young woman who experienced what she called the "hell of her overdraft (*l'enfer du découvert*)." In spite of the linguistic equivocation of the French word *découvert*, she herself meant it in the most realistic sense, as related to banking.[16] This object was watched over by her husband and led to almost daily disputes with him. Since she had monthly revenues, the overdraft also was part of a monthly cycle, which went from obsessive fear to the payment; the squabbling that went on within the couple oscillated between admonitions and reproaches. It can be guessed that the husband was called on to act as the supplier in charge of restocking the bank account. He did not shy away from this task, but did not act without protesting, without making her ask for help, without leading her to make a request, and all of this usually ended in tears and in love. This game lasted for a certain time, until fate intervened and a small inheritance came to fill in the overdraft and disorganize the couple's life. I will pass over the details. "Now, you're the arrogant one," the husband said to her. He then became the complainer ("I'm no longer of any use") and refused

---

16. The author is playing on the similarity between the words *découvert* (overdraft) and *découverte* (discovery) (Translator's note.).

her good offices. The patient ended up saying something rather strange: "I knew very well that he couldn't know about my money." It turned out that this woman, since she had come of age, had always had two bank accounts, only one of which had been known about, first by the father and then by the husband. In the secret account, she had what she called her "little nest egg," for since the age of seventeen, she had regularly deposited into it all the money that she could subtract from the Other's gaze, which allowed her to hide what she was earning and to play the poor woman. This masquerade, which went to the point of a true simulation, used the pretense of a lack of money as a metonymy of the lack of the phallus, which had a seductive value. We should not, however, suppose that she had a miserly jouissance of having the phallus, for she gave no other index of this; what ravished her was, instead, the secret character of having it.

The logic of the masochistic masquerade is not difficult to grasp: it is what could be called an unconscious adaptation to the implication of castration in the field of love. Since the object's imaginary trait of castration is one of the conditions for object choice in man, everything happens as if an unconscious guess imposed something like a calculation: if he loves the poor, then let's make her poor. We should not, however, believe, contrary to what my preceding example allows us to suppose, that there is only simulation here, for accommodation can go up to the point of actual sacrifice. What the masquerade has in common with masochism is that it makes the underside of the *agalmatic* object shine forth. It brings out the lack that founds the brilliance of this object, and that may announce the fate that has been promised to it in love: the reduction of the other to a surplus jouissance.

IMPRESSIONS OF WOMAN

Lacan, in saying that feminine masochism "is a fantasy of the desire of the man,"[17] gives us the key to the situation. This situation is produced in the intersection of two factors: on the one hand, the conditions of man's desire require the object to have the signification of

---

17. "Guiding Remarks for a Congress on Feminine Sexuality," p. 92.

castration, Women's famous accommodation to the masculine fantasy, which pushes them to the unlimited "concessions" that Lacan stigmatizes in *Television*, engenders, among other effects, the masochistic masquerade and makes its meaning clear to us: the traits of suffering and lack that are exhibited are paid into the account of what Lacan called "the misfortunes of *vers-tu*,"[18] in order to designate the tribulations of what is sought for in the desire or jouissance of the Other.

Apart from the role played by the semblance, the masochistic masquerade differs greatly from the perverse scenario. In masquerade, a woman submits to the conditions of the Other's love in order for man's fantasy to find "its moment of truth" in her. Yet because of repression, the masquerade proceeds blindly, "completely by chance," as Lacan says, since the particular motive forces of the desire concealed by the unconscious are not known. We can see what favors the masochistic slope of masquerade: since castration is the only condition of desire that is valid for all, this masquerade is the least risky of all masquerades. It remains, however, at the mercy of fortune, good or bad, since castration only takes effect for each person in very particular forms.

The masochist himself leaves nothing to the *tuché*. On the contrary, he imposes a contractual relation on jouissance. What he claims to establish, more than a right to jouissance, is a regulated duty of jouissance, from which improvisation has been excluded, and of which he makes himself the master. Nothing can be more opposed to the feminine position, which is always located in the time of the Other. There can be no possible pact with the moment of truth. The sexual object, whatever may be the more or less typical parameters of an age's sex symbols—parameters that are sustained by an industry—is not contractual. This is why Lacan notes that "the social instance of woman" remains "transcendent to the order of the contract."[19]

Another, more essential opposition, is situated at the level of what the two of them are aiming at by means of—and through—the

---

18. Jacques Lacan, *L'envers de la psychanalyse*. Paris: Le Seuil, 1991, p. 75. *Vers-tu*, which can be translated as "toward you," is a homophone of *vertu* (virtue), and thus recalls the title of Sade's novel *Justine, or the Misfortunes of Virtue*. (Translator's note.)

19. "Guiding Remarks for a Congress on Feminine Sexuality," p. 98 (translation altered).

semblance. We must distinguish what they show about what they want. There is a simple opposition here: we certainly do not know very well what a woman is looking for, but let us admit that she is looking for it through love. On the contrary, it is well known that the true masochist, who is almost always a man, is aiming at the point of anxiety in the Other, the point where the semblances fail, the point before which, precisely, everyone recoils, for no one places himself willingly at the edge of pure anxiety. The masochist knows this, and founds the calm assurance of his "simulation"[20] on it, a simulation in which he shows himself as the cast-off object; this, at least, is how I understand Lacan's qualification of him as a "phony."

This is the point that the neurotic in general, especially the hysteric, carefully avoids, by choosing the lack of desire in order to guard against the possibility of the real of jouissance. In showing a strongly affirmed will to jouissance, which claims to be realized by pain, the masochist realizes in fact a desire that he does not know about, and that aims at the anxiety of the Other, the point where the mirages of the semblance disappear. Let us say that he makes himself the cause of the anxiety of the Other, as the only signal of what is real about the object, beyond the semblance that misses this real. The transgression of jouissance, which he programs, remains within wise limits, which do not extend beyond the fragmentation (*morcellement*) imposed on him by the signifier.

We can now see why women, as such, are not at all masochists. They do not at all aim at the Other beyond the semblance, a semblance to which their charms owe so much—almost everything. Feminine masquerade is neither the masochism that aims at the Other beyond the semblances, nor the lie that ungrateful people impute to it. It is, instead, an accommodation with the semblances; there is no limit, as Lacan says, to the concessions that a woman is ready to make for a man: of her body, her goods, her soul, everything that is good for her—in order to adorn herself so that man's fantasy can find its moment of truth in her.[21] The note of derision that she often brings to this, even if it is genuine, is also

---

20. Lacan, "La psychanalyse dans ses rapports avec la réalité," p. 58.

21. Jacques Lacan, *Television: A Challenge to the Psychoanalytic Establishment*, trans. Denis Hollier, Rosalind Krauss, and Annette Michelson (New York: W. W. Norton & Company, 1990), p. 40.

on the surface, although it marks with a touch of protest the alienation of her being to which the structure of sexuation condemns her. Yet to pass beyond this would be to sacrifice the semblance of woman herself. Experience shows that most women maintain this semblance.

To locate women's concessions as part of a masquerade is to mark the conditional character of their sacrifices, which are only the price paid for a very precise benefit. Let us say, in a condensed form, that a woman sometimes takes on a masochistic appearance, but only to give herself the appearance of a woman, by being a woman for a man, for want of being Woman. The love that she calls upon as a complement of castration in order to locate her being defines her subjection to the Other and her alienation; this alienation intensifies the alienation that is characteristic of the subject. Yet this is also the field, which feminists would almost make us forget, of her power as object-cause of desire.

Here also, however, she is obviously aiming at something beyond the semblance. Even more than an aiming, there is an access (see *Encore*) to an Other jouissance, which itself extends well beyond the discontinuities of phallic jouissance. The being-effect that is gained in love at the price of many concessions must be distinguished from the jouissance that is obtained as an addition and that itself goes beyond the semblance; this jouissance makes us relativize what her masquerade makes her renounce. The only disadvantage is the hazards of love.

"MORAL MASOCHISM"?

Here we can rethink the feminine position in respect to what Freud first called moral masochism. If Freud did not argue that women are masochistic, he did, on the contrary, discover and affirm a universal masochism in civilization. The taste for pain that seems to animate the perverse masochist interested Freud so much only because it works against the homeostasis of pleasure, and for this reason it came to shore up the 1920 hypothesis on what is beyond the pleasure principle. He returned to it in *Civilization and Its Discontents* in order to say that civilization educates people for the sacrificial position through its ever more unrestrained requirements to sublimate. What he formulates in this way is the sacrifice of the drives to the ideals of civilization. This is obviously a forced choice.

This theme of sacrifice merits further examination, and the current political situation gives it a renewed acuteness. There is a sacrifice in subjectivity as such; in order for the subject to arise, being must be sacrificed to the signifier. The sacrificial position, however, is something else. It is judged less by the objects that it immolates than by the motive force of the act itself—let us say the cause of the sacrifice. The objects that are to pass by profits and losses are more varied, since they have only a single trait in common: to represent for the subject any value of jouissance whatsoever. From this fact, what is to be sacrificed is related to the subject's singular interests and is not universal. Most often, the subject sacrifices one bit of surplus jouissance for another. These are "conditional" sacrifices necessitated by structure. Since an infinite jouissance has been excluded, the speakingbeing is condemned to conflicts of jouissance. (There are no other conflicts.) Everyone thus spends his time sacrificing one thing to another: the family to ambition, love to one's profession, happiness to knowledge, the child to the beloved man, the poor woman to the rich woman. Let us think of Marx and the hellish life that his surplus value cost him; let us also think of Oedipus and of the price to which he consented for his passion.

Concerning women's sacrifices, there is a well-known scenario, specified as such in the history of psychoanalysis: a woman's withdrawal in favor of the object, in subjects who renounce all personal ambition for the beloved man, whom they devote themselves to supporting. Helene Deutsch gives a rather exalted description of this type of abnegation, which she did not at all exemplify in her life, but in which she believes that she can recognize true femininity. This is, however, only a conditional sacrifice, which is subordinated to the narcissistic satisfaction of realizing herself by the other's authorization, as "the wife of. . . ." Here we are, when all is said and done, in the register of the calculus of satisfactions. Men and women do not, however, make the same use of these conditional sacrifices. Women ordinarily make a lot of noise about the price that they have had to pay in order to attain their ends. Men are usually more discreet, even modest, but this is doubtless because complaining is not compatible with the parade of manliness, whereas it is propitious to feminine masquerade.

What Freud describes in Chapter VII of *Civilization and Its Discontents* goes further. It is the true sacrificial position: it transforms the conditional sacrifice to the level of an end in itself, in an infernal logic that *wants* the ego to be "masochistic"—wants, in reality, jouissance to be derived from sacrificing the drive's satisfactions—in order to feed and maintain the ferocity of the gluttonous superego. In "Kant with Sade," Lacan echoes Freud's *Civilization*; in his imposing *Critique of Practical Reason*, Kant advocates that all that is pathological in our sensibilities must be sacrificed to the universal quality in the law,[22] and once this has been done, what remains is the hidden object: the booming voice that commands the sacrifice. Although this morality belongs to the age in which the voice of the prophets has fallen silent and wants, like science, to reach the universal, it remains no less fierce than that of earlier ages. The ruses of renunciation—it would be better to speak of jouissance by renunciation—make the civilized person, contrary to appearances, into a being who is fond of the lack of jouissance (*manque à jouir*) and the question is to know whether women contribute to this in "competition" with men.

The existence of such a competition is not Freud's thesis—far from it. His *Totem and Taboo* had already presented a society of brothers in renunciation, brothers in the jouissance of the lack of jouissance, which did not include women. When he claims that the superego's requirements are looser in women—and from his pen, this is not a compliment—he concludes logically that she is less inclined to sacrifice to civilization, and that she remains more rooted in primary satisfactions.

Haven't our own elaborations brought up to date the idea of a specifically feminine dose of contempt for having the phallus, a contempt that would go beyond its importance as masquerade and reach true sacrifice? Haven't I myself emphasized the superb detachment of Paul Claudel's Ysé in *Break at Noon*? Ysé, a true woman, according to Lacan, sacrificed everything to a fatal absolute. Madeleine, Gide's wife, in whom Lacan recognized Medea, has also been mentioned in this series.[23] What all three of them have in common is an absolute act, which shatters the half-measures of any dialectic, and which inaugurates a

---

22. I am using here the term through which Immanuel Kant isolates the subject's field of "pathological" interests from the unconditional imperative that confers upon the moral law its universal value.

23. Jacques Lacan, "Jeunesse de Gide, ou la lettre du désir," *Ecrits* (French Edition), 1966, p. 761.

point of no return. One, in her agitation, burns a group of beautiful love letters. The second will sacrifice even her beloved children in order to strike her partner and assuage her rage. Ysé does not fall completely into a series with the two others.

This theme of the sacrificing woman was not accentuated in preanalytic culture—quite to the contrary. The Old Testament has brought the sacrifice of Abraham into our own age; in this sacrifice, everything is played out between father and son. The judgment of Solomon certainly points to a woman's sacrificial renunciation, but like Norma, she is only there as a mother. As for Medea, who has been given so much attention, she illustrates, in fact, the contrary of feminine sacrifice: a woman's absolute vengeance triumphs over the mother's sacrifice. Where would we find a true feminine sacrifice? Iphigenia, Alcestis, Antigone: a daughter, a lover, and a sister could perhaps help us find the specific trait.

Madeleine and Medea are both characterized by their extreme vengeance. If Lacan recognizes the sign of woman in the bleak figure of Madeleine, this is not so much because she accepts losing the precious letters as because she strikes straight to the heart of the "exquisite pain," through an act that traverses the semblances. What was aimed at there was not having the phallus, but being, which cannot be substituted and is unique. This is what Gide confirms, when he mentions the black hole left in place of his heart by these lost letters, which, as Lacan notes, had no more of a duplicate copy than does the object a itself. It is not certain that for Madeleine, the trait of the loss that she herself undergoes, in the form of the precious letters, is dominant in her act. For her, hadn't these famous letters, which Gide saw as being identical with his being, been brutally dispossessed of their agalma, when she discovered how the all-inclusive vileness of jouissance challenged the discourse of exalted love?

Ysé is different. She abandons everything but sacrifices nothing, since for her, the only thing that still has any value is the jouissance of love that she encounters. Just as mourning concentrates all of the subject's libido and estranges it temporarily from the world, her love has taken her away from the world. This annihilation has its own logic: if love annuls the castration-effect for a time, and does so especially if it is absolute, then as a correlate, it empties the objects that respond to it of their value. This is why Lacan, when he wants to evoke the jouissance in woman that has no relation to the phallus, examines mystical experience, It is well known, indeed, that the mystic's ecstatic love subtracts her from her creaturely interests and from all common desires. This extraction has nothing to do, however, with the masochistic passion for sacrifice. The mystic testifies that she renounces the world joyously, not from a taste for suffering, but because what captivates her is the Other thing: the temptation—perhaps the dream—of abolishing oneself in the jouissance of an infinite love. This is the far-away, quasi-divine horizon, where what is resolved, beyond its significance as masquerade, is the masochism that is wrongly imputed to those whom Lacan names "the claimants of sex."[24]

Ysé, Madeleine, and Medea are not sacrificial figures, in the common sense of this term. It is true that they prefer the jouissance of being to that of having, the absolute to the countable, but only the ideology of having can interpret this as a sacrifice. Freud read such situations better when he recognized, instead, a refusal of the civilized superego. Perhaps this is one key for understanding what is being announced to us with so many statistics: that women today, in the age of the capitalist discourse, are more depressed than men.

---

24. Lacan, "Guiding Remarks for a Congress on Feminine Sexuality," p. 97.

6

A Feminine Affliction

For a certain time, if we have been listening to the voices of doctors as well as statistics, we have been hearing the news that, in modern civilization, women are more depressed than men. Whether true
or false, this little mystery is worth being explored.

THE QUARREL OVER DEPRESSION

There is a quarrel over depression. It involves a larger quarrel between psychoanalysis and psychiatry; the latter, in the name of an approach that claims to be scientific, proceeds more and more by foreclosing
the subject. This quarrel has already been going on for some time. Against
a psychiatry that believes that it is as modern as its pharmacopoeia, owes
its allegiance to an outmoded empiricism, and short-circuits the dimension of the subject whenever that is what is in question, we can
rightly denounce both the "conceptual misappropriation" of the term

"depression" and the inconsistency of the phenomena that it is supposed to subsume.

This conclusion has been reached so unanimously by so many studies that I will take it as established: depression, in the singular, simply does not exist. Depressive states certainly exist and can be described and inventoried, but their degrees and variations defy any unification of the concept. We can say "psychosis as such," "obsession as such," "hysteria as such," but we cannot say "depression as such." We cannot even say "depressions," as we would say "perversions," since we cannot describe the types that would give the term its consistency. At most, we can isolate, in a variety of phenomena, the consistency of melancholic psychosis, but on the condition that we do not reduce it to the mood of sadness.

Some new data must, nevertheless, be taken into account. As Lacan affirmed, facts do not exist outside language. On this account, we cannot doubt that the facts of depression are being multiplied in the discontents of civilization. We may deplore and denounce this, but it remains the case. The "we" that I am mentioning is that of the multitude, which is always nostalgic, and which dreams of other, more heroic or more stoic, or in any case more thrilling ages. Yet the fact remains in the complaints of subjects and in the diagnosis made for everything by physicians and psychiatrists. This new vogue of depression has already been criticized, but such criticism, unfortunately, has no chance of putting an end to the phenomenon. The psychoanalyst himself is concerned, for the complaint addressed to him is formulated ever more frequently in the vocabulary of depression, which both motivates the demand for an analysis and which often objects to the rule of being well-spoken (bien-dire).

We can insist that people are making this new reference to depression because they have been influenced to do so. The argument is pertinent—the more we diagnose depressed patients in the name of the physician's supposed knowledge, the more there will be subjects who say that they are depressed—but it is also empty and undiscriminating. Isn't this what usually happens? Except for the specific inventions of particular subjects, doesn't everyone speak a language (une langue) that comes from this Other, which he has been influenced into using, since from this Other he receives "his own message in an inverted form"?

What is true is that, as psychoanalysts, we can no longer speak the language of today's psychiatrists, even if our diagnostic categories come to us from classical psychiatry.

The types of symptoms that we continue to talk about, following Freud's and Lacan's examples—hysteria, phobia, perversions, paranoia, schizophrenia, melancholia, mania—were described for us by the psychiatry of the beginning of the century. Neither Freud nor Lacan challenged their pertinence, and both of them recognized the consistency of these types. Freud, at the end of Chapter 17 of the *Introductory Lectures on Psycho-analysis*, entitled "The Meaning of Symptoms," is clearly instructive on this point. Beyond interpretation by historical and singular meaning, he wonders about the interpretation that is to be given to the fact that there are types of symptoms. He sees only a recourse to the typical experiences of humanity—phylogenesis—to explain them. What makes this obscure reference superfluous is the bringing to light of structure, which was mentioned in another introduction, that of the German edition of the *Ecrits*, where Lacan posits that the clinical types, although they were set forth before the appearance of analytic discourse, participate in its structure. Only this reference to structure allows us to conceive both of the consistency of the phenomena described by classical psychiatry, and of something else, which has also been noticed: that symptoms change, and have changed, and that they are, as Lacan says with a calculated neologism, "hystorical." They are historical in their manifestations because they are a function of the language (*langue*) and the discourse of the time, but are transhistorical in their structure; this fact alone saves us from having to remake our vocabulary at each turning point in history; it also shows us the importance of recognizing the same structure beneath its changing pictures.

This inconsistency of the notion of depression should obviously not discourage us from thinking about depressive phenomena. They are to be included in the composite whole of the sufferings that are addressed to the psychoanalyst. We find them again in transference, when there is a lack of progress in the analysis, and up to its final phase. Both Freud and Lacan testify to this: Freud, by stumbling upon the serious depressions of certain feminine subjects at the end of the treatment; Lacan, by assimilating the moment of the pass to a depressive position. Neither recoiled from the phenomenon, but the problem in confronting it is to know, in each of its occurrences, to what causal structure it refers.[1]

A SIGN OF THE TIMES

The question of what the phenomenon owes to our age has been raised. Our period has certainly registered a rise of new discourses about depression. The multiplication of depressed people is its major theme, one that is diagnosed as a sign of the times, a costly symptom that leads, in Freud's terms, to a hemorrhage of energy and money, burdening society and challenging health policies.

These new patients have not been generated spontaneously. It is obvious and even common today to locate the first cause of the modern subject's fate in our civilization: one conditioned by the discourse of science and the globalization of liberal capitalism that follows from it. Reality, indeed, has changed: the superegoistic standardization and anonymity of lifestyles, the deterioration of social bonds, world catastrophes, and so on.

For subjects, the experience of the death, dereliction, and anxiety of the Other leaves them lacking not only in the great causes of the past but in their former beliefs. Thus we see on the literary scene, from Kafka to Beckett and passing by Pessoa and many others, the new figures of nonsense, the laughable characters who grope through situations in which they have lost their way, and who thereby reveal the hidden side of the expansive, inspired, and conquering vitality of Walt Whitman, in the last century.

No ethics that is supposed to be contractual will succeed in quenching the protest over this abandonment, *hilflosigkeit*, as Freud said. As a good logician, our age will surely not write "Gödel and Heidegger with Habermas," as Lacan could write "Kant with Sade." In this crisis of semblances—the most important of which is that of the father—the subject is distraught, and seeks a new desire that will lift him up from the lonely, taciturn satisfactions of the drive. God is no longer part of the business, nor are the masters of knowledge. We can doubtless wager

---

1. On the question of depressive phenomena in transference, see Serge Cottet's article "La belle inertie," *Ornicar?* 32.

on the return of the little gods and their cults, if hysteria is going to play its part, for the hysteric does not go without the Other. While waiting for all of this, however, we can see its logic in a world in which people have ceased to raise their eyebrows about anything; in our age, indeed, all the scales have fallen from people's eyes and the result is that all values have fallen under the suspicion of being fake. In such a world, the old utilitarianism of Bentham, as Lacan reread it, has regained its vigor and the general cynicism of jouissance is reigning as master. In this age, it is logical that neurotics, who always have a bit of a "beautiful soul," are depressed; indeed, a long analysis does not always succeed in making them look directly at what Lacan designated as the "cynical balance" of any elaboration by means of language.

WHY DEPRESSED PEOPLE AREN'T LOVED

It is obvious that these new tests have been accompanied, perhaps as a compensation, by new places to which one can turn as a resort. Since the right to good health has been extended to the psyche, a growing legitimation of subjective complaints has made itself recognized. Psychoanalysis has contributed in large part to this legitimation, although it is not the only practice that collects sighs. One could believe that much has thus been gained in the struggle against the foreclosure of the dimension that is specific to the subject in scientific civilization. Yet as if by the cunning of pseudo-scientific civilization, with the category of depression we have refused to accept the meaning of the complaint that has been addressed to us. When subjects deplore their pain, we do not know how to read what they are saying about their intimate experience of the end or of loss, and therefore we reduce their complaints to the supposed dysfunctionings of illness.

What strikes me is that nothing in current discourse allows a humanly positive value to be attributed to depression. Other ages knew how to give a meaning, even at the price of what appears to us as an illusion, to the various ways of putting life in question. The theme of faith and the call to God sheltered many mortifying aspirations, and piety sublimated a disgust with the world. (See Donne's *Biathanatos*.) Romantic idealization knew how to absolve the self-absorption of a broken man as the despairs of love, and even to make them into a seductive pose. As to the morbid, Baudelairian taste of spleen, wasn't it authorized by a supposed protest against stupidity? These are only a few dispersed examples, borrowed from the field of religious or literary sublimation, but they allow us to measure how much—and how curiously—contemporary discourse dislikes depression, even while talking so much about it.

Incapable of elaborating it in sublimated forms, this discourse considers it as a deficit and never as a value. It is a defect in relation to health when the physician is speaking, but it is also a fault, and it is not only the psychoanalyst who takes it in this way. It is certainly a modern fault, in the eyes of our civilization's obscure imperative to optimism, against the commandment to "face up to things." Subjects themselves perceive it as a giving up and often refer to it as a renunciation of the fight.

Of course, there is always, especially thanks to hysteria, a special empathy for the subject who no longer succeeds in something. We may admire or envy the joyous and dynamic man, but it is rare for him really to arouse sympathy. On the contrary, we give in more willingly to the contagion of the beaten man's sadness, and compassion always lends itself to devotion and support for him. Nevertheless, among us today, the "blues" do not unify us, and a civilization that valorizes competitiveness and conquest—even if, in the final analysis, it is only that of the market—cannot love its depressed people. It fails to love them even while it is engendering more and more of them as the illness of the capitalist discourse. The empathy that I mentioned is, furthermore, very often mitigated, for the subject who does not give up on his/her depression irritates us and sometimes makes us run away. (Winnicott would tell us that we do so under the influence of a maniacal defense!) It is not only that this subject brings even the most devoted efforts to nothing. What s/he does is to make us experience something else: beyond the impotence of arguments and the inadequacy of the attempts at persuasion—whether the cognitivist likes this or not—s/he unveils the reasonlessness of our attachment to the world. Such a reasonlessness is not, however, without its cause: S(A). Testifying to the radical contingency of what we believe to be the meaning of life, she solicits in us what Lacan called the "inmost juncture of the subject's sense of life."[2]

2. Jacques Lacan, "On a Question Preliminary to Any Possible Treatment of Psychosis," Ecrits: A Selection, p. 191.

The depressed person disquiets us because, by her very existence, she threatens the social bond. Thus there is condemnation. It is not new, but today it is unanimous, although it has many different motivations. The ages of religious fervor could read it as an insult to faith, an attack on the bond with the divine Other, and made it into a sin. The modern age sees it as both an illness and a surrender. When Lacan situates sadness as a moral cowardice, relying on references from the age that preceded science—Saint Thomas, Dante, and Spinoza—he is certainly in a state of rupture with everything that has been said about it elsewhere, but he is judging sadness no less than the others did. Thus it becomes necessary to grasp what distinguishes the verdict of psychoanalysis from that of common discourse.

WHAT DEPRESSION SAYS

Psychoanalysts are acquainted with subjects' depression only through what their patients say about it. The practicing analyst knows only what is confided to him/her about what it is like either now or in the past. This path leaves an entire clinical space on its margins, for it does not encounter those who have passed over to the other side of the wall of language, and who are received by the psychiatrist. I am referring to the melancholic states in which the subject is frozen in silence or in petrified pain, and is inaccessible to any appeal from a fellow person. Like both Freud and Lacan, the psychoanalyst must learn about these extreme cases, and can even throw light on them with his knowledge, but they remain outside the grasp of the analytic process; the latter cannot receive those who, walled in by pain and wordless petrification, refuse to exercise speech. At this point, one could wonder whether, between psychoanalysis and the consistency of the depressive states—to the extent that such a consistency exists and supposing that the expression has a meaning—there is not a relation of mutual exclusion. Where depression is spoken, however, let us trust what is said of it, both inside and outside psychoanalysis.

It seems to me that the depressive state is reduced too easily to the affect of sadness. Perhaps we make this reduction because we are approaching sadness with Lacan's verdict on it: it is moral cowardice. Yet the depressive state is not reduced to this affect as a feeling. Whoever says, "I am depressed" certainly implies pain and sadness here, to the point that a happy depressed person would be nearly a contradiction, but the reciprocal is not true. The unhappy subject is not always depressed, and a depressed person can be indifferent to his feelings. As proof of this, one can speak of a subject who has never been depressed, but one cannot imagine a person for whom the word "sadness" would have no meaning and who could not refer any of his own experience to it. There is, indeed, a generic sadness, which means that it is virtually inevitable, even universal, for it is connected with the status of the speakingbeing. Freud situates it in this way, as the normal result of certain avatars of the libido—even if it has pathological forms.[3] As effect of language, the subject is saturnine in essence.[4] Lacan's thesis that sadness, in the context of a psychoanalytic ethics, is a form of cowardice does not contradict this. He makes this affect into the specific fate of the one who resigns from his duty "to find one's way in dealing with the unconscious."[5] Sadness is thus a fault, a sin, "which is situated only in thought," but as is the case elsewhere, no one can find himself completely in the unconscious, and consequently a place is given over to what is structurally irreducible in the sin of sadness.

When someone affirms that s/he is depressed, there is, in fact, always more than the sole dimension of affect: the subject speaks of it as a loss of interest or capacity, and uses formulas such as, "I no longer have any . . . strength, courage, vigor, and so on"; sometimes it is life itself that seems to him/her to have no more meaning or taste. This is more than sadness, which uses different words. This is something that touches on the subject's very animation and that has unmistakable repercussions, at the level of what s/he undertakes, in effects of inertia; beyond the coloring of the feelings, these effects touch the very principle of interest and action. We would be tempted to conclude that one speaks of depression when sadness has passed to the act, to the act of inhibiting the dynamism of the will; to say this, however, would be to fail to recognize that sadness is itself only an effect, and that we must seek elsewhere the cause of the libidinal deflation that leaves the subject not

---

3. Freud, *Introductory Lectures on Psycho-analysis*, SE XV, pp. 215–216.
4. For the history of the notion, see *Saturn and Melancholia: Studies in the History of Natural Philosophy, Religion and Art* by Raymond Klibansky, Erwin Panofsky, and Fritz Saxl. Revised with the collaboration of Raymond Klibansky. London: Nelson, 1964.
5. Lacan, *Television*, p. 23.

only sad, but as if s/he had "no motivation." With this expression, doesn't *lalangue* record an implicit reference to the cause? I have found the same reference in a subject, who, when emerging from a depression that could rightly be called melancholic, testified with remarkable accuracy: "I wasn't suffering, but I no longer had my commandment," and insisted that he could not say it in any other way than with this expression, which he devised himself. Such expressions are in astonishing harmony with Lacan's statement that the melancholic subject attempts to reach the object *a*, "whose command escapes him."[6]

In fact, in common parlance, the depressive state is formulated in bodily metaphors. It is enumerated in images of the body as arrested, immobilized, a body that "doesn't work any more," which "can't face anything." Isn't pain evoked in an image of petrification and of impeded movement, as Lacan noted in his seminar on anxiety? All these expressions, which have been deposited in the language (*langue*), are only scraps of subjective experiences, but as degraded as their metaphorical power may be, they still leave a trace. The last recourse of the laziness that cannot speak well, they are generally supplanted by the words that each subject draws from his stock, in order to say both the vacuousness and the inertia, since the statements of depression always designate an intersection where sadness is combined with inhibition.

THE CAUSE OF DESIRE INSIDE OUT

Today's psychiatry attaches great importance to this dimension of inhibition, which allows it to misunderstand the subjective touch in favor of a supposed deficit of the ego. We do not understand it in this way, but that is no reason to minimize this dimension. Freud himself saw in it an effect of the division of the subject, and imputed it either to the paralyzing defense against the return of the repressed or to the punitive prohibitions of the ego and the distribution of the investments commanded by the two.[7] He had clearly already recognized it

---

6. Jacques Lacan, *Anxiety*, unpublished seminar, July 3, 1963.

7. Sigmund Freud, *Inhibitions, Symptoms, and Anxiety*, trans. Alix Strachey. *Standard Edition of the Complete Psychological Works*, Vol. XX. (London: Hogarth Press and the Institute of Psycho-analysis, 1959), pp. 89–90.

as a subjective phenomenon and he connected it explicitly with depression. It is true that in his celebrated triad, inhibitions, symptoms, and anxiety, as well as in Lacan's discussion of it in his seminar on anxiety, the term "depression" shines by its absence and its difference. Depressive sadness, indeed, is not anxiety, the typical affect of a relation to a real that cannot be assimilated. It is, on the contrary, a "senti-ment,"[8] which deceives concerning the cause; it is also not a symptom—it has neither structure nor consistency—but rather a state of the subject, which can undergo fluctuations and is compatible with different clinical structures.

Neither a structure nor an affect of the real, depression participates, however, in the figures of inhibition. This is the way that Freud understood it, when, speaking of the latter at the end of his first chapter, he specifies that in "the depressive states," inhibition is "general,"[9] freezing the whole of the libidinal functions. From this, it appears that the depressive states, as varied and fluctuating as they are, can all be located within a unitary formula. I will call it the suspension of the cause of desire; the apathetic and painful lack of appetite that can be called depression finds its structural condition in the fall of the effectiveness of the cause of desire. Thus, to speak of depression is nothing other than to approach this cause of desire inside out, by means of its failures and vacillations.

I will note, moreover, that this thesis immediately explains what I will call the antidepressive effect of psychoanalysis. As limited as it may be, this effect is no less obvious, and derives its power from the fact that from beginning to end, psychoanalysis operates through the cause of desire. At the beginning of an analysis, first of all, it introduces the subject into a temporality of expectation that sustains or restores the vector of desire; the conclusion, if it has taken place, marks out what is beyond the depressive position.[10]

This formula is valid for all the structures: it is true for both the vacillations of the cause in the neuroses and for the sidelining of the

---

8. The author here makes an untranslatable pun. "Senti" means "heartfelt," while "ment" is a form of the verb "mentir," to lie. (Translator's note.)

9. *Inhibitions, Symptoms, and Anxiety,* p. 90.

10. See "Leçons cliniques de la passe," drafted by Colette Soler for cartel A, 1990–1992 (Serge Cottet plus-one, Pierre-Gilles Guéguen, Herbert Wachsberger), in *Comment finissent les analyses,* Paris: Editions du Seuil, 1994, p. 181.

cause in melancholic psychosis. On the one hand, the foreclosure specific to psychosis and its correlate of an overflowing of jouissance explains the sidelining of the cause. This may take multiple forms, which are not always spectacular or pathetic: the most unobtrusive indifference, apathy, and apragmatism—which can sometimes be confused with the "normal"—up to the most extreme paroxysms of pain and melancholic inertia. On the other hand, with the neuroses there are also numerous occasions in which what Lacan called "the power of pure loss" fails for a time.[11] This expression, which summons up the vital effectiveness that Freud himself located in the lost object, indicates quite well that it is "death as it is actualized in the signifying sequence"[12]; this power presides just as much over the feeling of life and its dynamisms as over its depressive consequences. As a result, the latter are a matter of more contingent conjunctures, which are situated at the joint of the relation with the object.

THE EFFECTIVENESS OF CASTRATION

If one asks, "Are we depressed by what is intolerable in castration?" the answer can only be negative. Castration, if this is the name that we give to the loss, engendered by language, of the thing, may always be implied in the depressive affect; if castration is its condition, it is far, however, from being its cause. The opposite thesis can even be accentuated: the cause of desire only takes on its function from the effectiveness of castration, which is what Lacan's expression "the power of pure loss" means. What is this power, if not what impels and maintains the dynamisms of all orders, their conquests, and their undertakings? What is it, if not what gives to the subject, who has already been killed by the signifier, the anomalous and paradoxical vitality of a decisive desire?

If there is an affect that belongs to castration, it is not depression but anxiety and even horror, which are quite different. Isn't there a sad truth, as our language (la langue) suggests? Truth is not sad; it is horrible,

---

11. Lacan, "The Signification of the Phallus," p. 276.
12. Jacques Lacan, "The Direction of the Treatment," p. 253.

inhuman, and horror does not depress us; instead, it awakens us. An analysis, far from resolving castration, reproduces it. (At one period, Lacan called it, in the vocabulary of the transformation of the subject, the "taking up of castration" and he later set it forth through the propositional function $\forall x.\Phi x$, which rewrites castration in terms of the logic of set theory.) Thus it is conceived that an analysis resolves what can be called the temptations to depression and that it sometimes succeeds in reversing them into an effect of enthusiasm, without there being any need for exhortation or any other suggestion.

Depression is not produced directly by castration, which is perhaps our only universal, but rather by the singular solutions that each subject brings to it, which vary according to contingencies, but which always imply the ethical dimension. In this sense, the statement that the subject is "structurally depressed"—with the implication that this is because of castration—is imprecise. It would be more accurate to say "subject structurally to depression," a depression that always arises in relation to the avatars of the junction with the object.

The clinic of the cause, inasmuch as it articulates the lack in castration with the object as surplus jouissance that responds to it, takes place between two boundaries. At one extreme, castration founds the desiring power, erecting the object in its *agalmatic* power. Alcibiades, the "epitome of desirousness,"[13] a figure who is very far from us, illustrates this, since for him, castration is included in the object $a/-\varphi$. At the other extreme is the extinction of the fires, the loss of the relation with the world, the stasis of the melancholic's petrified being, which itself becomes the rejected object, incarnating a jouissance outside the phallic reference: a/φ_0.

Between the two are to be found all the ambiguous phenomena of neurosis. They are ambiguous because the neurotic subject's depressive states are figures of desire as well. They are what remains of desire when, untangling itself from the drive, from what Lacan calls its heavy soul, it detaches itself from the "hardy offshoots of the wounded tendency,"[14] and tends to reduce itself to the negative instance of the drive. In this case, one could say that such a subject has everything that could

---

13. Jacques Lacan, "The Subversion of the Subject and the Dialectic of Desire," *Ecrits: A Selection*, p. 310.

14. Jacques Lacan, "The Direction of the Treatment," p. 253.

make him happy, but instead of being so, he challenges and denounces all the surplus jouissances that have been actualized. This is not the zero degree of desire, but its more or less achieved reduction to the foundation of the (-φ) of castration. The subject in this state gets jouissance from something, for his/her rejection of what life offers stirs up the empty utopia of the nothing—the nonexistent other thing—about which Paul Claudel, in *Le soulier de satin* (*The Satin Shoe*), makes the marvelous statement: "And is it nothing other than this nothing that delivers the all?" And, indeed, doesn't it allow the subject to get off on the consistency, which can be called a-corporeal, of castration, and which can be written as (-φ≡a)?

From hysteria to obsession, the different forms do not exclude all kinds of combinations with the sad pleasures of autoeroticism or even the taciturn jouissances of the drive, but what is important here is the curve of the whole on which the phenomena are divided up. Such phenomena go from conquering desire to the melancholic's abolished desire; they include the neurotic's problematic or doubtful desire, object-love, self-hatred, and narcissistic self-investment. The relation between this desire and jouissance must be articulated: from the moment that desire itself becomes a defense, wherever it falls, jouissance rises. It is therefore exactly right to say also that the depressive state is a mode of jouissance, but this formula will only operate if we succeed, in each case, in giving it its singular coordinates.

A DIFFERENTIAL CLINIC

Here I encounter once again the question of whether and why women are more frequently depressed. The most recent statistics claim to establish this, whereas for manic-depressive psychosis, there is no significant variation between men and women. This point is not astonishing if we consider that the empire of foreclosure knows no border between the sexes. As for the statistics on depression, psychoanalysts, who hardly trust statistics, could neglect them and see them only as an artifact. What is seen today as a distinguishing trait of depression is the complaint.

The propensity to complain, as well as the toleration of it, varies according to sex. If women complain more easily, it is because confessing the weaknesses of being, sadness, pain, discouragement, in short, everything that can reduce one's vigor and combativeness, is more compatible with the standard images of femininity than with the ideals of manliness. In addition, the complaint itself is feminizing, so those located on man's side learn to contain it, whereas on woman's side, nothing objects to its use, and it can even become part of the art of pleasing.

> A little air of doubt and melancholy,
> You know, Ninon, makes you even prettier

as Musset said in an invitation.

One cannot forget that Freud himself, connecting women's depression with their position toward castration, makes penis envy the predisposing factor. We know the fearsome feminine itinerary that he describes for us in light of his experience of transference: beginning with envy, it continued in the expectation of a substitute, and ended in serious depression, in despair before what is impossible. These three phases are not without an homology with the three moments of erotomania, which a certain psychiatry described shortly afterwards, and empirical findings do not contradict this itinerary. It even seems that we gladly admit that feelings of inferiority, of a negative value, a deficit in self-esteem, as people say today—feelings that are so propitious to the depressive state—are more frequent in women and are very much in harmony, indeed, with envy. Envy brings to life the experience of powerlessness, which each subject encounters in the register of devalorizing comparison, a register in which one imagines that others are less exposed to this experience than one is oneself.

The question is obviously not statistical. It is rather a matter of knowing what could found the dissymmetry between men and women in relation to depressive states. Why would the "holders of desire" be less subject to it than the "claimants of sex"[15]? Since it is a question of the cause of desire, let us seek the answer in the misfortunes of love, which could very well program for women a mourning that has no equivalent in men. I am referring to sexed love here, leaving aside what is addressed to the child. Motherhood also includes its share of worries,

---

15. "Guiding Remarks for a Congress on Feminine Sexuality," p. 97.

suffering, and renunciations, but I believe that it leads more to torments than to depression.

Love, as we have always known, is the spontaneous, almost natural treatment for sadness and despondency; the affects of plenitude and joy that it arouses are completely opposed to the feelings of unhappiness and vacuousness that characterize the depressive position. Here, there is, curiously, a dissymmetry between the sexes, one that is rather homologous to what is observed in homosexuality: men's is connected with the impasses of desire, whereas women's is engendered by the failure of love. I will take up this aspect of the problem.

A SURPLUS OF MELANCHOLY

Freud recognized the phallic value of love, since he posited an equivalence between men's castration anxiety and women's anxiety of losing love, but Lacan's formulas, which distinguish being and having the phallus, allow us to formulate this value better. This is the dissymmetry: being the phallus, the only identification that sustains being a woman, takes sustenance from love. This is not the case for a man, whose virility is affirmed on the side of having, by sexual potency and its multiple metonymies. Being a woman is doubly sustained by love: inasmuch as "being loved" is equivalent to "being the phallus," but also inasmuch as one only loves on the basis of one's own lack. It can thus be said that love is feminine.

This is what led Lacan to affirm, in a formula that is as provocative as it is perfectly rigorous: when a man loves—which happens of course—it is as a woman. It is inasmuch as he is himself subject to lack, since, in terms of his being as man, he understands nothing of love— as everything indicates—because he "is sufficient in his jouissance."[16] Women love therefore, but because they call for love. Love is called for because it is a gift, whereas desire is "taken." From this we can understand the antidepressive effect of encountering love, which, although it includes body-to-body contact, cannot be reduced to it, for love is

---

16. Jacques Lacan, Seminar, *Les non-dupes errent*, the session of February 12, 1974.

addressed to saying (*dire*), thus bringing about the enigmatic recognition of two unconsciousnesses.

Love, unfortunately, is risky and ephemeral, as we have always known. This is why it aspires not to cease being written; it wants to elevate itself to the necessary. Exalting when one succeeds in encountering it, love is also depressing when it is lost. Placing the cause of desire in the Other, it leaves the subject at the mercy of the caprices of the Other's response, and threatened with its absence. This alienation also operates in men, of course, except that their being is nourished by something other than love. Women more frequently make love into a cause, and when it is missing, either contingently or through the acts of civilization, which is in crisis today, they are left stranded. What is worse, love, when it does not disappear, can by its very presence overwhelm the subject with the weight of an Other; what makes the weight even more crushing is that the cause of desire is attributed to the Other. Freud recognized this, emphasizing that love and melancholia are two cases of being "crushed by the object." Lacan does not recoil from saying in Seminar I that love is a kind of suicide. The elation, plenitude, and joy of love disguise the handing-over of oneself to the Other, the degrees of which are varied, but which can go to the extreme of voluntary self-abolition in certain kinds of mysticism. Thus, whether it lends itself or disappears, love always programs a bit of disenchantment, and by putting herself into its hands, each woman always becomes a bit of a widow! The consequences of this are varied: they include acute mourning—which is so frequent—a deflation, at the very least, of the joy of life, or unforeseeable metamorphoses, such as the typical reduction onto having, which, sometimes, in the course of time, transforms a young woman disappointed by love into a shrew. Well, who will tell us about the motive forces of certain kinds of feminine avarice, that, for example, of Balzac's Eugénie Grandet or Buñuel's Tristana?

A HINT OF SADNESS

Until now, I have discussed the effects of love and its consequences only on the level of the phallic identification with being. They must, however, also be connected with the field of jouissance. Lacan marked out a precise articulation that connects, first, what is insatiable in love

with the sexual nonrelation and, second, the properly feminine requirement with her status as absolute Other, a status that is not completely
in the phallic function.

It is noteworthy that, concerning women, Lacan was never in complete agreement with Freud, and he brought something new concerning sexuation and its consequences. He maintains Freud's accent on
feminine lack by formulating that every subject as such is inscribed in
the phallic function of castration; when it comes to situating difference,
however, he recognizes it on the side of a jouissance that is supplementary and "not completely" phallic. This is a jouissance foreclosed from
language, which the unconscious does not know, which cannot be assimilated, and which is rejected and expelled to the limit of the series,
and thus segregated. It is in excess of the possible ways that it can be
ciphered. We see the problem: if the remedy for sadness is to "refind
oneself in the unconscious," in its signs and its fictions, what will be
the affect of the jouissance that is not inscribed there and for which
woman, inasmuch as she is Other for herself, is responsible?[17]

Here we can return to the problem of guilt. Freud, as we know,
connected it with the father of the Law, the dead father of *Totem and
Taboo*, whose murder never ends: the father of monotheism. Obviously,
this is only a myth, but it provides an irreducible knotting of guilt and
the love for this dead father, who has become the Name-of-the-Father,
and to whom we remain forever in debt. On this question, there is a
perceptible gap between Freud and Lacan.

Lacan does not connect guilt with the father but with jouissance:
to jouissance inasmuch as it ex-sists in relation to the symbolic and is
marked by the symbolic. As for the first of these, it is the defect of the
symbolic that makes jouissance at fault, a fault that includes existence
and sex.[18] Jouissance, however, can be said to be faulty not only because
it does not exist, but also because it is wounded, even gored by the signifier. The original sin is double: because of both the jouissance that is

---

17. This is the expression that Lacan uses in "Subversion of the subject and the
dialectic of desire" for jouissance, "whose lack makes the Other inconsistent" (p. 305).

18. The references to this point are multiple. See especially, "Remarques sur le
rapport de Daniel Lagache," in the French edition of the *Ecrits*, pp. 666–667 and "The
Subversion of the Subject and the Dialectic of Desire," in *Ecrits: A Selection*, p. 305.

there and of what is there no longer. In this respect, the Name-of-the-Father, whose "true function" is "to unite (and not to oppose) a desire to the Law," far from engendering guilt, blots it out.[19] This is the only thesis that really explains the fact that (guilt is raised to delirious certainty only in the case of psychosis, precisely where the paternal mediation is lacking.)

Furthermore, Freud's thesis, which attributes melancholic guilt to an identification with the primal father, does not contradict this, if we recognize in the latter, not the Name-of-the-Father, but rather the father as *jouisseur*, from before the murder. I would like to direct your attention to Freud's final remarks, nine in number, dating from June 1938, for they signal an approach that does not go by way of the father.[20] The series itself indicates a gravitation in Freud's thoughts, since four of them deal with feminine inferiority, guilt linked to unsatisfied love, inhibition, and mysticism. I will examine only inhibition, since as I have said, it is correlated to depression. He situates its first cause in infantile masturbation inasmuch as this jouissance is "unsatisfying . . . in itself."[21] This, it seems to me, is a way of saying that phallic jouissance, indeed, is unsatisfying. It is the jouissance "that shouldn't be/could never fail"[22]; it is guilty by definition, and the depressed inhibition of it exposes and rejects its nonsense.

The being of the jouissance that is not identified by any signifier, not even the phallic signifier, can only be aimed at in discourse through the insult; the latter, which is "the first and last word of any dialogue,"[23] is located at the edge of the ineffable. This brings me back to woman, who is defamed.[24] This is not just because of mean-spiritedness, but because one cannot *say* her with the words of phallic jouissance) What is important here is that this ability to encompass her in words is also impossible for her as well as for a man, and as experience shows, she defames herself more often than men do. Let us recognize, in her trait

---

19. "The Subversion of the Subject and the Dialectic of Desire," p. 309.

20. Sigmund Freud, "Findings, Ideas, Problems." SE XXIII (London: Hogarth Press and the Institute of Psycho-analysis, 1964), pp. 299–300.

21. *Ibid.*, p. 300.

22. Lacan, *Encore*, p. 59.

23. Lacan, "L'étourdit," p. 44.

24. Lacan, *Encore*, p. 85.

of melancholy, an attempt to speak of herself as Other. Her jouissance is unciphered and goes beyond her because it does not pass into the unconscious; it is impossible for a woman to "find [her] way in dealing with the unconscious."[25] Thus a surplus of sadness is always possible, one that is "unmotivated," if we wish to use the term that Guirault applies to certain murders, in which the subject aims straight at the *kakon* of being.

This has nothing to do with the feelings of insufficiency mentioned above: this trait and this affect may not exclude the experience of "inferiority," but in themselves they refer to neither phallic lack nor jouissance, both of which instead generate anxiety and inhibition. The delirium of melancholic indignity—which is something else, of course—is revealing in this context: going to extremes, it shows that the rejection of the foreclosed jouissance in the insult aimed at oneself is the final verbal rampart before this jouissance is expelled in a suicidal passage to the act. More commonly—outside psychosis—the rejection into the insult is like the first degree of a paradoxical sublimation coming from this place of jouissance, the place "from which 'the universe is a defect in the purity of "Non-Being"' is vociferated."[26]

This status of jouissance gives meaning to the specifically feminine call for a chosen love. This requirement will not be able to resolve the disharmony of jouissances; rather it will repeat their disunion, which in bringing the sexes closer together, gives existence to the absolute Other, making woman always Other: Other to herself. Love therefore will not leave her alone with her *heterity*, but will at least be able to index it with the name of the lover: such is the case with Juliet, made eternal by Romeo, Iseult by Tristan, or Beatrice by Dante. What can be deduced from this is that for a woman, the loss of love exceeds the phallic dimension to which Freud reduced it, for what she loses in losing love is herself, in the form of the named Other. For Freud, the work of mourning always allows an irreducible kernel of "inconsolable" fixation on the lost being, a kernel that is all the more unforgettable since it is radically foreign and impossible to assimilate.[27] Lacan, however,

---

25. *Television*, p. 22.

26. "Subversion of the Subject and the Dialectic of Desire," p. 305.

27. See Michael Turnheim, *L'autre dans le même*. Paris : Editions du Champ Lacanien, 2002.

makes us perceive another side of the phenomenon, in which what is unforgettable for a woman is what love turns her into: the Other whom, by the same movement, it institutes and . . . rehabilitates. This is what the lesson of mystical loves teaches us.

BENEFITS OF THE WELL-SPOKEN

Does psychoanalysis depress women, as Freud thought that it did? In fact, the question comes back in another form: To what extent can the ethics of the well-spoken (*bien-dire*), which is specific to psychoanalysis, lighten the subject's burden of jouissance, especially the burden of those who are not wholly in phallic jouissance?

Psychoanalysis, which operates precisely *by* transference love, does not work *for* love. Instead, it takes the spontaneous solution offered by love and drives it to despair. It is amusing to note that Freud asked himself this question around 1914, in the texts that he devoted to transference, and hesitates over what should be accorded to love. His response, as we know, was categorically bad-tempered. Contrary to what one wants to expect from it, an analysis assures us of nothing about love.

The well-spoken will spare no one from being affected by the paradoxes of jouissance, in terms of both phallic limitation and the supplements that sometimes come back to women. Yet psychoanalysis is the only contemporary discourse to offer us a cause that is . . . other, and, if the subject is this "logical analysand" whom I mentioned in the past, there will be a gain in knowledge. Now this knowledge is not without both therapeutic and subjective effects; by elevating the incapacities that are experienced into structural constraints that transcend them, knowledge touches the very principle of the horror of castration, sometimes to the point of producing an effect of enthusiasm. Thus it can be concluded that the sadness that falls short of well-saying can legitimately be stigmatized as a fault. As for love, although none of its contingency is reduced, it will not be lost, and, if we are to believe Jacques Lacan, could even be made "more worthy than the proliferation of chattering that it has constituted up to today."[28]

---

28. Jacques Lacan, "Note aux italiens," *Ornicar?* 25, p. 10.

IV

THE MOTHER

7

The Mother in the Unconscious

It is hardly news that the empire of the father has fallen. People like to say that this is the fault of the effects of science and indeed it is. Yet what can the family become outside this empire? Doesn't the position of the mother take on a weight that is in proportion to the effect of molecular disaggregation that has marked the past century, the final residue of which is the individual, much more than the family?

Lacan said that we could do without the father, on the condition of using him (*s'en servant*). Perhaps we could also do without the mother, and we would like to, but we begin to see a dissymmetry here, in the condition that *she* was of use (*servait*) first of all, at least in producing our body.[1] The dream of Frankenstein confirms this, and the progress of techniques of artificial reproduction has not invalidated this,

_____
1. The author is alluding to the session of April 13, 1976, of the seminar *Le sinthome*, where Lacan says of the Name-of-the Father that "one can do without it [*s'en passer*] on condition of using it [*s'en servir*]." The passage also contains a pun on *s'en servir* (to use it) and *servir* (to serve). (Translator's note.)

at least not yet. Lacan happened to designate women with the term "breeders" (*pondeuses*). This derogatory reference to animal reproduction says quite well that the mother, the female parent, is not a semblance. The disjunction between the functions of real reproduction and symbolic semblance are exactly reversed with the father, who, as Name, is a semblance, but not a male parent.

Apart from this limit point of reproducing bodies, the function of mothering can be substituted. The old practice of using wet nurses, as well as the more current one of adoption, testifies to this. Moreover, there has been no lack of historical attempts to replace mothers, whether in fantasy or reality. Let us recall Rousseau in *Emile*, where the concern with putting the mother aside forever is so pressing that he makes it the condition *sine qua non* for making a man. Except that, according to Rousseau, she must, first of all, breastfeed him! Let us also not forget the various nonmaternal, collective attempts to bring up children, which marked the last century and emerged in the most opposed ideologies.

However, in the current social bond the mother, or her substitute, is becoming in an ever greater number of cases the child's preponderant, and even exclusive partner, or at least the only stable one. Thus there is a configuration that has become common: a mother with her child or children, plus possibly a man—or a series of men who succeed each other—and who is called "my mother's boyfriend." The concrete configurations are obviously multiple and varied, but the mobility of social bonds and of the bonds of love give a new weight in history to the child's face-to-face relation with the mother; this new weight cannot be without subjective consequences.

THE DEBATE OVER THE MOTHER

What part does psychoanalysis have in this change of deal in civilization? This is a double question. It concerns analytic discourse itself, what is said or not between the analyst and the analysand in an analysis. It also concerns the theoretical elaboration that gives an account of this practice, an elaboration not without responsibility for the facts that are collected there, for practice and doctrine are in harmony with each other.

It is a curious fact that the question of the mother's function and place in subjectivity is coextensive with the history of the doctrines of the symptom. It is well known that analytic theory has played a lot on papa and mama. The essential question concerns, in any case, the cause of this central subjective fact, which Freud named castration, and which, in essence, means the lesion of jouissance, which, unlike the Oedipus complex, "is not a myth,"[2] and which requires some objects to compensate for it. Freud constructed a structure that divides up these functions: on the one hand, there is an object of primary satisfaction, and on the other a limit-function. Thus, in the child's oedipal romance, there is a confrontation between the object-mother—an object of love, desire, or jouissance—which is to be lost, and the Freudian father, who carries the prohibition.

After this father of the oedipal myth, the post-Freudians brought the mother onto the stage as cause. There have been several mothers, in fact: the one whose body is full of objects (Melanie Klein), the care provider (Winnicott), the giver of primary love (Balint). In each case, the cause of the subject's misfortune is identified with the failure or the limits of the maternal function: if she is full of objects, she will be guilty of receiving stolen goods; as the unconditional envelope, she will lack an absolute presence; as love, she will sin through her incompleteness. Thus, blurring Freud's elegant distinction, we have weighed the mother down, not only with the bid for jouissance (l'offre à jouir) but also with the first limitation of jouissance, substituting the defect in maternal love for the principle of paternal legitimacy.

Some light can be thrown on this return to the mother by its context. It is connected with problems of development in the history of psychoanalysis: on the one hand, its extension to children and psychotics, and on the other, its stumbling against the limits that Freud himself encountered. We know that, after the golden age of the first discoveries gleaned by the method, he was forced to notice that the symptom was only partially docile to the operation of deciphering, and he had to take into account and conceive of the resistant element in structure. He responded through his formulations on the death drive, what is beyond the pleasure principle, the negative therapeutic reaction, the interminability of analysis, and finally, the discontents of civilization.

---

2. "Subversion of the Subject and the Dialectic of Desire," p. 305.

The symptom was certainly there from the beginning to testify to a certain gap in jouissance, but at first it was possible to believe that it was contingent and could be imputed to some individual distortion or other. Instructed by experience, Freud concluded that it is irreducible and even double: something in it is not quite right, partly because of what is lacking—through castration—and partly because of an excess: the imperialism of the drives, which are always partial, but which never give up, even at the price of displeasure. In other words, there is a jouissance that is impossible to reach, but also a jouissance that is impossible to reduce.

In the context of the paradoxes of jouissance, post-Freudian psychoanalysts called upon the mother. They were pushed by a secret logic: with the mother, in any case, the first object of impossible jouissance is elevated to the status of the one who is guilty of limiting it. Nothing, indeed, was simpler than to authorize oneself on this point by what analysands said, for they were the first ones who, when left free to say what was always going on in their heads, could do nothing other than to return, again and again, to childhood and its first objects. That speech within transference seems to be magnetized by the primal figures is a fact, even if we must quite obviously go beyond this if we are to situate the category of causes. In the analytic complaint, which is the form that transferential speech takes, the mother, first of all, is unmistakably called up, and is inscribed at the heart of the most vivid memories.

Does this mean that the family is to be blamed? This is not the postulate of psychoanalysis. It is certain that many things pass between the generations, but surely not the cause of symptoms. To speak of the family's causality at this level would make the therapeutic effects of transferential speech unintelligible, for such speech takes place entirely in the subject's space. This does not prevent each person, however, from carrying, in the most intimate part of him/herself, the mark of the "primordial Other." On this point, psychoanalysis is syntonic with the father's decline in civilization, in the sense that it has put an ever greater accent on the mother's role.

We can trace the curve of this debate over the mother's structuring function.

Concerning the outcome of the castration complex, Freud accented unambiguously the essential, central function of maternal castration for both sexes.

Some fifty years later, Winnicott, Balint, and the English "middle group" passed resolutely to "something else": the unsubstitutable role of the mother's presence and her love. In the space between the two stands Melanie Klein, who emphasized less the mother's castration than her good and bad objects.

Lacan, first of all, brought attention back to her desire. Where others had been concerned with the mother and her love, he reminded us of woman. This woman was, first, the woman attached to the father—the father of the paternal metaphor; he thus returned to a Freudian Oedipus that had been rationalized in terms of language. He did not, however, stay in this position; he passed beyond the Oedipus complex, and in this new place, he situates woman as barred, as Other, a figure who is not completely occupied with either the man or the child.

This is our question: What is to be said of the mother from the point of view that includes what is beyond the Oedipus complex? It is not only society that has changed, although it is true that it accentuates ever more strongly the mother's preponderant and sometimes exclusive role in relation to the child. Psychoanalysis has also changed with Lacan's teaching, with his formalization in the 1970s of a logic that is not the unary logic of the Oedipus complex and that implies new advances concerning femininity. I note, moreover, that for Lacan, as early as 1958, psychoanalysts' accent on the deficiencies of maternal love or the imaginary of the maternal body needed to be interpreted: he recognized in it, indeed, "a conceptual foregrounding of women's sexuality,"[3] thus directing our attention back toward the economy of desire and jouissance. In fact, what we—Lacan's students—are doing today is accentuating the function of her jouissance. We still need to know, however, which jouissance is in question.

REPROACHING THE MOTHER

There is obviously a prior discourse on the mother that makes her the vital object par excellence: the pole of the first sensual excitations, the figure who captivates the speakingbeing, the very symbol of love.

---

3. "Guiding Remarks for a Congress on Feminine Sexuality," p. 87. (Translation altered).

Echoes of this come back in what analysands say, but for the most part, they foreground something else: anxiety and reproach. To situate the distance between these discourses, I am going to give two examples, which have the merit of staging, in very different ways, the imaginary of castration between the mother and her child.

On one hand, there is the saying (*dire*) of a female analysand who remembers the girl that she was for her mother, and on the other, a son's tender memory of an exceptional mother. The female analysand remembers that when she must have been eight or nine, she had a magnificent head of hair with two long pigtails. That day, her mother announced to her that "we're going to the hairdresser to get your pigtails cut off." She begged to no avail; her mother's astonishing intention was to have them made into a wig, which she could wear as a chignon! Today, having now become a mother herself, the analysand still keeps this chignon in the top shelf of an armoire: it is the *agalmatic* object that the mother had finally never dared to use. The other anecdote is the opposite of the first. The son was not an analysand, but the famous Catalan musician, Pablo Casals. He remembered a shattering instant in which he saw something (*instant de voir*). He was then living in Paris, through the determination of his mother, who although she had no resources, wanted him to go to schools that were worthy of his genius. One day, she returned home in an unrecognizable state, having sold her abundant and beautiful hair, which she had willingly sacrificed to her son's vocation. In this case, what suffused his memory was an idealizing gratitude and a nostalgia for the lost object.

In free association, on the contrary, whatever the individual variants may be, the mother is, instead, the defendant. Imperious, possessive, obscene, or, on the contrary, indifferent, cold, and lethal, too often present or, too often away, too attentive or too distracted, force-feeding or depriving, caring or neglectful, refusing or giving, she is, for the subject, a figure of his first anxiety, the place of an unfathomable enigma and an obscure threat. At the heart of the unconscious, the mother's lapses always have their place, and as Lacan says, will sometimes go to the point of "ravaging" the child, when this child is a girl.

It is not enough to make a survey of these grievances, like good empiricists. We must construct the structure that contains their many varieties. It is striking to notice that analytic doctrines about the mother most frequently relay the neurotic's recriminations, which remain in the memory as traces of the drama that Freud designated with the term "infantile neurosis." In these recriminations, we do not hear the mother's voice; instead, what comes through in what the analysand deplores is the infantile complaint, and no further light is thrown on the true cause. This simplistic transposition of what analysands say makes the doctrine itself into a product of neurosis. For this reason, Lacan qualified Melanie Klein as an "inspired tripe seller," as a "diviner of entrails for children."[4]

It is a fact that there is a wide distance between the mother who is spoken of and the mother who speaks. The first is an object, seen through the prism of the speaker's fantasy. The second is a subject, possibly an analysand, and as such, tortured by the division of the speakingbeing. The problem is to grasp in each case "by what paths the fantasies pass in order to go from the mother to the child,"[5] for we cannot doubt that the fantasies that she arouses owe something to her own subjectivity, to her lack and her way of filling it up.

MATERNAL POWER

These paths can only be those of discourse. It is as a being of speech that she leaves her mark on her child. Speech hits the body as an arrow hits a target, but it is able to bring its effects to bear upon the child only because it is incarnated; there is therefore no contradiction in invoking the weight of maternal jouissance.

Lacan had to enter into a polemic with the proponents of the silent two-body relation that is supposed to conjoin the mother and her product within a primary unity—whether or not one wants to call it undifferentiated. The text "Remark on Daniel Lagache's Report" echoes this, but the debate aims, beyond the man whom he was speaking to at that moment, at all the partisans of a preverbal causality for psychic reality. One certainly cannot deny that the mother, as parent and parturient, is a corporeal entity, but one also cannot deny that the reproduction of bodies is entirely organized, and even programmed, by discourse. We cannot fail to be aware that at the level of the organism's first vital needs and the care it calls for, what occurs is what Lacan calls

---

4. Jacques Lacan, "Jeunesse de Gide," p. 750.
5. *Ibid.*

an "object relation *in the real*."[6] The analytic question, however, concerns something else: the emergence of the subject and the imprint that it receives from the Other.

It is certain that the body is concerned here. First of all, if the child who is to be born already figures as a subject in the sayings (*dires*) of its parents, when it comes into the world it is as a body, a sexed organism. It is an organism that is to be given life, but also one that is to be civilized and bent to one's own prescriptions. The mother, or her substitute, has to lend a hand: voicing the first imperatives concerning regulation and support, she is, in this respect, the first to mediate what could be called the policing of the body. The latter could not take place only through the silence of regulated habits, although the child cannot be unmarked by them. There must be language in order for the demand to be articulated, and this articulation alone allows this body to "be made into a body by the path of the signifier." Winnicott, Balint, and a few others can dream of a prior time in which the child is enveloped mythically by a wordless presence that makes no requirements. This time, even as a supposition, however, would concern only a subjective limbo into which nothing that is analyzable could be placed.

The powers of the word go very far—to the point of regulating jouissance—and the mother is the first representative of these powers, from the moment that she introduces the child to the articulated demand by imposing the bid in which the child is alienated: a double bid, of the language (*la langue*) in which the demand can be made, and also of the response that comes from the Other.

THE CHILD AS OBJECT

It is here that the mother's will sometimes disputes with her love and the child must undergo her iron rule or her caprice. I am thinking, for example, of the mother who made it a point of honor that by their first birthdays, each of her children would have acquired control over their sphincters! The great modern, anti-Sadian principle that no one has the right to dispose of the other's body hits a stumbling block in

---

6. Jacques Lacan, "Remarque sur le rapport de Daniel Lagache," *Ecrits* (French edition), p. 654.

this limit-zone of mothering: the first humanization of the body is open to excesses and transgressions. Even before the child begins to apprehend the difference between the sexes, these excesses and transgressions already trap him in the "sexual service of his mother,"[7] in the position of fetish, and sometimes of victim.

The decline of the paternal third term has been accompanied by the rise of all kinds of specialists, as if we understood that mothers cannot complete the humanizing of their child by themselves. Such specialists are legion, and they offer to interpose themselves within the primary couple in order to tell mothers what they should and should not do. Sometimes even the child analyst does not recoil from committing himself/herself to being what could be called the Other of the maternal Other, in order to give advice to mothers! The examples of Winnicott and Françoise Dolto come readily to mind. In fact, this process can be read as early as Freud's case history of little Hans, where, in a family that is coming apart, the "Professor" is called upon because of the father's deficiency.

These deviancies of mothering indicate how strongly the mother's division and the place that she allows the child are determinant. This, indeed, was already Freud's thesis, although he formulated it differently: he recognized a structuring function for the phase of the "castration complex" and the specific anxiety that is manifest in it. The latter becomes significant in his eyes only on the basis of the discovery of the mother's lack of a penis, which Freud identifies with her castration, and which engenders the subject's symptomatic responses. To speak of the division of the subject—here that of the mother as the child's Other—is to designate both the lack that founds desire—which is inscribed by the symbol $(-\varphi)$—and the object that responds to it in the fantasy. Each child is in a position to experience and be marked by it. A French proverb has noted one of these connections: for every saintly woman, there is a perverse son. Psychoanalysts themselves have gotten into the habit of speaking of mothers of psychotic, backward, sick children.[8]

---

7. Jacques Lacan, "On Freud's '*Trieb*' and the Psychoanalyst's Desire," trans. Bruce Fink, in *Reading Seminars I and II*, ed. Richard Feldstein, Bruce Fink, and Maire Jaanus (Albany: State University of New York Press, 1996), p. 418.

8. See, on this subject, Jacques Lacan, "Note on the Child," trans. Russell Grigg. *Analysis* 2, 1990:7–8.

Is motherly love thus an empty word? Certainly not, but like every other love, it is structured by fantasy. This is not to say that it is imaginary—far from it—but that in a very real way, it reduces the partner to being only the object that the subjective division calls to. Furthermore, the mother–child relation carries to a higher power the alienation inherent in love, since the newborn is not first a subject, but an object. The child is a real object, in the hands of the mother who, far beyond what is required by her care, can use him/her as a possession, an erotic doll from which she can get jouissance and to which she can give jouissance. Freud had already emphasized the erotic ambiguity of maternal care, from which the subject will have to emerge as the effect of speech. This is the step that the autistic child never takes, and that, for all others, is only the first on the path toward separation.

THE CHILD AS INTERPRETER

A lot will depend, therefore, on the place that the maternal unconscious gives to an object that has arisen in the real, if, indeed, it does give a place to it. There are mothers who are only breeders of objects with which they feel no connection; for them the child, for want of being a phallic substitute, is merely a piece of flesh. This was Lacan's hypothesis about schizophrenic children. Most often, what will determine the child's fate is the mother's solution to phallic lack and the way that the child is placed within it.

One must also recall that the constancy of the mother-subject's fantasy does not exclude the impact of the conjunctures of life and also leaves a place to the little subject's own reading of it. Let us not forget that for the mother, as for everyone else, the desire sustained by the fantasy and the jouissance ensured by it participate in what is impossible to say; therefore, they can be approached only by means of the little subject's interpretation of the discourse that envelops it.

It can thus be understood why the castration complex is present in a temporality that occurs in phases. There must be a certain maturing of the organism, but there must especially be a crucial moment in which circumstances actualize the enigma of the barred Other for the subject. Such an encounter can occur on the slope of the mystery of her desire or on that of the opacity of her jouissance. The birth of a new child, mourning, a separation, a departure—all the accidents that touch the mother's, or the parents', libido are propitious occasions for it.

It must also be concluded that the hackneyed notion of the desired child must not be handled too simplistically, and that the desire for a child (*désir d'enfant*) is not identical to wanting a child (*une envie d'enfant*): psychogenic sterilities point to this distinction and analysands' words often demonstrate it. The birth of one such subject, which had been awaited joyously and eagerly by the entire family, was immediately darkened by the death of the mother's own father. This woman may have had a pathological fixation on her father and she said, "My son killed my father." Because he experienced her depression for the first three years of his life, the subject, in the "unfathomable relation that unites the child with the thoughts that accompanied his conception,"[9] became unable to identify with the signifier of life. He interpreted his coming into the world not as that of the desired child that he was, but as a child dedicated to death, which he became.

Conquering, by his very demand, the mother's presence and love, the child offers himself in the lures of seduction, as what can make real whatever he perceives—on the basis of the mother's words and conduct—to be the object of her desire. In the process, the mother is raised to the status of symbolic power, the holder of the powers of speech; this speech is, first of all, the primal one of the first verdicts. "What is first said (*Le premier dit*) decrees, legislates, aphorizes, is an oracle; it confers its obscure authority on the real other."[10] It leaves a trace in the memory, where we find the sometimes ravaging and persecuting voice of its unforgettable words, imperatives, and commentaries.

Yet this grip stumbles when it hits another side of the powers of speech: it signifies, beyond what she says (*ses dits*)—through her contradictions, her silences, her gaps, her equivocations—everything that she does not say of her desire, but that she allows the young subject's eager ears to hear. This desire may be inexpressible, but it gives itself to be read, while the opacity of jouissance, on the other hand, can only be surprised in furtively perceived scenes. In deciphering this enigma, what the child is seeking is the very place of his being and his final

---

9. Lacan, "Jeunesse de Gide," p. 754.
10. *Ibid.*

identification; he scrutinizes and interrogates the maternal Other in a way that is all the more insistent since he expects to find in her the key to his inexpressible and "stupid existence."[11] He seeks the answer to the question of what he is for the Other. Love, as much as desire, begins with lack.

If I have accentuated Lacan's reference to Léon Bloy's *La femme pauvre*,[12] it is because, for a woman, there is an opposition between being a mother and a woman. The mother, through the child, gets back the object that she is lacking; she is a woman inasmuch as her libido is addressed to a man and she posits herself as dispossessed of what she is looking for in him. One of them has, and is thus rich, and the other, the poor one, does not have, in terms of the metaphor of the ($-\varphi$). What is missing in the mother is the *dit-mension*[13] of an other desire, other than the one that is satisfied in her relation to her child; the child will be doomed to the maximal alienation of making the mother's fantasy come into existence, and if it is signified to him that he fulfills her, he will be trapped entirely in his being as object, as the mother's possession.

It is not the lack of love but too much of it that is harmful and that calls for a necessary effect of separation. This is why Lacan accentuated the mother's desire. This is to be understood as the desire of a woman *in* the mother, a specific desire to limit maternal passion, to make her *not completely* mother: in other words, *not completely* concerned with her child, and even *not completely* concerned with the series of children, the sibling rivals. The paternal metaphor already implies this, for the operation that substitutes the signifier of the father for that of the mother has the result of specifying the maternal lack as a phallic lack, and of instituting the father as a partner outside the series. A mother is not completely concerned with her child because her phallic aspiration is divided between the man and the child. It is good that this is the case: it is woman's desire, or more generally, a desire that is

---

11. Jacques Lacan, "On a Question Prior to Any Possible Treatment of Psychosis," p. 183.

12. See Chapter 2, "A Woman," above.

13. Lacan's pun on "dimension" carries a reference to "*dit*" and to both a dwelling-place and the act of mentioning. For more information, see the translator's note in *Encore*, p. 21.

other, maintained beyond the gratifications of maternity, that introduces the child, via castration anxiety, to a dialectic of contradictory
identifications. Through these identifications, he will be able to lose
his fondness for the passion of being the mother's object—a passion that
would render him passive—and will, in the end, take up his own sex.

THE MOTHER, OTHER

What can be said of the mother as absolute Other? The 1958 text
on feminine sexuality does not exclude her from the relation with the
child. Lacan notes explicitly there that we must ask "whether phallic
mediation drains off the whole force of the drives in women, and no-
tably the whole current of the maternal instinct."[14] It is not by chance
that, for once, Lacan uses the term "instinct," which he challenges
everywhere else, preferring, as a translation of Freud's *trieb*, the French
term *pulsion* (drive), which is more disjoined from any connotation
of the natural. What are the repercussions on the child of what it is
possible for a woman to make real, on the margins of every phallic
inscription?

Desire that is specifically feminine makes the mother absent to her
child, but for the child there will be a big difference in whether this
absence is deciphered within the phallic order or whether, on the contrary, it will obscurely exceed this order. From the fact that phallicism
speaks and is conveyed in signs, it establishes between objects an order
in which the child tries to situate him/herself, even if only as a negative value. On the other hand, the *not-whole* remains, by definition,
silent; it is an absolute silence that haunts everything that is ordered
in the phallic series. I have mentioned, at one of the poles of maternal
harmfulness, the mother who is entirely engaged by her child. On the
other pole must be situated the mother who is not engaged by her child
at all, and we can contrast the hostage-child of the first with the neglected child of the second. The latter has no recourse when confronted
with the power of an unfathomable silence, which is equivalent to a

---

14. "Guiding Remarks for a Congress on Feminine Sexuality," p. 92. (Translation altered).

point of foreclosure. This does not at all imply an abandonment by the mother, or if so, it would be necessary to speak of a subjective abandonment, through the failure of the only signifier that can serve as signifier of jouissance: the Phallus.

Thus the variety of figures of the mother fans out between the two extremes of the too-mothering mother, who has the child in her clutches, and the too-womanly mother, who is occupied elsewhere, to the point of being sometimes so Other as to be unrecognizable. A number of nuances should still be added. Lacan said that there are several ways "to cherish a child too much." Indeed, certain differences—whether it is the child's body or his/her being as subject that is in question, or whether the child is a boy or a girl—will change everything.

We know, for example, Freud's astonishment on discovering, at long last, the strange consistency of the bond uniting the girl to her mother. Lacan confirms this when he notes, in the 1970s, that it seems very much as if, in light of analytic experience, the daughter expects more "support" from her mother than her father, but that the mother is, for her, what he calls a "ravage." This term, through its connotation of an erosion of any reference point, goes well beyond the discords of rivalry that belong to the phallic register; in strict accordance with the notion of the barred woman as absolute Other, it is not far from raising the mother to the place of what cannot be thought.

The daughter, however, is not the only one who sometimes has to pay the costs of the mother's extremism. The French writer Romain Gary testifies to this in his autobiography, *Promise at Dawn*. A fatherless only son, he bore the boundless expectations of an unstoppable mother. Promised to various exceptional destinies, he was neither the inspired violinist whom she dreamed about, nor the gifted prodigy at tennis for whom she obtained, by a bluff, an encounter on the Riviera with the king of Sweden, who was quite amused by his adversary's mediocrity. However disappointing his performances may have been, he could always count on an unshakeable mother. When the war came and he flew for the allies as an aviator, he continued to receive loving letters from her, although he would never see her again, for she was already dead! In her love, she had anticipated this incredible posthumous dialogue: she had given these letters to a chargé d'affaires in the hope that they would sustain her son in his time of trials! This shows how little such a mother's letters had to concede to the current situation, even when she was preparing to meet her fate. Thinking of Romain Gary's tragic end, I cannot keep myself from believing that more than any other he was cradled at dawn, according to the beautiful expression that Lacan applies precisely to the mother, by the "false promises of her true despair."

In every case, it is by speech that the mother leaves her mark. Lacan recalled, in his seminar *Encore*, that a woman as mother makes the little human speak, and that, as soon as he, in turn, transmits "*lalangue*" back to her, "[s]he has unconscious effects."[15] This transmission is not a cognitive exercise, for *lalangue* is not only the idiom of each person's region; it is, first of all, the private language of the primal couple—the mother and her little "premature child." It is the language of the Eros of the first body-to-body connection, whose words leave a trace of the jouissance that they have harbored.

Yet the mother is no less the mediator of a discourse in which she cannot fail to leave her marks. It is here that the rise of her dominance can be diagnosed: in the fragmentation of contemporary social bonds. The more the intergenerational transmissions are reduced to the implicit prescriptions of her desire alone, and especially to what she desires for her child, the more the child will see his/her subjective options in relation to the desire of the Other reduced to an alternative: either take up the maternal mandate and follow the vocation to which one had been promised by her wishes, or reject it and mark oneself as excluded from it. To do the latter would be to affirm the little freedom that is left in the form of the negative. Twenty years ago, Lacan prognosticated that this growing power of "being named to" something by the mother will become a relay for the social. The course of events has hardly contradicted his prediction.

---

15. *Encore*, p. 99.

8

The Mother's Anxiety

Psychoanalysis has asked the question: What is a mother's love worth? The child, at first, is nothing more than an offshoot of her body. How valuable is her love in humanizing it?

QUESTIONING MATERNAL LOVE

People have been questioning the value of maternal love for a long time. We can see a double movement in our own civilization: one idealizes maternal love as if it were all-sufficient and one suspects that mothers are always unequal to everything, in the name of the widely shared feeling that between the mother and the child there must be a third term. As proof of this ambivalence, I will mention two opposed but converging facts. First, the "utopian communities" that marked the last century. Whatever the larger significance of their efforts to subtract the child from the singularity of a family, they all supposed that individual differences—which are odious to all forms of collectivism—are rooted in the marks left by infantile love. Next, in a register that seeks to be more scientific, I will note the striking fact that the "decline of paternalism" has been accompanied by the rise of all kinds of specialists—pediatric and early-childhood specialists, educators, psychologists—who offer themselves, as I have said, as the Other of the maternal Other.

In psychoanalysis itself, questioning the maternal libido has become a general phenomenon. This begins, indeed, with what analysands themselves say. Despite the big differences between one analysand and another, the mother figures most often in free associations as the one who is accused. What *isn't* said about her? Too present or too absent, too concerned or too negligent, she appears as the figure of the first anxieties, the place both of an obscure threat and an unfathomable enigma.

The mother's lapses are also always present at the heart of the discourse of the unconscious, and even when the subject does not have any reproaches to make against her, this lack will itself become one of them: she is unforgettable, sometimes to the point of "ravage" for the daughter, since the partiality of sexual difference is not unmarked here. Freud himself perceives this; although he is severe toward women—he has been reproached often enough for it—with the mother, he is more positive than any of his successors have been. Making the bond of love with the first object the irreplaceable experience that is the root of the subject's later capacity to love, he even thought that he could recognize the only unambivalent love in the attachment to the son, and he had to struggle to admit what time ended up imposing on him: for the daughter, the verdict is darker, and perhaps even without appeal.

It is still necessary to grasp the logic that orders these various experiential data: the logic that Lacan brought to light in re-examining the Freudian Oedipus complex, accentuating the "desire of the mother" as distinct from her love, a desire that is to be understood as a sexed desire, or in other words, a woman's desire.

Freud, in forging the myth of Oedipus, cast the mother essentially as an object. By "object," he meant an erotic object, one that is coveted and is to be lost. Following this thread, a certain orientation highlighted her body rather than her speech. Something, however, remains to be clarified here. Certainly, the figure of the mother is always bound up with what is unthinkable about the reproduction of living bodies, the question about which, "Where do children come from?" haunts the imagination of Freud's little Hans, and of many others. It is certain, besides, that the relation between a mother and her child really begins with a body-to-body contact, in which, because of the infant's prematurity, the nursling has not yet become a subject. Yet once Imaginary, Symbolic, and Real have been distinguished, one notices that this object is also the Other, the symbolic strength that holds the power of the bids of speech. These are the mother's words, her imperatives and her commentaries, which inscribe in the memory the sometimes ravaging and persecuting voice that the analysand mentions so often: "My mother said that. . . ." Also, to echo the formula about the father whom one could do without, one would say about the mother, instead, that one must do without her. And why, then, other than to serve her no longer?

MOTHER, WOMAN

In one way or another, the entire analytic movement recognizes the necessity of the separation-effect. Yet it is at this level that the risk of failing to recognize the true cut is situated, for the cut that separates the mother and the child must be referred to another cut, which Lacan brought to light: that between the living, even animal, organism and the subject as effect of the symbolic. As we know, this thesis rejoins the Freudian discovery called castration: it is the symbolic that, ensuring its grasp on the living being, introduces into it the lack that Lacan differentiated as the lack in jouissance (*manque à jouir*) and the lack in being (*manque à être*). In doing so, it confers a fundamental role on the lost object in humanizing this offshoot of the mother's body. We could follow this theme in psychoanalytic literature. It oscillates between two poles: the mother herself as lost object, the grounds for a fundamental nostalgia, and the child as an object that must be subtracted from the mother's grasp, for if there is no such subtraction, he remains attached "to the sexual service of his mother."[1]

---

1. Jacques Lacan, "Of Freud's '*Trieb*' and the Psychoanalyst's Desire," trans. Bruce Fink, in *Reading Seminars I and II: Lacan's Return to Freud*, ed. Richard Feldstein, Bruce Fink, and Maire Jaanus (Albany: State University of New York Press, 1996), p. 418.

In this operation of separation, what acts as mediator is not the mother's love, but her division by an object that causes her desire. This is why Lacan, in his *Seminar IV*, going against the supporters of the "object relation," placed such an accent on the notion of object-lack and the necessity for the child to encounter—beyond the mother as a power (*puissance*) that can fill up or be filled up—the mother as desiring: the mother in whom the lack of the phallus is in its place as cause of desire. It is here that the divergence between her being as mother and her being as woman is introduced. Both certainly refer to phallic lack, but in different ways. Her being as mother resolves this lack by having, in the form of the child, a substitute for the phallic object that is missing in her. As I have said, however, the mother's being as woman is not entirely resolved in this substitute for having the phallus. Precisely inasmuch as her desire diverges toward man, it is rather to being or receiving the phallus that a woman aspires: to being it, by the love that phallicizes her; to receiving it, by means of the organ from which she gets off. The price of both aspirations is that of not having the phallus. Feminine poverty indeed!

THE DOUBLE ABSENCE

Feminine desire as such makes the mother absent. This absence is to be symbolized, but it is quite necessary, for it opens onto the dialectic of separation. To the extent that she is a woman, a mother is not completely (*pas toute*) oriented toward her child. Since her relation to the phallus is divided, the child does not saturate it. This, however, is only one aspect of things, for a supplementary question is raised by the formulas of sexuation. The latter inscribe another division than the one —internal to the phallic register—that I have just mentioned: the division between her relation to the phallus (-φ) and what is absolutely Other [S(A̶)].[2] One can therefore distinguish in the mother's absence —in feminine desire inasmuch as it makes the mother absent—the element of this absence that is inscribed on the side of the phallic symbolization and, on the other hand, what is indicated as Other without being inscribed. The possible consequences for the child of this lack of inscription remain to be explored.

---

2. See the schema from *Encore*, p. 78.

A woman's phallic desire doubtless subtracts something from the child, but it also, as I have said, has a separating effect. Indeed, phallicism speaks; it is conveyed in signs and can be read. The child does not fail to interpret them, and this pinpointing of something of her desire helps prevent him/her from being captured in an immediate identification with the phallus. On the other hand, the silence of the not-completely phallic, absolute Other, who has a relation with an other jouissance, which Lacan qualifies as mad and enigmatic, is not written and remains undecipherable. It makes the mother, in her unconscious wishing, a woman who is not at all occupied with the phallic child. The mother's harmfulness, of which so much has been made, is divided between two poles: between possessiveness, which is so often denounced, and neglect, which is less often perceived. Completely occupied with the child, she makes him/her into her phallic hostage; not at all occupied with him/her, she leaves the child with no recourse when faced with the power of her silence, a silence that is not speech but foreclosure.

This subjective state of leaving the child high and dry has nothing to do with abandoning him/her at the level of corporeal reality and can be accommodated to the mother's presence, even to something like a paradoxical, almost indifferent love, one that has been reduced to the possession of the body as real. What makes this possible is the fact that, in every case, the child is not only a phallic symbol. S/he is such a phallic figure, but is also a real object, one that is impossible to cipher, "appearing in the real,"[3] in the place of the S(A). We can try to seek the indices of this.

ANXIETY

I am going to take maternal anxiety as an index, since, according to Lacan, it is "not without an object": this object is the real, outside signification, of the phallus. It can obviously be approached, classically,

---

3. Although this expression was first reserved for psychosis, Lacan uses it about the child in his two notes to Jenny Aubry. See "Note on the Child," trans. Russell Grigg. *Analysis* 2 (1990): 8. As early as 1977, within the Freudian School of Paris, I highlighted this theme of the real child, in the text that can be found in the Appendix, entitled, "The Difference between the Sexes in Analysis."

as castration anxiety, which can take various forms. There is, of course, the anxiety of losing the child and we know the strength of the fantasies that aim at the death of the child; another form of castration anxiety is that of depriving the child, of imposing requirements upon him/her: of being the one who is in charge of what I have called the first "policing of the body," since it is up to her to make the child enter into the limitations programmed by discourse. And so on. Yet anxiety before the real of foreclosed jouissance is something else; it exists on the edges of castration anxiety properly speaking, but is to be distinguished from it.

I will mention some clinical facts, which are discrete, but which seem to me to be good indications. I will start with the "softest": the always somewhat dumbfounded side of a young mother when she has just given birth. Confronted with this note of stupor, which oscillates between fear and ravishment, and which can make her flee from her analysis and grant herself a holiday from speech, we cannot fail to recognize that all of it cannot be attributed to the idea that the phallus has been given back to her!

There is also the affect of pregnancy that reacts to the parasitic relation to the body of this foreign element, the fetus. Reactions to this are quite varied, and are not always those of anxiety. They can go from a sense of euphoric fullness, produced by having the equivalent to the phallus, to true horror, which one mother was able to maintain for nine months at the level of the purest hypochondriacal anxiety.

Anxiety about the care to be given to the newborn is also worth examining. It is a terror of not knowing what to do with this living thing, this baby who does not speak, who is not yet subject to repression, and who therefore stands in greater proximity to the jouissance of life, a jouissance that is still unmarked in the child. Some mothers are terrified of this object and imagine that they do not know how to do what all mammals know instinctually: how to carry it, feed it, keep it warm, and so on.

In such cases, the young mother usually turns toward her own mother, a fellow creature, as it were, even if her anxiety is matched by her reproaches toward her mother. What is mobilized here is the relation to living jouissance, a relation that, in all cases, is a function of the mother's own repressions. I will note, furthermore, that such reactions toward babies extend well beyond mothers, and take forms that always stand in very lively contrast with each other: they go from taste to distaste, from an anxious malaise to a fascinated passion, from willed indifference to a sustained vocation, and so forth.

Finally, I must mention the puerperal psychoses, which do not exclude taking care of the child, but which show that for a mother, a birth can be the encounter with a real that is capable of causing a delirium, by making a point of foreclosure present for her.

"THE SERVICE OF HIS MOTHER"

How does a mother make use of her child—for there is more than one way of doing so? The "sexual service of his mother," when it is not at the level of the pure real, is understood as phallic service, but is itself stratified.

The distinction between the organ and the signifier can be used to distinguish two poles of this use of the child. The child as organ—in Freudian terms, one would say the "penis-child"—is the body taken as an erotic doll. At this level, many abuses are permitted; the anti-Sadian principle that no one has the right to place the other's body at his/her disposal encounters a certain limit here, for this relation, under the cover of love and upbringing, is open to excesses, as I mentioned above. Analysis gives us many examples of this, but I would like to refer today to a text that comes from elsewhere, from a man who had a horror of all the jouissances that are not those of the organ itself: Henry de Montherlant.

In a little satiric text, written in a rather extreme style, in which he describes a Spanish train, he portrays, "screaming at the top of his voice, the babe-in-arms, the international crybaby who haunts trains as a bug does beds." You can already get a sense of the text's tone.

Glued to him like a ghoul to the corpse, his mother sucks on his neck, his ears, his hair, imitating with her kisses the noise of falling pieces of dung, infects him with the germs of her mouth, speaks even more stupidly than he does when he speaks, messes her pants when he messes his, puts her hand on his bottom, excites him with all her strength to scream more loudly. . . . The whole car goes into a delirium about the fetus. . . . The whole car goes inane with him, and is no more than one vast *yummm-yummm*. (This means "mommy" and has no more importance morally

than the braying of an ass.) Papa, caca . . . (these two words mean almost
the same thing) tries to vanquish him in stupidity, while the convulsed
being projects his saliva, his urine, and his mucus everywhere, which those
present receive religiously.[4]

We are very far here from the "ideal of the angel" and the "sacrifice of
jouissance" characteristic of Gide's mother![5]
    The child, however, can also be used in other ways than this body-
to-body contact. The child as phallus is something else. As a being of
discourse, s/he is not so much at the service of the mother's eroticism
as of her narcissism, fashioned as s/he is by her/his mother's signifiers,
destined to take upon him/herself her chimeras and her dreams, even
to the point of assuming the secret prescriptions of her discourse. These
two uses are to be distinguished but are not opposed to each other, and
can obviously be combined. Sometimes great vocations, particularly in
the field of sublimation, result from them. When the link between them
is broken, when the first is practiced exclusively, erotic possession does
not exclude leaving the subject high and dry in the silence of the Other,
as is the case with certain schizophrenic children.

A NAMEABLE LOVE

What, then, is a mother's love worth in humanizing her child? The
phenomena of institutionalization show us that taking care of the body
is not everything: the little person is humanized by a desire that is not
anonymous. Let us conclude that for a child, maternal devotion is worth
more if the mother is not everything to him/her, and if she is also not
located in an unfathomable elsewhere: it is still necessary for her love
as woman to refer to a name. As Lacan said, there is only the love of a
name: here, the name of a man who could be any man, but who, from
the sole fact of being nameable, will set a limit as much to the metonymy of the phallus as to the opacity of the absolute Other. Only on
this condition can the child be inscribed in a particularized desire.

---

4. Henry de Montherlant, *La petite Infante de Castille*. (Paris: Gallimard. Collection Folio), pp. 18–23. Originally published in 1929.
    5. Lacan uses these expressions about Gide and his mother.

9

An Infantile Neurosis

INTERPRETATION INCARNATED

It is obvious that the child is interpreted very early in his life, but who is the interpreter? It is certainly, first of all, the Other, and then, very soon, the unconscious. Yet the child is also an interpreter, and is perhaps even interpretation. This is Lacan's implicit thesis in his two notes to Jenny Aubry, when he situates the child either as the truth of the couple or as the truth of the mother alone.

Here is the great distinction, which, in its simplest and most condensed formulation, refers to a structural opposition that can be written with the two signifiers of the paternal metaphor. To say that the child represents a truth that is not his own but the Other's, and that he is either the couple's or the mother's truth—doesn't this mean that the child is an incarnated interpretation? Doesn't this mean that the child's symptom enables what neither the mother nor the couple decipher in their unconscious or their union to appear in the real, in a form that is enjoyed (forme jouie)?

In other words, to use Lacan's later formulas: like adults, children have symptoms, which are very polymorphous and often transitory—and which are thus more difficult to diagnose—but by their symptoms, by the symptoms that they have, they are symptoms, symptoms of the Other. They lend their body to the truth of the Other that gets off through them, just as Lacan can say that a woman is a symptom for a man, or that the analyst him/herself is a symptom. Obviously, the question is to know how, for each child, at each moment, her "symptom-being" is articulated with her own symptom, a symptom that would give her the proper name of her jouissance.

Now I come to the interpreted child. When does such interpretation begin?

Let us not forget that the child appears first of all as an object, but that s/he does so in various ways. When s/he comes into the world, s/he is first real, a living doll, a little erotic thing, a body enjoyed by the other. This goes far, and perhaps to the point of serving as an exception to the absence of the sexual relation. Lacan stated this once, at the very end of his teaching, in a truly astonishing sentence, one that retains its enigmatic element for me. Recalling his statement "There is no sexual relation," he added, "except between the generations." It is true that for a woman, the child that Freud reduced to its phallic value is also real. With this offshoot from her body, a woman sees appear, in the very real of life, S($\bar{A}$), the equivalent of her own lack.

A clinic of the everyday life of maternity could be grafted on here, one that would study the way that women live through their pregnancies. We know its poles: on the one hand, it goes from euphoria to blissful ecstasy, and on the other, from the horror of the parasitic connection to the feeling of mutilation in postpartum depressions, not to speak of puerperal psychoses. There is an entire series, a whole range of phenomena, that testify incontestably that the mother's body-to-body connection with her child is a jouissance-relation. This, however, does not exhaust the status of the child-object. S/he is also an object in the sense of being an image-child, an image that is moving for some and repulsive for others. Think of the passion with which we photograph the newborn, of all the films that follow his/her growth, sometimes step by step, and which we watch nostalgically twenty years later! I will leave aside the best-known situation: the signifier-child suffused with the phallic value in which the parents delight.

Whatever the case may be, it is not the object-child who is interpreted. Interpretation supposes a missing element, and therefore the appearance of the interpretable child, and not simply the child as an object that is enjoyed—whether really, imaginarily, or symbolically—can be dated from the first appearance of the minus-one of the subject. The latter emerges with a cry, the first manifestation of the living being that hollows out its hole in the Other. In the supply of signifiers that covers over the child even before it is born, the cry brings into existence the empty place of the subject, which can function, from then on, as an x interpreted by the Other's response. The child's interpreted being begins here, and is manifested clearly in the clinic of mothering, where we note every day the interpretative activity by which mothers lend their voices and words to the baby's still inarticulate manifestations, which they raise to the value of a signifier. This *Che vuoi?* that comes from the maternal Other and that finds its first responses there, generally in terms of the drives, makes the interpreted child a preliminary of the child as interpreter.

For the child is also the interpreter, the decipherer. To become this, s/he must enter into the structure of speech, and the interval between signifiers must hollow her/him out enough to make its bid precisely for interpretation. The encounter with the enigma of the Other is decisive here and if it is not saturated, each child endeavors to establish her/his own reading of the Other's—and principally the mother's—saying (*dire*). We know the attention that even the youngest children pay not only to what the Other says (*dits*), but also to her silences, contradictions, lies, in short, to all the gaps in her discourse. The child is obviously concerned in her very being, since what she is seeking to pierce through is the mystery of her conception as well as of her sex. The interpreter thus finds herself again as interpreted, and the secret of all her interpretations resides in this knot of interpretations. We can see what is missing to the child in the institutionalization syndrome mentioned at the end of the two notes to Jenny Aubry. Her vital needs can be satisfied with relatively anonymous care, but for want of this "particularized interest" that Lacan mentions, the child lacks the Other as interpreter, as well as the other who is to be interpreted, through which she could herself come to being in a non-anonymous desire.

LOOK FOR THE INFANTILE NEUROSIS

To throw light on the question of the child as interpreted and interpreter, I have chosen a case of a child who is not psychotic: Winnicott's Piggle.[1] In institutions for children, analysts certainly deal with an enormous number of children who are not neurotic, but I believe that infantile neurosis remains an essential reference point, even in the sometimes thorny matter of adult diagnosis. It is easy to conceive of cases where we do not succeed in saying with certainty whether a particular adult is psychotic or neurotic, since, in neurosis, the consistency of a fantasy can saturate the subject's question, and a psychosis can have remained untriggered. Such cases have led to the use of the terms, "borderline" and "narcissistic personality," and they do not present paradigmatic effects of foreclosure, for there are no major phenomena of language and no pathognomic triggering. When confronted with such cases, we should seek major neurotic phenomena: not only subjective division within transference, but also the traces, the scars—this is Freud's term—of infantile neurosis. I therefore adopt the clinical watchword "Look for the infantile neurosis," as people say, in other contexts, "Look for the woman."

To look for the infantile neurosis is, first of all, to "look for the castration complex," which, as we know, is a complex organization; far from being reducible to the presence of images of mutilation, it is an elaboration of the major affect of castration anxiety and is confused with what Freud called infantile neurosis. On this point, I will follow Michel Silvestre's thesis that the infantile neurosis and the adult neurosis are not homogeneous and symmetrical. As he said, the second cannot be resolved, for it makes up for what is impossible in the sexual relation. On the contrary, it is almost necessary, for any subject who is not going to be mad, to pass through the first, and for each of these nonpsychotic subjects, we can recover its marks, as well as its solution. To say that it is a necessary passage also indicates that it is an evolutionary phase. We no longer use the term "development," but when all is said and done, there are, nevertheless, a diachrony and typical phases.

---

1. D. W. Winnicott, *The Piggle: An Account of the Psychoanalytic Treatment of a Little Girl*, ed. Ishak Ramzy (New York: International Universities Press, 1977). References to all quotations will appear in the text.

To begin, I will remind you of the structural and separating effect of the castration complex. This is a classic thesis, but one that remains with us. Lacan, in rethinking the Oedipus complex, never questioned castration—far from it. His seminar on *The Object Relation* accentuates the object-lack in the mother, almost ironically, it should be said, since the notion of the object relation was then in vogue. The castration complex is the child's response to his/her encounter with the mother's phallic lack, for castration is not registered directly on the side of the subject. It has its impact only on the basis of the actualizing of the lack of the Other, here the mother, and of the question concerning the object that responds to this lack.

I have therefore chosen the case of a little girl who was tortured by the castration complex: Winnicott's Piggle. In this case, the little analysand, the Piggle, interests me more than the analyst, Winnicott himself, for it seems to me that he lags a bit behind her.

PIGGLE AND HANS

One could linger a bit on the couple of the Piggle and Hans. There are many analogies between them, and also some differences. First of all, these are two children who would be called normal, if you will allow me this term, which is not much approved of nowadays. Winnicott himself uses it, and he is not far from thinking that the Piggle, if need be, could have done without a psychoanalyst. This is what he believes, and he says in the text that her capacities to evolve could be counted on: the dynamism of her unconscious work would resolve the question that was presented to her. Little Hans also has a very ordinary little symptom, which is frequent in young children. Until its appearance, he was a little boy who enchanted everyone and who had nothing in particular wrong with him.

They have a second point in common: they have something to do with analysis only because their parents are adepts of psychoanalysis. Hans's father is a follower of Freud, one who is only too happy to say to the Professor, "Finally, here is a child who can be lent to your doctrine and confirm it." The Piggle's parents are also converts and, indeed, speak "Winnicottian." It's quite astonishing! We come up against this tendency of theirs when, after having read the case for a first time, we go back to it later. Certain assessments stay in our memory, but we no longer know whether they are Winnicott's or not, and they must be checked if we are to see whether they come from the parents' letters or from his own text. They are really speaking the same tongue and we perceive a transference onto Winnicott that is easily as powerful as that of Hans's father onto Freud; indeed, just as he spoke of *Professor* Freud, so they speak of *Doctor* Winnicott. This nuance does not escape the Piggle, who, at the moment when her transference begins to be marked by some doubts, asks, "Is it *Doctor* Winnicott? Does he make people better?" (p. 133).

Something else brings the two cases together: the intervention of the parents in the treatment, by their accounts, their questioning of their children, and their collection of a large part of the data. For little Hans, this is very clear. We can wonder what kind of analysis this child has, since he only sees the psychoanalyst once or twice. For the Piggle, the situation is different: she does at least see him sixteen times, even if these sessions take place over a period of two and a half years. This too is hardly very intensive. Winnicott, indeed, raises the question in his brief preface: he wonders whether, in a method that is so far from the classical one, it is really possible to speak of a psychoanalysis at all.

Here, I believe, is a question that we do not ask ourselves, since we do not have a classical method. For us, it *is* an analysis; Winnicott doubts this, but we do not. He considers it audacious that there are not three or four regular and obligatory sessions each week. Not only is the timing of the sessions very spaced out, for reasons of distance, but they are also sessions on demand. The child must insist on going to see Dr. Winnicott. This process takes a certain time. First of all, she must say, "Take me to Dr. Winnicott," then the mother says, "Yes, soon," and she waits for the child to ask a second time. Then she writes to Dr. Winnicott, "Doctor, she has asked twice," and finally there is an appointment. It is thus a very particular method, which they want the child to make her own. Of course, we understand that the child's demand, even if it is perfectly authentic, is nevertheless, especially at the beginning, a repercussion of the parents' demand, which has the effect of suggestion: they get it said through the child's mouth that they would like Winnicott to see her.

These sixteen sessions are spread out between February 3, 1964, and October 28, 1966. Coincidentally, they begin in the same year as the creation of the École freudienne de Paris; this did not happen such a long time ago. The Piggle is two years and four months old. Her major problem, which she shares again with Hans, is anxiety. There are many other possible infantile symptoms—anorexia, agitation, insomnia, and so on—but for both, the pivot of the problem is anxiety. What occasions this anxiety for the Piggle is perfectly identifiable: it is the birth of the little sister. With Hans, there are also other factors in the triggering conjuncture, but here, it is only the birth of the little sister: the appearance of a new object for the Other. We see immediately that maternal castration is not mentioned directly but indirectly, as what this new object implies, since its very appearance allows the Piggle to suppose that something is missing for her mother.

There is another common point in the curve of the two treatments: where they start and where they end up. I will come back to this.

I am not forgetting that there are also differences. First of all, in age: five years for one, and two years and four months for the other—the ages are very different; their sex, of course, and then, especially, their symptoms. Piggle does not have a phobia, whereas Hans, with his horse phobia, has raised his anxiety into a symptom.

What makes up for the lack of a phobia for Piggle? She has nightmares, which make her want not to go to bed, want not to sleep, which make her wake up screaming, and which make the nights especially turbulent. Obviously, this places her in more difficulty, in a certain way. Phobia, as a symptomatic elaboration of anxiety, is comforting, if only because it localizes anxiety, thus displacing it from its point of origin—the face-to-face relation with the mother—onto an object that is further away and possible to avoid. This is a very big benefit for the subject. The poor little Piggle, on the other hand, has manifestations that complement her anxiety, which the parents diagnose at the level of mood: sadness, apathy, tears, fragility, in a little girl who is described to us as having been fearless and brimming with vitality, until her little sister was born.

There is yet another big difference: the parents. For the little Piggle, we speak of "the parents." With little Hans, there are the father and the mother, who are quite separate in every sense of the term. We can speak of "the parents" because, while there was discord between little Hans's parents, here there is a manifest harmony, although the mother, in passing, mentions a moment of tension. This is an occasion for us to note that this latter situation is not better, and that finally, it is not at this level that things are played out! This is not the structurally determinant element, and Winnicott, indeed, is so far from finding anything strange about this rather striking unity that he notes: "letter from the parents, written by the mother" (p. 5). Only once is there a word from the father. This is a little symptomatic trait of this couple, and perhaps of Winnicott himself. We could say that these parents are a bit fused, at least in this narrative.

Perhaps this tendency goes even further, for despite several calls to order that the Piggle—or at least her unconscious—directs at him, Winnicott considers that the father, at certain moments, acts as the mother, and is equivalent to her. It is striking to see, in fact, that both of them lend their bodies to the little girl. I do not know whether this is the effect of an inclination or of their Winnicottian training, but both of them consent to a certain type of body-to-body relation with this child. We see her ask to suck the "yams," as she calls her mother's breasts, and the mother ends up allowing her to do so, after hesitating a bit, because she does not know whether this is quite orthodox. Homologously, she wants to suck her father's thumb, and there is a description of a trip in which she sucks his thumb throughout. This fact has its importance. In the case of little Hans, the phallophorous element was reduced by the discord between the parents: by the father's powerlessness to get his wife, who neither loved nor desired him, to hear him. Yet we see here that with this good understanding, the phallophorous element is still elided. It is not absent, but it is reduced, and when it is mentioned, nevertheless, in certain interpretations, it is never without confusion.

PIGGLE PRE-INTERPRETED

Before she comes to see Dr. Winnicott, Piggle has already been interpreted in terms of the commonsensical understanding of the Oedipus complex, which can be found everywhere now: she is described at the beginning of her life as a little girl who is very attached to her daddy and behaves high-handedly toward her mother. The change, once noticed, is also seen in oedipal terms. The anxiety that appears is interpreted as a disappointment in her father, who, it is inferred, gave a child to the mother (as they do not take long in saying to her explicitly). In sum, the appearance of anxiety and her troubles of mood are taken as a regression to the baby stage. You see that there is a response in the mother's first texts. To the question "What is happening," she responds that her daughter is suffering from abandonment by her oedipal objects and that she wants to regress, out of rivalry with the baby, to the nursling stage. We sense that the mother is very touched by the fact that her little girl has lost her obvious joy, her autonomy, her equilibrium. She says, "Her balance had been excellent always, but since the change in her she had been falling and crying and feeling hurt" (p. 14).

How, then, does the Piggle, who has already been interpreted and even indoctrinated, enter Winnicott's consulting room? Notice her vocabulary: a little girl who is so young—less than two and a half—who says that she has worries. Yet we have seen in the mother's texts the phrase "She has worries" (p. 5). She arrives at Winnicott's office with the idea that he knows something about the babacar and the Black Mummy. This has been said to her, and has inspired her transference. What does she do when she enters? In the first session, she begins to take out the toys that are in a box and says, "Here's *another* one . . . and here's *another* one" (p. 10). Winnicott, reasonably, says to her, "Another baby" (p. 10). Why not say this? The context calls for this remark. Taking another toy, she asks, "Where did this come from?" (p. 10). Winnicott then recognizes here, obviously, the Freudian question par excellence, which as we know, is knotted to castration anxiety: "Where do babies come from?" This is really the question of the symbolizing of existence, one that also made Hans stumble, along with the question of his sex organ.

The Piggle's question is, indeed, a foundational one. She enters with a question and not a complaint. I do not know whether it can be said that "nothing is without reason"; this would be an Hegelian thesis par excellence, but for us, in any case, what is without reason cannot be said not to be inserted into reasons and we are dealing here with a subject who is seeking reasons. What is stupefying is to see the ingenuous confidence with which Winnicott commits himself to giving the answer. To the unanswerable question, "Where do children come from?" Winnicott responds. He responds, obviously, as an empiricist: the man puts something in the woman, and it makes a child. Piggle, having been interpreted by her parents, is now interpreted by Winnicott, and in a way that is extremely naïve. As for the Piggle herself, she places herself, for the moment, beside this question, which is still there, awaiting an answer.

THE WORDS OF THE UNCONSCIOUS

Piggle also has her words from the unconscious. She does not sleep, does not want to go to sleep, tosses and turns, wakes up, and talks during the night. These are not what could be called classical nocturnal terrors. She has nightmares that speak. Even before she arrives, we have a minimal text at our disposal. There is nothing equivalent to Hans's horse, but there are, nevertheless, the words of the anxiety. A word, rather, and then a sort of nocturnal phantasmagoria. The word is "the babacar," a sort of childish neologism. It can make us think of "car," of "baby." Yet these are not what the "babacar" is: it is a word that means nothing. The little Piggle is more specific: "because of the babacar" (p. 21). We remember Hans's formula, which Lacan emphasized: "'Cos the horse." Here, it is because of the babacar. Of course this babacar arises in a dialogue with the parents because, when we read the text, we see that the parents press the child, observe her, scrutinize her, question her: "What is wrong? Why? . . ." It arises, thus, in a dialogue. She leads them on a bit of a wild goose chase, as Hans had done with the horse. Nevertheless, this is serious: the "babacar" is the signifier without a signified, without any signified other than the enigma, without a signification that would ward off anxiety. The babacar is not as effective as Hans's horse because it has the virtue of ubiquity: it is always everywhere.

"Babacar" is the name of the cause of anxiety, not of the cause of desire, and it never lets go. I am not saying that Piggle never forgets it; it is the "babacar" that never forgets her. The parents note in passing that when all is going well, she will suddenly become immobilized, say "the babacar," and then everything is ruined. She gives, indeed, some astonishing replies. Once her mother says to her, "Don't worry," and she answers, "But I want to worry!"

The other verbal element is a sentence. There are some variants, but its matrix is, "The Black Mummy says: 'Where are my yams?'" (p. 36). This is powerful as a formula, and there are a lot of things in this sentence, produced by the unconscious of a little girl of two years and four months. The Black Mummy is, rather clearly, the name of the—threatening—barred Other. There is a whole semantics of blackness in our culture—blackmail, black magic, black widow, and so on. Let us say that black is the color of *kakon,* and also the color of mourning. Here it is the name of the bad, dangerous Other. We will see, throughout the case, that the black can circulate and we will see the successive appearances of the black baby Sush—the little sister—and then the black Piggle herself; in each case, "black" means "bad."

"The Black Mummy says: 'Where are my yams?'": can we find anything simpler as the name of the barred Other than "black mummy," or anything more condensed to illustrate the dream that interprets what she wants: her "yams." The dream interprets desire in terms of the oral object; the "yams"—quite simply—give the name of the object as desire of the Other.

Some Commentary

There is no doubt that this object—which the black mummy wants as a possession that has been stolen from her—also designates the little Piggle's own being. We have a precise index of this: at the moment when the "babacar" and "the black mummy" who "wants her yams" appear, the parents—and this is what worries them the most—indicate that problems of identity also arise.

A large part of the parents' interpretations is formulated in terms of infantile jealousy, in terms of what Lacan calls *jalouissance*: jealousy of the other object, which is to be situated on the imaginary axis. Yet there is more. From the moment when the "babacar" and the "black mummy" arise with the little sister, Piggle no longer wants to be herself; she no longer wants, in any case, to be called by her name. She claims that she is the mummy or the baby, but she is never Piggle any more. Her mother, indeed, notes that she changes her voice and intonation and takes on a little high-pitched, artificial voice, which disturbs the parents. We see quite precisely here how the birth of the other child has shaken the only child's assurance, which may not yet be an assurance that comes from the fantasy, but which is certainly its embryo; the birth has shaken her to the point of producing what must be called an effect of depersonalization. The little Piggle no longer knows who she is.

This is a wild dis-identification as a reaction to the sister's birth. It proves that for her, the question of her place in the desire of the Other has now been raised. Before, she had a sense of assurance concerning her unique place and could identify herself as the family's little marvel. Because of the new object, however, she no longer knows either what her place is or what she is worth. What results is the call to interpretation and the call, as well, to a new identification. Therefore, when the dream interprets the desire of the Other in terms of orality, it is also a way of naming her being as object or, as Lacan said, "her erection [of herself] as living being (*son érection de vivant*)." Winnicott, indeed, understands it in these terms. He does not use the same language, but he takes it in this sense.

He does not doubt that these "yams" also designate her own object, and that they interpret her desire and a part of her jouissance. In the narrative of the little Piggle, there are two oral trances. Winnicott emphasizes one of them: he says that "it is a generalized orgasm" (p. 118). This is produced in the ninth session, but already in the second consultation, she and Winnicott had begun to communicate, as he says, by noises of the mouth and movements of oral sensuality. Winnicott specifies: "She moved her tongue around; I imitated, and so we communicated about hunger and tasting and mouth noises, and about oral sensuality in general. This was satisfactory" (p. 25). This was its first, rather discreet occurrence, and then there is the ninth session, where he says that it is a general orgasm.

THE QUESTION OF TRANSFERENCE

What is the signifier of transference? There can be no doubt about this: it is "babacar." She arrives with her "babacar," presents it to Winnicott, who—she has been told—is the one who knows about "babacar" and the "black mummy." "Babacar," therefore, can be written, without any forcing, in the matheme of transference as Lacan writes it in 1964.

It is the signifier of the enigma, which represents for Winnicott the little s of the unknown subject, and one must wait to find out what it is, since the parenthesis of supposed knowledge is still empty.

$$\frac{\text{Babacar} \longrightarrow \text{Winnicott}}{\text{S} (.........)}$$

Furthermore, and this is very striking, after the first consultation, when she goes back home she comments, "Dr. Winnicott doesn't know about the babacars" (p. 15). This is really extraordinary! At the second consultation, Winnicott questions her about the "babacar," setting her up as the subject who knows about it, and then he attempts an interpretation: it is the black that causes fear. The result is not very clear, but in the third session, she clarifies her position again: "I came on a train to London to see Winnicott. I want to know why the black mummy and the babacar." He answers that "We will try to find out about it" (p. 40).

We really have here, in a purified form, the entry into transference, and it can be followed throughout its evolution. Winnicott comments a great deal on it at the level of trust and love, but in fact, things happen on another level. The major session—the turning point of the treatment—is the ninth, which also opens out onto the exit from the treatment, and in it, there is a precise testimony of the weakening of Winnicott's position as the subject supposed to know.

"WE GIRLS . . ."

What is the curve of this analysis? I have emphasized what is analogous with the case of little Hans: it begins with the words from the unconscious—"babacar" and "the black mummy"—and finally it ends with a little family romance. We also have this with little Hans, whose case started with the horse-anxiety and ended, doubtless influenced a bit by Freud's suggestions, with his invention of the fiction that resolves his oedipal impasses: his father will have the grandmother and he will have the mother. The little Piggle also makes up her own fiction. This begins with the eighth session, but its culmination is the ninth. I will deal only with what seems determinant for my purposes. Winnicott has made various interpretations, about oral voraciousness on the one hand, and especially about the rivalry with the sister. We arrive at the eighth session. We have seen the blackness circulate among all the characters; she speaks again of the little sister, and he interprets in terms of love/hatred, on the imaginary axis a/a'. He tells her, "You love and hate Susan, both at the same time" (p. 103). Then she gives him a little lecture.

In an immediate reply, she explains to him that she and her sister are counterparts and distinguishes between liking and loving. She tells him, "When we play with mud we are both black. We both bathe, we both change our clothes" (pp. 103–104), and then she says, in the central passage: "I like Susan. Daddy likes Mummy. Mummy likes Susan best. Daddy likes me best" (p. 104). This is very precise and very striking. It would be too much to say that this is an inverted paternal metaphor, but if we graphed the vectors of love that she designates, we would find that one is missing: (the one that goes from the mother to the father) For the little Piggle, it is clear that the father's love goes toward the mother, and secondarily toward her, but the mother's love goes toward the child, and more precisely, toward the sister. This is a second interpretation of the desire of the mother, which is no longer for "yams."

The ninth consultation confirms this. She already feels less anxiety and everything is going better. In this consultation, she begins to describe a kind of fistfight with the black mummy, but we are no longer in a climate of anxiety; the atmosphere is more that of a squabble. She says that the black mummy "comes every night. . . . She gets on my bed" (p. 113). "I am being forced out of my bed by the black mummy and I've got such a nice bed" (p. 114). There is a page and a half on the fight with "the black mummy." All of this is relatively playful; she is mumbling and playing. Winnicott says that it is becoming "indefinite," and he feels himself getting drowsy (p. 115); he always takes his drowsiness as an important sign of what is happening on the patient's side. It is here that Piggle brings out her little family romance of the future, with its promises, like those of Hans, who told his father, "You are going to live with grandmother, and I'm going to live with mama."

These promises of the future are preceded by a short preamble, which is itself valuable. She says, "For a long time, mama didn't want a baby, then she wanted a boy, but she had a girl" (p. 115). The mother is very bothered and protests. The Piggle knows very well, the mother says, that it didn't matter whether the first child was a girl or boy, and that for the second child I would have wanted a boy, but not for the first. The little Piggle, in any case, does not believe this at all, and continues, and it is here that the family romance begins. According to it, "We are going to have a boy when we are grown up. Me and Susan. We will have to find a daddy man to marry" (p. 115). Here is the romance:

girls will have a boy, but the necessary preliminary condition for doing so will be to find a daddy man to marry.

Here we can make a certain number of comments. First of all, this romance confirms and clarifies what was said in the eighth session: papa loves mama, who loves the . . . little boy. We see that the phallus is in the picture. She thus has a very clear interpretation of women: they are mothers, and men are in the place of the instrument. Indeed, it is even more precise: a mother wants a boy. In other words, one seeks the phallus not on the man, but on the son. The man is a "daddy man to marry." This expression is interesting and is worth pausing over. Perhaps it comes from Winnicott himself, for, at one point, he says that in transference, he is "a daddy person" (p. 17). The division of a woman into a woman-mother and a woman-woman is a classical element of the unconscious, but the division of a man into a daddy man and a man as such is a novelty of the case of the little Piggle and of Winnicott's text. He is apparently always careful to reestablish the equality of the sexes; it is very clear that everyone has two sides! His approach to castration, indeed, would merit a study in itself.

I will summarize Piggle's romance: "We girls will have a boy." Here is a solution to penis envy. Winnicott does not make a move; he says it: he dozes. She asks playfully, "Did you hear what I said, Dr. Winnicott?" (p. 116). As she calls out to him, "Did you hear what I said?" he interprets, and in a very surprising way. I have studied the material carefully and I do not understand what is the basis of his words. Whereas she says, "I'll have a son," and even, "We girls will have a son, on condition of finding a father," he tells her that she takes the position of boy in regard to her sister. This interpretation by identification with the boy is not what is imposed by the material at this moment. She does not reply explicitly, but it is here that we see the appearance of what I announced a while ago: the little Piggle's transferential doubt.

First, she had begun the session by telling him that if he would be quiet and listen, then it would go well. She continues her game, speaking to no one in particular, and says: "This is my bed, so I can't go by train to Mr. Winnicott. No, you don't want to go to Mr. Winnicott. He really does know about bad dreams. No, he doesn't. He does. No, he doesn't" and so on (p. 116). She has a whole conversation about Mr. Winnicott's doubtful knowledge. Next, she even writes to him for his birthday: "We'll send Dr. Winnicott a knife to cut his dreams up " and many other replies coming from a gently negative transference; this is a de-supposition of knowledge (p. 162). Piggle, in any case, has found a solution to the desire: having passed from her interpretation by means of the oral object—the "yams"—to her interpretation by the phallic object—the boy as bearer of the phallus—and she now has her formula for men and women. The man, the father, likes mummy. I can translate this by saying that man is looking for a woman. The woman, the mother, is looking for a son. This is very clear.

Now we see the results. Along the path that goes from the words of the unconscious to the solution, by means of the family romance, of "we'll have a son," what has happened to the anxieties?

They have been reduced. "The black mummy" and "babacar" have been gotten rid of. The latter has quite simply disappeared from her discourse, without having taken on any meaning; she simply does not talk about it any more. This is one way of resolving the enigma. The "black mummy" also disappears, but in another way: she is killed. The little Piggle recounts a dream in which she kills the black mummy. She has seen murders on television, with guns and things of that kind. She was a little anguished before talking about it, but everything goes well and the black mummy has died in one of her dreams. Even before this, there had already been a change: the black mummy had become less real. Winnicott says that this is not the only thing: at first, she was ever-present, and later she was only present in the dream. In other words, he perceives that an effect of symbolization has been produced. A clinical trait signals this effect: one day, at the very beginning, her mother asks her, "Did the black mummy come?" She answers, "The black mummy doesn't come; she is in me," that is, she is always there. In this session, on the contrary, she states specifically, "The black mummy doesn't come any more." She has thus begun a movement of presence/absence, and finally the black mummy has been killed, which is a way of making her into a signifier; from now on, only her memory will remain, for her consistency as anxiety has been stricken from the record. The symptomatic benefit is thus also very clear: it is the gain over the anxiety and the clarification of the anticipated position of being a woman-mother. She has many other moments of anxiety, but it is no longer massive. There is one other effect: the fall of the superego-effect.

THE SUPEREGO

One of the most interesting aspects of the case is the emergence of the superego. The "black mummy" who wants her "yams" is a figure of the superego, a voice that requires an object and demands that the child give up the object of her jouissance. It is very striking, and the parents observe painfully the appearance, in such a young girl, of guilt, self-accusation, and self-reproach.

The case of the little Piggle shows us how the superego is linked to the object of love, and arises when the enigma of the barred Other emerges from love. The obscene and ferocious figure of the superego is not engendered by the violence of the Other, of which it would be a transposition; Freud noted this a long time ago. It is linked, on the contrary, to the sweetness of love, which misleads us about desire and jouissance. With the little Piggle, we can perceive this without any difficulty: when the bar over the Other is made present, because of the appearance of the sister, then the persecution begins, the superego proffers its requirements and guilt rages. First of all, she tries to be a model little girl: she arranges things, she scrubs, she cleans up, although the mother does not require this at all, and does not do it herself. Then she changes her mind, says "I won't do it any more . . . ," and even invents some faults. The mother notes that once, a long time ago, in a shop, Piggle had pulled up the mother's skirt a bit—a very instructive gesture—and then the mother had turned around and given her a little slap. A few months later, she says, "Mummy, I won't lift your skirt again" (pp. 51–52). Pathetically, she accuses herself, "I'm bad; I am naughty."

Finally, with the treatment, the vise of the superego begins to loosen. Winnicott notes the progress in this respect. First of all, she stops putting things in order; she leaves them in complete disorder in his office. Then she begins to get things dirty, to mess things up everywhere with glue. He is very happy because the audacity of the drive is gaining the upper hand over the jouissance of renunciation. Finally, there is a big oral trance in which the sucking of the object engages her whole body in what Winnicott calls an oral orgasm that comes just after she announces that she has killed the black mummy in her dream. Winnicott obviously recognizes in this the triumph of the drive over the morbidness of the superego.

WINNICOTT AS INTERPRETER

I do not want to skip over Winnicott's own original trait: the playing out of interpretation. Doubtless all child-analysts use games, but only Winnicott practices what I am calling "playing interpretation." This can give us some comic scenes: one day, he starts to play a baby. He is the black Piggle, who is furious because he wants all the "yams" for himself, and he starts stamping his feet, jumping up and down, and kicking. The little Piggle is both delighted and terrified, then she talks about it to everyone: "Baby Winnicott was very angry. . . ." This is a trait of his singular practice: interpretation is played and acted. The mirror-effect is obvious, but it serves to bring out, to designate the subject's—here, the Piggle's—drives. There are also obviously interpretations that are proffered classically. They are varied: they aim either at love/hate on the a-a' axis or at the drive—especially the fury of oral voracity—or finally at the phallic referent.

Winnicott's weak point is his way of treating the problem of castration and the phallus. What is most missing in him is precisely the dimension of object-lack. Winnicott, however, had read Freud, and refers to him explicitly, speaking of penis envy in the little girl, but this is almost a penis envy without the phallus. He sets up a realist equivalence throughout between what he calls the "wee-wee" and the breast, both of which are taken almost as objects of perceptible reality. The wee-wee and the breast are treated as two equivalent partial objects, just as the father and the mother are precisely two mirror-figures, both of whom, as I have said, lend their bodies. Thus, when Piggle plays at being born between her father's legs, Winnicott has no idea that the signifier of the father introduces something here. For him, it is the same as being born from a mother.

Finally, he ends up making an interpretation that is properly scandalous in what it suggests. It is an interpretation in which he gives his version of the sexual couple, of what, for him, is in the place of the paternal metaphor. He tells her, in substance, that the man takes the woman's "yams," but that afterwards he returns them to her in the form of something that he gives her so that she will have his child. In other words, the man is a thief—as Piggle formulates it at one moment—but a repentant thief. This effects a reversal: it is the mother who has, and when she does not have, it is because it has been taken from her, and therefore it can be returned to her. The reduction to the register of frustration is complete, explicit, and massively formulated, and its correlate is a true negation of the mother's lack of the phallus. He is not even Kleinian in this respect, since Melanie Klein, from the beginning, makes the penis enter the circuit of objects.

What is encouraging is that this does not seem to cause any great damage, because Piggle has already given her own interpretation. It can be said that it is the unconscious that wins in the end. To repeat Lacan's expression in *Television*, where he says that the joke "wins the hand with the unconscious," here it is the little Piggle's unconscious that wins the hand with Winnicott. I rather have the impression, subject to every reserve, that Winnicott's interpretation is not harmful so much as empty, although it goes in the same direction on one point: the fallacious promise of getting something back.

V

WOMEN IN CIVILIZATION

10

The Hysteric in the Time
of Science

The master/hysteric couple can be found throughout history, and the clinic of the individual involves diagnosing the present state of discourses. Since the symptoms of hysteria vary from period to period, she is "hystoric" with a "y." Yet doesn't history also owe something to her?

HYSTORY

If the hysterical subject "is the unconscious in practice," it is not only in the modern age that she has begun to make her presence felt in culture, since the unconscious is inherent in the very fact that there is a speaking being. Hysterical subjects are not alone in giving voice to this being, but more than any others they bear its leitmotif. The effectiveness of this presence could be the origin of the desire that gave birth to science itself in the movement beyond the Greek *episteme*. This, at least, is the thesis that Lacan developed in his seminar *L'envers de la psychanalyse* and "Radiophonie." It gives no place to the Hegelian master/slave dialectic and instead, makes science the shepherd's response to the shepherdess: the progression goes from Socrates, the perfect hysteric, to Newton, from Anna O. to Freud, inasmuch as the discourse of the master "finds its reason in the discourse of the hysteric," as Lacan says. The ancient master depended on the slave's artisan-like knowledge to produce a surplus jouissance, and left any desire to know out of the picture. It took Socrates to question the master about his desire, to call upon him to justify his powers as master, and finally to inspire in him the desire to know from which Galilean science arose; this movement involves a mutation of the artisan's know-how into the formalized knowledge of a mathematical apparatus.

In what way has the hysteric succeeded? This resurgence of desire has produced the new knowledge that operates in the real, but it still leaves in a curious hiatus the subject who is confronted with the sexual impasse. Even more than ancient discourse, science excludes this impasse from consideration: "science is an ideology of the suppression of the subject."[1] Considering this situation, it is not surprising that post-scientific hysteria has ignited one more blaze in history, on the basis of the failure of the enlightenment; the result is the emergence of psychoanalysis, through which Freud objected to the medical foreclosure of the subject.

The question is thus what becomes of hysteria some hundred years after Freud accepted the challenge, after psychoanalysis appeared within science in order to take on, both practically and theoretically, the hysteric's entreaty, and after it has succeeded in establishing an enclave within the dominant discourse. Thus we are examining hysteria in science, as it exists after a century of psychoanalysis.

REPERCUSSIONS OF SCIENCE

The repercussions of science in our world are manifest in an effect of globalizing universalization, which can be seen everywhere today and which is beginning to be deplored widely. Its correlate is the reign of the modern economy's products over subjects' lives, and the ques-

---

1. Jacques Lacan, "Radiophonie," p. 89.

tion is to what extent this is the effect of globalization. Yet whatever may be said of this double result—universalization and the tyranny of products—it is only indirectly concerned with the sexual couple, which is what fascinates the hysteric.

The mortification conveyed by language has now passed into the real of instruments, which instrumentalize us. They do so to such an extent that, in our everyday lives, we even forget their effects, and there has to be some accident—or the phantasmagorias of science fiction— to remind us of this instrumentalization. Today, what we call our life, which we lend to our body, is totally fitted out with these machines. Yet there is even more. As Lacan noted, in the final part of his teaching, to have a body "is to be able to do something with it"[2]—especially in terms of using jouissance. There are many ways of doing this: a body can be lent, sold, offered, and refused.

A new avatar has appeared in capitalist discourse: our bodies are now inspected and inventoried by a great production machine. The phenomenon is not new in itself, but it is so at the level of its mass application, which goes well beyond the circle of the proletarians to which Marx circumscribed it. At all levels of social labor, bodies, which had already been instrumentalized, have themselves become instruments. Don't we keep them up as we do machines: with check-ups, diets, gymnastics, and beauty treatments? Not all of this can be put down to narcissism. In fact, we make calculations about the resistance of the material: our leaders' health bulletins have no other meaning. Why did Yeltsin, speaking recently on French television,[3] let us know about his cold shower in the morning and the number of hours that he sleeps, if not to reassure us about the instrument that he is in charge of?

For all of us, the body has now become a part of our capital, and we treat it as such. How would this not be to the detriment of jouissance, if the very definition of capital is that it is subtracted from such jouissance? It is certain that love is lost here. Think, for example, of the patience and industry required by courtly love or the maps of

---

2. Jacques Lacan, *Joyce avec Lacan*, p. 32.

3. This reference is from 1992, but the same could be said today about Putin, whose daily schedule is also reported.

tenderness[4]; such practices were for lazy people, who did not have desk diaries or answering machines! Can we imagine a troubadour with a fax machine? While family ties may have become independent of the transmission of goods, love has come to speak of itself more and more in terms of having. We count its occurrences, its products, its gains; we make calculations that anticipate its profits and losses and legislation ratifies them. Thus the capitalization of the body goes along with a general debasement—and not only among neurotics—of the problems of love.

This new realism is accompanied by an even more remarkable effect, one that has been unheard-of until now, and that I will call the *unisex* effect, generalizing thus the expression that advertising applies to clothing. By means of this effect, sexual difference is now being covered over rather than being made manifest. It will be said that this general transvestism goes hand in hand with the ideology of equality between men and women. This may be the case, but isn't this transvestism also in harmony with science and its correlate, the subject in its Cartesian definition, which does not know sexual difference? Science accommodates itself very well to a world that reduces all subjects to potential workers and consumers.

The immediate result is especially perceptible for women. For centuries, they saw their jouissances confined within the home. Now the labor market has emancipated them from this closed field, but not without alienating them in the imperatives of production. For this reason, the feminist movement hesitates, oscillating between the contrary claims of equality and difference; through the latter, it expresses the protest of particularity. What is certain is that, today, there is no field to which women do not have access. Although this movement has not yet accomplished its goals completely, its effects are becoming more and more general, and its triumph seems irreversible to me. Marguerite Yourcenar has succeeded where Marie Curie failed with the French Academy. In the last few months, we have seen the first woman in Formula One racing, the first to climb a difficult mountain alone, and even a pioneer fourteen-year-old chess champion. There are still, of

---

4. The map of tenderness is to be found in *Clélie*, by the *Précieuse*, Madeleine de Scudéry. (Translator's note.)

course, a few bastions of male supremacy. A woman's recent attempt to join a company of the national police provoked an outcry among them! Here we will have to wait a bit! Concerning this evolution, psychoanalysis as such does not have to take a side. Its consequences for both sexes must not, however, be misunderstood.

How can we understand the subjective impact of these reshapings of civilization? They concern phallic jouissance itself, inasmuch as its field is located not only within the framework of the sexual relation, but supports, as I have said, the whole of our relation to reality. This phallic jouissance is capitalizable jouissance par excellence. Unisex is the regime of phallic jouissance, and all its forms are offered equally to all. It is not that women have been deprived of this jouissance, but for a long time and without exception, they could only encounter it within the limits of their destinies as wives and mothers. This restriction—not to say prohibition—has now ceased to exist, to the profit of a competition that is also general.

Let us not think that it was merely by chance that Freud came to accentuate the scandalous phallic phase—with all that it implies of an inequality between the sexes in the unconscious—at a certain historical moment of capitalism. The context of his discovery is the ideology of human rights and the ideals of distributive justice, which have repercussions, in the field of ethics, on the universality of the subject of science. It must be said, with Freud and with all of common discourse—they are on the same side on this point—that boys and girls are far from being born "free and equal under law." The liberalities of discourse credit boys with a bit of extra capital: that of having the phallus. It is therefore logical for woman to feel that she is poor and to dream of enriching herself. This is all that Freud discovers and explores: the feminine unconscious! There was a time when she could only do so through the husband, the bearer of the organ, and then through the children, who were substitutes for it. Today, beside the endearing realities of married or maternal love, the whole field of what Lacan calls the "most effective realizations"[5] are open to her: goods, knowledge, power, and so on.

---

5. See the "Note aux Italiens."

It is a fact that the civilization of science has changed women's reality. Analysis has seen this, and this change has not necessarily made women happy: it has been accompanied by anxiety, inhibition, guilt, and feelings of a lack of accomplishment. The first psychoanalysts, especially Joan Riviere in discovering masquerade, supposed that if women sometimes feel that phallic jouissance is forbidden to them, it is because they are afraid of losing their feminine essence. Is it not, perhaps, instead, that phallic jouissance in itself engenders guilt—in men as well, although under different forms? As a limited jouissance, it is always at fault, and is ready to support the superego's imperative: once more, one more effort. Thus, along with these new possibilities for women, there are also new torments.

TODAY AND TOMORROW

What is happening, then, specifically for the hysterical subject? As I have said, hysteria and femininity are distinguished and even opposed. If they are sometimes confused, it is because both of them are mediated by the Other. Yet where woman exercises this mediation in order to realize herself as a symptom, the hysteric uses the desire of the Other and identifies with its lack.

It happens that, in its current state, our civilization has become the accomplice of every possible identification with masculine possession. Thanks to the resources of metonymy, a career is open to everyone, to our modern hysterics as well as to others; they don't lack talent for it, and we can expect that they will make a lot of noise about it, since discretion is not their strong point. Nevertheless, this offer leads in a direction that is the contrary of her desire, as analysis in all of its forms attests: unlike what is sometimes imagined, the more the hysterical woman succeeds in her phallic conquest, the less she can get off on it and the greater grows her feeling of disappropriation. Karen Horney saw this very well. An hysteric can certainly take part in the various competitions that are offered to her, but as soon as she succeeds in proving herself, her profit disappears. It is not jouissance that is a necessary part of her true question. This question is at play elsewhere, in the closed field, as Lacan says, of the sexual relation [relation]. It is only here, indeed, that sexual difference, repressed everywhere by the regime of unisex, remains impossible to eliminate.

The hysteric's strategy is remarkable at this level, for she is very far from seeking her jouissance as woman in the way that Charcot imagined. She exalts femininity in the form of the other woman, not in order to be feminine but rather to bring into existence the Woman whom man lacks. The hysteric is an activist for what does not exist! The result of this is clear: in her sexual relation with a man, the man whom she loves—for she loves men, that is, she is hommosexual with two m's, as Lacan writes the word—what is most precious to her is the Other's castration. Without this castration, the *agalma* of her partner, femininity, would be nothing. I could almost say that in this field, she makes the unisex of castration reign—but this is because she is only interested in the object that is its correlate and that she exalts.

To the hysteric, who is a being composed of a lack in being (*manque à être*), contemporary discourse offers conquests based on possession. We can see how great the misunderstanding is! In this respect, psychoanalysis is really what was necessary for the hysteric, since its mechanism is willing to recognize the enigma of sex and to take responsibility for it. The difference between psychoanalysis and Charcot is enormous. The latter imagined, a bit stupidly, that what the hysteric needed was an artisan of sex. This, at least, is the implication of the formula that so struck Freud, and that prescribed, as a remedy for all the hysteric's ills, repeated doses of the penis. The same echo recurs, indeed, in the impudent expression "not getting the right stuff." What the hysteric is looking for is not the artisan of sex, someone who would do her some good, but someone who is learned about sex, one who would say what exquisite jouissance woman carries, beyond that of the organ. If this exquisite jouissance cannot be said, its place can be marked only by leaving phallic jouissance unsatisfied: the hysteric's faithlessness is not without its logic. Freud accepted her challenge and invented a procedure which, by prohibiting body-to-body contact, excludes the artisan of sex and thus obliges us to make the Other respond, to make him produce a knowledge homogeneous to that of science, one in which logic plays a major role.

Psychoanalysis has thus satisfied the hysteric's entreaty that she be given knowledge about sex. This knowledge, however, is surprising in relation to the aspirations that gave birth to it, for it is made only of a "negativity of structure," according to Lacan's expression, and thus leaves the hysteric's wish unsatisfied. She had expected the unconscious to deliver a science of the cause of jouissance inasmuch as it would be sexual, and what has been discovered is that the unconscious knows only phallic, asexual jouissance. Knowledge can only delimit the other jouissance by logic and approach the real as what is impossible to say.

The question of whether hysteria will be contented with this arid response remains unanswered and must be left to the future. There is little chance that she will give up on the challenge that it presents. Instead, she will continue to use her body as a way of going on strike, offering the fragmented body of her new symptoms to the scientist (neuropsychiatrist, cognitivist, or any other) who makes a profession of knowing nothing about the mysteries of the sexed subject. It is always possible that she will be tempted to inspire a resurgence of religion. We know that Lacan was worried about this. It must be said that a part of what analysis unveils also lends itself to this, since as far as jouissance is concerned, psychoanalysis also highlights that the last word is not castration for everyone. Not only is there a surplus jouissance that plugs up castration, but there is also something of the Other: a jouissance that objects to unisex. The analysand certainly consumes and consummates phallic jouissance, but the analyst incarnates what remains, the complement that is irreducible to the phallic One. We can easily see that this irreducible element lends itself to various subjective uses.

Woman's supplementary jouissance has been newly accredited as the limit of knowledge; this recent alliance with Teiresias is already engendering new clinical facts in the field of analytic discourse. There is certainly a question about this jouissance, but there is also a wish that, if not new, is being deployed in a new way. The envy of other jouissance is becoming the rival of penis envy: there is a wish for it, but also a fear, and even a denunciation of it. We can find its traces in men as well as women, and can discover the amusing use that women make of it in renewing the resources of their masquerade. The cult of its mystery could very well make her exist, as it makes God the father exist. In short, the religion of woman could use the not-whole in order to authorize itself. Would this be a new negative theology? That will depend on whether or not the hysterical discourse gives in to the analytic.

11

New Figures of Woman

In 1834, Balzac wrote a novel entitled *A Woman of Thirty*. In 1832, curiously, Freud ends his lecture on femininity with some considerations on the thirty-year-old woman.

Balzac and Freud were writing a century apart, in two different languages, were living in two countries, although they were both Europeans, and operated within two different discourses.

The title Lacan gives to his seminar, *L'envers de la psychanalyse*, is an allusion to another title by Balzac, *The Reverse of Contemporary Life* (*L'envers de la vie contemporaine*).[1] Balzac, obviously, writes from the point of view of the reverse (*envers*). As for Freud, in 1932, when he gives his final assessment of his analytic experience of women, his message is radically opposed to Balzac's.

---

1. *Envers* can be translated variously as "reverse," "back," "underside," and "wrong side." Balzac's novel *L'envers de l'histoire contemporaine* has sometimes been rendered as *The Seamy Side of History*. The expression *à l'envers*, which appears later in the chapter, means "inside out," "upside down," or "back to front." (Translator's note.)

The implicit message of Balzac's novel, seen from today, is one of progress, which anticipates something of the evolution of women's conditions. Balzac writes to say that at the age of thirty, his heroine, despite her misfortunes, has her life in front of her. In this case, the future means love, and also the possibility of determining her own life. As the jacket of my copy of the novel says, "She is not forbidden from becoming a human being."

This has nothing in common with Freud's final sentence, which although well-known, is still very striking:

> A man of about thirty strikes us as a youthful, somewhat unformed individual, whom we expect to make powerful use of the possibilities for development opened up to him by analysis. A woman of the same age, however, often frightens us by her psychical rigidity and unchangeability. Her libido has taken up final positions and seems incapable of exchanging them for others. There are no paths open to further development; it is as though the whole process had already run its course and remains thenceforward insusceptible to influence—as though, indeed, the difficult development to femininity had exhausted the possibilities of the person concerned.[2]

This paragraph comes after some considerations on the drive, in which Freud emphasizes that women's drives are less plastic than men's. He gives two well-known examples as proof: the lesser aptitude of women's libido to be displaced onto compromise formations—especially the sense of justice and fairness—and to be sublimated into the creations of civilization. Freud's thesis is categorical: the drives have been fixed immovably. Is this a simple prejudice on the part of the very traditional Freud? Perhaps. This is the mainstream opinion. I do not doubt, furthermore, that every enunciation bears the mark of the subject's sexual inscription; nevertheless, I do not think that we can get rid of Freud's thesis by positing simplistically that he was more prejudiced than other people. We know at least that his prejudices did not prevent him from inventing psychoanalysis, and this is enough to indicate, as Lacan said, that he had a "sense of orientation."

---

2. Sigmund Freud, "Femininity," *New Introductory Lectures on Psycho-analysis*, trans. James Strachey. *SE* XXII, London: Hogarth Press, 1964, p. 119.

If I tried now to draw a portrait of a thirty-year-old woman of today, in 1995, I believe that it would be different once again: she would be neither Balzac's nor Freud's woman. In the discourse of the reverse, it is indisputable that many things have changed since the 1930s. Women are no longer as they were, and if we were to rewrite Balzac's novel, it would have to be very different. These mutations of reality are not enough, however, for us to discard Freud's thesis. It seems to me that today, the question is the following: How and to what extent have these changes at the level of the discourse of the reverse, by obviously modifying women's desire, also modified the economy of the drives, and especially of the part of jouissance that does not proceed by phallic mediation, the part that is *"not whole"*?

In his final paragraph, Freud, conscious of the malaise that he is going to produce, tries, in order to make his judgment more nuanced, to introduce a distinction that is not unrelated to the one that I mentioned earlier. He says, "[D]o not forget that I have only been describing women in so far as their nature is determined by their sexual function. It is true that that influence extends very far; but we do not overlook the fact that an individual woman may be a human being in other respects as well" (p. 119). The German text can be checked: the expression "human being," used in the French and English and suppressed in the Spanish translation, is correct. Thus Freud establishes, concerning woman, a cut between what can be called her being for sex—as one says, "being for death"—and her belonging to humankind: the universal of the speakingbeing.

CHANGES INSIDE-OUT

The institution of the family, the semblances, and the discourse on sexual jouissance are no longer what they were several decades ago.

Lacan, at the end of his text on feminine sexuality, asks himself whether it is not women who have maintained the status of marriage in our culture. Today, this remark from 1958 seems largely irrelevant. Numerous indications—at the level of statistics, the evolution of legislation, and so on—indicate that the status of marriage has changed radically in the last two or three decades. The disturbance of this status, which reaches an extreme in the dissociation between marriage and sexual life as well as maternity, has not yet become general, but can be seen quite clearly, at least in the United States. To bring up a child alone, or in a homosexual couple, or in a partnership between a woman and a homosexual, and so forth, are configurations that are not only possible, but ever more frequent and legal. They are especially symptomatic of changes in discourse that have taken the scandalousness out of the category of unmarried mother. Couples who do not want to be married can obtain the legal benefits of marriage; homosexuals of both sexes can be married, and as a correlate, the status of the family is changing with surprising speed. People are obviously asking questions about the long-term subjective repercussions of these changes on children. The structure of the traditional family is not the necessary condition for the paternal metaphor, but when the effect of the fragmentation of social bonds touches the elementary cell to the point of producing single-parent families, and the individual becomes the last residue of this fragmentation, we must necessarily anticipate some consequences, as impossible as they may be to foresee.

For some time already, we have been talking, almost as a banality, about the fall of semblances, or at least their pluralization. It is obvious that the ideal of what a couple should be has been included in this general fall. Let us take, as our reference point, because of its dates, Léon Blum's book On Marriage, which was first published in 1907 and then reprinted in 1937. At the time, it was an ideological bombshell, a provocation: in the name of erotic satisfaction, he argued in favor of sexual freedom, fought traditional values linked to marriage, especially abstinence outside marriage, recommended, in order to forestall future disappointment, multiple sexual experiences before one makes any definitive choice. This struggle for sexual freedom has become out-of-date in the context of today's mores and we can sometimes find it amusing. When condoms are sold at the doors of high schools, when fidelity, which was once a value, is reduced more and more to a subjective requirement or to a personal disposition, when houses of prostitution are launched by having an "open house" for potential clients, when prostitutes testify on television, then exalting free choice no longer has any meaning. The "images and symbols" of women have changed drastically. The same semblances are no longer drawn on the masks: the place of the "girl phallus" remains, but Zazie and other Lolitas have been substituted for the virginal innocence that Valmont enjoyed despoiling in

Les liaisons dangereuses, and the femme fatale of the great age of Hollywood has herself been replaced by supermodels with empty gazes. As for man, the theme of the possible disappearance of manliness has been circulating for some time now. In short, therefore, and without a more ample survey, we can see that the semblances that ordered the relations between the sexes are no longer what they were.

As a correlate, the place given to jouissance in discourse about love has been modified greatly in recent decades. Whatever the causes may be, we are the contemporaries of what I would call a legitimation of sexual jouissance. This was not the case of the age in which Freud analyzed and wrote. Sexual satisfaction appears as a requirement so justified, a dimension so natural, an end in itself so independent of the aims of procreation and the pacts of love that not only has it become the object of a discourse that is public—and no longer intimate—but it has also become the object of attention and care for an entire series of therapists and sexologists.

Psychoanalysis may not be completely innocent in this evolution of mores, but something like a de facto right to sexual jouissance is added today to the list of the modern subject's rights (see all the polemics concerning female circumcision). Furthermore, sexual jouissance is subject today to the discourse of distributive justice. Everyone can now lay claim to his/her own orgasm, and sometimes even in court! All we have to do is to read the press in order to see how far this has gone.

What are the effects of these changes for women? What are their effects at the level of the economy of the drives?

THE "PHALLIC RECUPERATION"

As I have already said, all the new objects of the "recuperation of the sexual metaphor"[3] are offered to all people, without distinction of sex. In the field of reality that is founded on desexualization, when it comes to conquering knowledge, power, and more generally, all the products of surplus jouissance engendered by civilization, the arenas of

---

3. "Guiding Remarks for a Congress on Feminine Sexuality," p. 91. Translation altered.

competition are now open to women. It seems that the recognized and accepted substitutes for the lack of the phallus have themselves been multiplied: this is why I have spoken of a general unisex.

We can also question what happens at the level of the sexual relation. Lacan challenged Freud's belief that the child wanted by a woman, and who is the consequence of a man's love, is the only phallic substitute that is in harmony with feminine being. Today, with the discourse of the legitimation of the sex, it is clear that this substitute is not the only one. Depending on the case, the organ itself, discreetly fetishized, can be such a substitute, as can a more recent development, the series of lovers who dispense the phallic *agalma*, not to speak of women who become lesbians and those who disdain motherhood.

RETURN TO FREUD'S WOMAN

In the light of these changes, it is important to explain, or rather to interpret, Freud's position: Why did he think that the only positive evolution of the libido in a woman was her transformation into a mother? Lacan, we repeat, diverges on this point, but Freud's reduction of woman to mother does not seem to me to have been explained completely.

Freud affirms this thesis categorically throughout his elaborations, and it appears very clearly in his text on femininity. Not only does it destine woman to be the mother of her own child, but it also seeks to make her the mother of her husband. After some considerations on the bond with the child, he notes that "a marriage is not made secure until the wife has succeeded in making her husband her child as well and in acting as a mother to him" (p. 118). The context leaves no doubt about the fact that the child, especially the son, and the child-husband, have the function of satisfying, by proxy, the aspiration to have the phallus. In considering the husband as a reduplication of the child, Freud intensifies his reduction of femininity to the mother's phallicism. Not only does he say that a woman can have the phallus only through the bond with the child, but he effaces the phallicism of being, which is in play in love, to the profit of a single phallicism: that of having the phallus. This tendency is all the more noticeable since two pages earlier, Freud emphasized what women require from love. As a couple, the mother-woman and her husband, the child-man, make up for the more problematic couple of a man and a woman. This is a metaphor and the substitution can be written as

$$\frac{\text{Mother}}{\text{woman}} \diamond \frac{\text{child-husband}}{\text{man}}$$

From the structural point of view, it is obvious to us that the relative failure of Freud's efforts to find a satisfying conception of the avatars of the libido in women and his constant tendency to make other bonds the metaphors of the sexual bond carry an implicit enunciation, for which Lacan was finally able to give us the statement (énoncé): "there is no sexual relation." Despite all these considerations, however, the question of Freud's prejudices has not yet been settled.

It is difficult to say how far Freud considered his conclusions to be absolute, but I would like to emphasize that he introduces the solution of the child-husband as the condition for a marriage's stability. This fact relativizes his solution, for it connects the supposed norms of a woman's evolution—making herself into a mother—with the only socially acceptable outcome that Victorian society offered women. Perhaps my remark should itself be made with greater nuance, since it is based on an isolated indication by Freud; just afterwards, he adds some considerations on the erotic value of the mother-woman that go in a completely different direction and that are surprising since they come from the man who diagnosed the debasements of love life so well. This indication testifies, however, to the link between the clinical facts that Freud isolated and the state of discourse in his time, and thus leads us not to attribute everything to his own prejudices.

The lack of the phallus, which is Freud's sole reference, gives us only half of the phenomenon. The other half is the objects that arise as its substitutes. They function as social bonds and program certain arrangements between the sexes, arrangements that are now dated. They enable us to grasp why Freud's "impression"—this is his term—of the inertia of libidinal positions in his thirty-year-old woman would not necessarily be shared today, even from the analytic viewpoint. The historical definition of the kinds of surplus jouissance offered to women, or more precisely, the reduced series of objects compatible with the semblances of woman, accounts for a part of the libidinal blockage that

Freud perceived. It presents not only a woman who is completely in the phallic problematic, but who is also the captive of social conditions in which there is no safe point outside marriage; such a state condemns her to achieve her phallicism, with a few exceptions, only as a mother. Thus it is not so much a matter of questioning the phenomena that Freud perceived as of seeing what they owe, despite the universal of castration, to the bids of the discourse of his time.

NEW FANTASIES

Today, now that the whole field of phallic acquisitions is being opened to women, we need to ask where, outside the sexual relation (*relation*) properly speaking, the manifestations of the relation to the signifier of the barred Other and of other jouissance are to be found. We no longer have any mystics and we can wonder whether it is possible to identify the substitutes for yesterday's mystics.

I believe that the absolute Other, or more exactly, woman as absolute Other, is everywhere and haunts the figures of the same. Contemporary civilization no longer deals with the Other by segregation—at least in the West. Internal segregation was a simple, and perhaps effective, way of dealing with the Other. It plugged up problems by allotting spaces: to each his/her own perimeter, and as a correlate, his/her own tasks and attributes. To a woman the house, to a man the world; to a woman the child, to a man the career. The first could sacrifice herself through love and the second could exercise power, and so on. Today the situation is more mixed, and this, as Lacan said in *Television*,[4] produces new fantasies.

In fact, the rise in the past century of the theme of women seems to be a correlate of the extension of the discourse of human rights and of the ideals of distributive justice. The more the ideology—I think that this term is adequate here—of distributive justice triumphs, with all that it implies of a common measure, the more the Other and its opaque jouissance, a jouissance that is outside the phallic law, takes on existence. We can certainly speak of the modern subject, the Cartesian sub-

---

4. *Television*, p. 32.

ject, conditioned by the *cogito*, but concerning contemporary woman, to know whether she is modern is another problem: she is doubtless so as subject, like anyone, but could it be that she is not, inasmuch as she is Other?

The absolute Other of a jouissance that is not whole, not countable, can hardly be thought of as modern, even if it is foreclosed from a discourse that calls itself such. There may be something well-founded in the rather antiprogressive expression, the "eternal feminine." On this point, it is not impossible for psychoanalysis to make a contribution. By following Lacan's indication in *Television*, which establishes a link between the "racism" of jouissances and religion, in order to predict their revival, we can situate a theme that *Encore* develops more broadly, that of the two faces of God: the face of God-the-Father, but also the face of an Other god, who is completely other and absolute, and whom woman makes present. This is a very earthly god, but one that is capable nevertheless of arousing "fear and trembling."

In fact, we can note a certain "uneasiness"—this may be a euphemism—one that is discreet but obvious, toward modern women. It is an ambiguous disquiet, composed of phallic rivalry, but also and especially of frightened fascination, and perhaps even of envy for her Otherness, which unisex does not succeed in reducing. I would argue that this "envy" develops as the shadow of cynical discourse: the idea that women have a jouissance that does not fall within the discontinuity and short duration of phallic jouissance and does not call for a complementary object of lack. Women have an access to something oceanic, to borrow the term that Freud uses for religious aspirations. In lending our ears to this, we sometimes perceive a fascination with the jouissance attributed to women, a fascination that goes in exactly the direction indicated by Lacan: toward God, the god of jouissance, who takes up existence beside woman.

With this thread, we are very far from the classic theme of feminine penis envy. The latter can only arise from a lack, from a sense of frustration concerning something that an other is supposed to have at his disposal. Envy is the sister of the malady of comparison. It is intrinsically linked with the register of phallic jouissance, for the latter is an incarnate objection to any access to beatitude, about which it can, however, dream. Freud was right: envy is very much linked to the phallus. In other words, the absolute Other, as such, never envies.

What is amusing is that women who identify most with the phallus sometimes carry, as a pretense, the *agalma* of the ineffable other jouissance, and play at bringing about (*jouant à faire*) the Other, without actually being her. This is my explanation of the surprise provoked by that incredible diva, the divine Marlene Dietrich, when she confessed that she had always been frigid.

NEW SYMPTOMS

What about the new symptoms of contemporary women? I am not going to consider the most recent forms of the internal conflicts that women experience in their relation to the phallus, which have been diagnosed for a long time. Conflicts, tensions between the two types of phallicism—being and having the phallus—far from being reduced only to the opposition between being a woman and being a mother, also take on a new form today, one that has become banal: a tension between professional success and what is called the "emotional life"—let's say between work and love.

Debasement

I would like first to introduce the theme of the debasement of love life, which Freud diagnosed in men, but which does not spare women. In terms of the splitting between the love object and the object of desire, the evolution of contemporary mores has made new phenomena appear. Lacan, years after Freud, had already spoken in a more nuanced way. His 1958 text, "The Signification of the Phallus," seems first to adopt Freud's thesis, which he reformulates by noting that in women, unlike men, love and desire are not separate, but converge on the same object. On the following page, however, he introduces an important nuance: the division between the objects of love and desire is no less present in women, except that the first is hidden by the second.[5]

Well, what must not be hidden today is that, once liberated from the sole choice of marriage, many women love on one side and desire or get off on the other. They had to escape from the yoke of an exclu-

---

5. Lacan, "The Signification of the Phallus," pp. 278–280.

sive and definitive bond before we could see that their various partners are situated on one side or the other: on the side of the organ that satisfies sexual jouissance or on that of love. The convergence of the two on the same object is only one configuration among others. Here I see an obvious change in the clinic.

Inhibition

There is also another: the new feminine inhibitions. There is only inhibition when a choice is possible, or when there is an imperative. When women were not asked about their desire and were constrained to act in certain ways, they could hardly procrastinate in deciding or acting. Their emancipation multiplies what is possible for them; they can live in any way they like, can choose whether or not to have a child, whether and when to marry, and whether or not to work. This liberation shows that the drama of inhibition is not a masculine specialty. This is all the more true since, in discourse, everything that is not forbidden becomes obligatory. Consequently, we see women shrink before the act in the same way that an obsessional man would; they exhibit the same hesitations when confronted with fundamental decisions and definitive commitments, especially in the domain of love. In the clinic of contemporary life, we frequently encounter women who want a man and a child, but who must defer having the latter until they have met someone better; such situations are often the origin of a demand for analysis. The extension of unisex to the whole of social conduct goes along with the homogenization of a large part of symptomatology.

Women in Charge of Fatherhood

There is a typically feminine configuration that seems to me both frequent and quite contemporary. It can be seen not among thirty-year-old women, but rather among those who are approaching their forties, single, who usually work, who can choose freely whom to be intimate with, and who are beginning to notice that time is passing and that if they want to have a child, they are going to have to hurry. They are going to have to encounter a man who is worthy of being a father, at least if they have not chosen to be single mothers. Since contraception and the legality of abortion have disjoined reproduction from the sexual act more radically than ever, women are obliged not only to decide to have a child but often to take upon themselves the choice of a father; now only age or sterility remains to make the situation impossible. The conjunctures of the desire for a child have changed and have engendered new subjective dramas and new symptoms. They also, however, give women a new power, which, I would argue, could have massive consequences.

We could say that these women put themselves in charge of the father. Diogenes, in his ironic position, claimed to be looking for a man. Today, many women are looking for a father for the child who is to come. Now there are new choices, new torments, new complaints! Their configurations are multiple: "I am looking for a father, but I cannot bear to live with a man"; "I am looking for a father, but the men I meet don't want children"; "I am looking for a father, but I haven't found anyone." Let us also not forget the statement, "I immediately thought that he would be a good father!" The next step is to give the father a lesson about what a father should be, and this sometimes takes the new form of self-reproach concerning the man who has been chosen; she cannot forgive herself for having given such a father to her children.

I obviously do not want to call into question the freedoms that have been conditioned by the disjunction between procreation and love; it is also important not to misunderstand the small bit of freedom that the unconscious really leaves the subject in terms of what is to be chosen. We can, however, notice that these new freedoms place women in a new position, one that allows them, more than ever before, to make themselves the ones who judge and measure the father. Thus, we have seen the development of a discourse of maternal responsibility, one that has reached the point of triumphing over that of the father. This new discourse conveys something like an inverted paternal metaphor, or at least raises to a second power the paternal failure that is specific to our civilization, for it places the mother-woman in the position of a subject who is supposed to know about being a father. We perceive, indeed, that the statement "I am looking for a father," like Diogenes's "I am looking for a man," means "there aren't any": "There isn't anyone who meets my requirements."

In conclusion, we are not deploring the evolution of our civilization. A psychoanalyst has nothing to criticize: s/he can only report the facts within the perspective of the discourse that determines him/her. Perhaps, for the moment, we do not yet know what are going to be the consequences of the mutations of contemporary woman's status.

12

Sexed Ethics

Freud did not hesitate to repeat Napoleon's saying, "anatomy is destiny." Lacan challenges this idea and advances a formula that seems to mark the end of any norm coming from nature: as far as being a man or a woman goes, "they"—subjects—"have a choice."

THE APORIAS OF SEX

It would be easy to exploit the gap between the two formulas and make it the unchallengeable sign of the doctrine's inconsistency. Let us recognize the opposite here: it is the index of the aporias of sex with which psychoanalysis is confronted. They appear and remain on the surface of phenomena. Subjects identify so little with their anatomy that they are inclined to worry about their sexed being. The extreme cases of transexualist delirium or the luring games of transvestism are at one here with more common cases, in which someone wonders whether he is *really a man*, sometimes to the point of being obliged to show that he is. Meanwhile, another person is preoccupied with knowing whether she is *a true woman* and finds no better way to assure herself of this than the famous masquerade.

For a century, analytic theory itself has been confronting the problem of defining what makes a person belong to one sex or the other, for if anatomy decides one's legal status, it commands neither desire nor the drive; the existence of perversions could already have made us suspect this a long time ago. At the beginning of the child's life, anatomy is reduced to the presence and absence of the penis, which decides whether the baby is to be called a boy or a girl and how, in consequence, s/he is going to be indoctrinated. There must, obviously, however, be more than this simple opposition if a child is to be made a man or a woman. Now there is little chance that the gene for sexual normality is going to be discovered. Freud's saying itself, contrary to what it may seem to suggest, does not advocate any naturalism. It refers, rather, to this fact of "denaturing" by language, according to which the natural difference between the sexes has consequences only by being submitted to the signifier; it has repercussions at the level of the "speakingbeing" only by passing through the twists and turns of discourse.

IDENTIFICATION OR SEXUATION

The divergence of Freud's or Lacan's responses about what leads us to belong to one sex or the other can be given a condensed expression by the opposition between two terms: identification and sexuation. This conceptual reduction obviously sacrifices both the nuances and the stages of their respective elaborations, but it gives us, in my opinion, their major axis.

Freud, after having discovered the child's polymorphous perversion, invented the Oedipus complex in order to explain how the little pervert becomes unimorphically either a man or a woman. The oedipal phase is, according to Freud, what allows the polymorphic dispersion of the drives to be corrected by unifying identifications, at the price, however, of some sacrifices and failures. In other words, identification is the name that he gives to the process by which the symbolic ensures its grasp over the real.

With the Oedipus complex and the different identifications that it generates, Freud gives consistency to an Other of discourse: an Other who knots the norms, the models, the obligations and the interdictions of discourse to anatomical identity. The Other would thus impose a standard solution—the heterosexual solution—on the castration complex, and would reject any other solution as being atypical or pathological. This Other, as Lacan would say, tells you, by erecting the semblances that are appropriate for ordering the relations between the sexes, what you must become as a man or a woman.

Many nuances and distinctions are necessary here in order to be fair to Freud. First, he is not at all working only with the notion of identification; instead, in each case, he uses the trio of drive, identification, and object-choice. Next, he himself perceives the failure of his solution and the limits that it encounters in the resistance of the repressed drives, which never cease to return in the symptom and the inertia of the death drive. Nevertheless, one can say, in a condensed form that lacks certain nuances, that for Freud, according to the myth of Oedipus, becoming a man or woman, with the different modalities of desire and jouissance implied, is a matter of identification and therefore of assimilating social models.

In this sense, moreover, the notion of "gender," which is so dear to the English-speaking world, stands in the same path, despite the theoretical entropy that separates someone like Stoller from Freud. This is precisely the path that Lacan left behind when he passed beyond the Oedipus complex, after years devoted to reformulating and rationalizing Freud's oedipal problematic in terms of language.

The term "sexuation," which Lacan suggests, and the logical formulas that he gives for it in "L'étourdit," identify man and woman, in the final analysis, by their modes of jouissance. The formulas of sexuation note and explain what we observe every day: the reign of the Other's norms stops, it could be said, at the foot of the bed. As soon as what is in question is sexed bodies, the order inaugurated by discourse is unable to correct the denaturing of the speakingbeing; it has nothing to make up for this denaturing other than the phallic semblance. These formulas write the distribution of subjects between two ways of being inscribed in the phallic function; what is in question is nothing other than the function of jouissance inasmuch as, by the fact of language, it comes within the grip of castration.

A man is the subject who has submitted completely to the phallic function. Consequently, castration is his lot, as well as phallic jouissance, to which he accedes by the mediation of the fantasy. A woman, on the contrary, is anyone who has *not* submitted *completely* to the regime of phallic jouissance; she has access to an other, supplementary jouissance, without the support of any object or semblance.

This distribution, as we see, is as binary as that of the sex ratio, which, for reasons that we do not know, and until the situation changes, divides the species more or less equally, into male and female. According to Lacan, however, the binary quality of sex, far from being a simple effect of this natural division, depends on a completely different necessity; this other necessity is appended to the constraints of *signifiance*, and, curiously, reduces the artificiality of sex to the single choice between the phallic whole and not-whole.

The thesis therefore makes a strange homology emerge between two heterogeneous alternatives—male/female and man/woman—both of which can, however, be said to be real: one—that of the living sexed being—depends on nature and its recognized regularities; the other—that of the speakingbeing—is a matter of the logical constraints of language. Such constraints, which do not cease not to be written, are equivalent to the real in the symbolic.

THE CURSE

The claim that we can choose between being a man or a woman does not depend, therefore, on any reference to free will; it means first of all that the two alternatives are not isomorphic and that what slides in the gap between them is all the *discords*, attested to by the clinic, between our "official" sex and erogenous sex. We can verify, indeed, that anatomy is not the destiny of Eros, although for each "speaking-being," it is *a priori* an injury. In other words, there are "men" and "women," in our usual understanding of these terms, who are not men and women in the sense of sexed being—and thus there is a choice.

The term "choice," however, remains paradoxical, in regard to the most common experience, which would attest, instead, to the rigors of constraint; subjects either recognize themselves so fully in their sexed aspirations that they suppose that the latter come from nature, or on the contrary, they feel so much that these positions have been forced on them that they live them out only as a symptom and in a state of pain. In both cases, if there is a choice, it is very much a forced choice: the choice between the phallic whole and the not-whole. In reality, the one who is designated as the subject, far from being the agent of this choice, bears its brunt.

In authorizing themselves as sexed beings, according to an expression from the seminar *Les non dupes errent*, subjects are constrained by the fault of the speaking unconscious. This is a curse! It is a misfortune, for the unconscious speaks the Sex badly, without our always noticing it, since we know that it is structured like a language, "by speaking so much, this heavy step (*pas*) that is said of it."[1] The unconscious does not (*pas*) speak the Sex any better than does the phallic One, with its narcissistic adherence, which can say nothing of "what takes refuge from it,"[2]—nothing of the Other—who ex-sists all the more from it. Thus it is concluded that the unconscious is homosexual[3]; this is another way of saying, as Freud did, that there is only one libido. Such is the curse that leaves the Other of sex foreclosed. The statement that "there is no sexual relation (*rapport*)," by which Lacan formulates Freud's implicit saying (*dire*), means that in the physical sexual relation (*relation*) itself—despite love and desire—jouissance, as phallic, gives no access whatsoever to the jouissance of the Other.

GENERAL PERVERSION OR THE OTHER

Consequently, we perceive another disjunction, between the choice of jouissance and object-choice. Gide and Montherlant, to take literary examples, illustrate that, although they did not approach women, they were nevertheless men, since they were attached to the jouissance of the organ. More generally, beyond the limits of their respective masquerades, all gays are certainly not "drag queens" nor are all lesbians viragos. We are thus very far from the oedipal standard of

---

1. Jacques Lacan, "L'étourdit," p. 24.
2. *Ibid.*
3. This expression is Jacques-Alain Miller's.

heterosexuality that claimed that, except for a deviation, man and woman were made for each other, simply because their two signifiers, "man" and "woman," copulated in the place of the Other, like the king and the queen in Edgar Allan Poe's story. In other words, sexed identity is not effected through object-choice, and this fact can be said to equalize heterosexual and homosexual. It is a misunderstanding to impute any homophobia to Lacan. As to real perversion, which is not general, it is not decided at the level of choice.

If a man, because of the lack of the sexual relation, only has access to the partner through the fantasy, then it can be said that he is married to the object of his fantasy, with which he cheats on his partner, whether the latter is male or female. Thus, for each man, the real "lies" to the partner, as Lacan says in *Television*; the hidden object, the secret cause of jouissance, is substituted for the beloved. We see that this general perversion has the major consequence of relativizing the partner. The unconscious certainly imposes the male norm, which is the phallic norm, as Freud had already perceived, but this norm does not commit us to any norm for the partner, other than that of the surplus jouissance that is specific to each person; such jouissance is the true partner, as it were, of repetition. It is obvious that this surplus jouissance can be lodged just as easily in a woman (heterosexuality) as in a man (homosexuality); it can even, for certain mystics, be located in God. This is the case, for example, of Angelus Silesius, who, if we are to believe Lacan, is an example of the perversion mentioned a moment ago, since he imposes the gaze between himself and his God.[4] As for a woman, inasmuch as she is not completely destined to phallic jouissance and not completely caused by the object of the fantasy, she likewise finds an access to other jouissance through various partners who go beyond man in the sexual relation (*relation*): by means of another woman, as well as through God if she is a mystic.

It is thus not a contradiction that those who are men by anatomy and choice of jouissance can also be heterosexual or homosexual or mystical in their object-choice; that hysterical women who are completely concerned with the object of the masculine other can rank themselves on the man's side, in the phallic whole; that, likewise, heterosexual or homosexual women—but also other mystics, such as Saint

---

4. Lacan, *Encore*, p. 76.

Theresa, Hadewidjch of Antwerp, or Saint John of the Cross, or even psychotic subjects of both sexes—place themselves on the women's side. The variation in partners does not affect which sex the subject belongs to, a question that is decided at the level of the mode of jouissance; the consequence is that in each case, the true partner, which is jouissance, remains veiled, as if it is awaiting interpretation.

Freud recognized that this hiatus, which creates a gap between the drive and love, with their respective objects, is the foundation of all the debasements of love life; he formulated it, first of all, in terms of development, as the passage from autoerotic jouissance to the investment in the other as object. This certainly creates the most acute difficulties in the space of the relation to the sex, but beyond this, it brings into question the social bond itself and, more specifically, love, for we need to know how the drive, which never gives up, can be linked up with the well-ordered relation (*rapport*) to the counterparts.

Encore studies this question again, when it posits, at the end of the first development of its first chapter, that the "'Jouissance of the Other,' of the Other with a capital O, 'of the body of the Other who symbolizes the Other, is not the sign of love.'"[5] What is missing is the implication that would say, "I love him/her, therefore I get jouissance from him/her." Consequently, the formula opens up a double question: Where does what responds through jouissance in the sexual relation (*relation*) come from, and what is the true nature of love?

HOMMOSEXUAL LOVE

Lacan returns to love at the beginning, as at the end of the seminar, to remind us, first of all, that it is addressed principally to the specular image, which had long been recognized in his mirror stage; next, he adds, at the end, that it comes from the unconscious, and finds its motive force in the enigma perceived by the subject, who, because s/he speaks, is made the subject of the unconscious.

In a difficult passage, Lacan had already posited, in "L'étourdit,"[6] that whenever, in the two of sex, what would be the second is missing

---

5. *Ibid.*, p. 4.
6. Lacan, "L'étourdit," p. 24.

and inaccessible, the counterpart, the image of the mirror stage, *s'emble*,[7] or *s'emblave* (sows itself) thus concealing the libido, and does so *s'en ensemençant* (by sowing its seeds)—since such is the meaning of the two verbs *s'embler* and *s'emblaver*. Impregnated, the image is a substitute, let's say, an imaginary substitute (*suppléance*) for the inaccessible Other. This could be written as a metaphorical substitution: i(a)/barred A. In the same field of equivocations, why not evoke the *emblavure*, the sown field, if this deliberately neological term makes us hear, in this flight of the libido by the generic image of the species, a *bavure*, a flaw of structure. This is precisely the structural flaw that makes love "hommosexual," with the two m's that Lacan writes it with; he does so without betraying Freud, who already knew this. By giving too much love to the clothing constituted by the image, love remains "Beyondsex."[8]

This is the case even when it permits, on the basis of the lack of the sexual relation (*rapport*) and the contingencies of the encounter, a relation (*relation*) of subject to subject; this is the new definition of love suggested at the end of *Encore*. If we wanted to be sure that such a relation really exists, all we would have needed to do would have been to watch, this year, on Valentine's day, a special on French television about love at first sight,[9] and to hear a very diverse series of testimonies: a male/female couple who have nothing interesting about them other than the fact that they fell in love at first sight; two recently married black American lesbians; and as its high point, the narrative of a lifelong love, formed on the edge of death, just before leaving a Nazi extermination camp. In all of these testimonies, there was a single message: beyond the particular circumstances, the lovers said, while wrestling with the enigma of what cannot be explained, they had instantly become certain that they had recognized each other.

Lacan connects this recognition with the opaque perception of the way in which each person is affected by the solitude of his fate. Here again, love goes from the same to the same, and not from one to the Other. What is in question here is no longer the sameness of the image, nor even the common fate that the speaking unconscious reserves for

---

7. The verb *s'embler* is homophonic with *sembler*, to seem. (Translator's note.)
8. Lacan, *Encore*, p. 85.
9. A broadcast from 1997.

everyone, but something else, which is more obscure: the way in which each person responds to this fate and bears his destiny as a speaking-being. It is therefore an option that must be called ethical, one that is both singular and original, and that analytic discourse submits to its imperative of being well-spoken: speaking well what, from the fantasy and/or the symptom, makes up for the foreclosure of the sex.

We can wonder how much in tune these conclusions are with the spirit of our age. By the order that it inaugurates between the sexes, by the prejudices that it maintains, by the bids for jouissance that it tenders to its subjects, discourse tries to make both the sexual impasse and the defect of the nonexistent Other more bearable to us. Discourse stops, as I have said, at the foot of the bed, where the exploration of *Encore* begins, but it is able to surround the edges of this hole with its semblances, norms, and rules. Each subject encounters the latter as a kind of pretreatment, by civilization, of the deficiency in sexuality, since the unconscious is not completely individual, but is impregnated with the discourse that rules a community. Ours has promoted, along with human rights, the values of sexual equality, which coincide—by chance? —with the ever more unisexual lifestyles oriented by the market for new objects that can give jouissance to everyone. We cannot fail to recognize today that the way people conduct their love lives has been profoundly reshaped by this.

NEW MORES

Recent decades have marked, in fact, an unprecedented change in mores, which legislation confirms more and more, progressively legalizing sexual practices that would have been unacceptable only fifty years ago. Today, Claudel could no longer imagine that he was putting in a word for tolerance by saying that certain establishments exist for such and such a practice! I am not going to examine the question of what, in our civilization, conditions this liberalism, which is not complete, for it never ceases to arouse opposition. This liberalism, nevertheless, is an established fact, and I believe that the changes that it has brought about are irreversible. It is not limited, let us note, to granting tolerance to old-fashioned homosexuality—although the short century that separates Oscar Wilde's prison from our homosexual marriages allows us to measure the changes that have occurred; it no longer prejudges any practice, if the fantasy establishes it and the partner consents.

The various sexual scenes that Freud describes as being at the heart of the unconscious are exhibited today before the eyes of all, children as well as adults, and the *Three Essays on the Theory of Sexuality*, which created a scandal in 1905, now seem too ordinary. The supposedly perverse theories of the child, who invents an answer to the mystery of the parents' carnal union, are illustrated on our screens every day; the whole panoply of such fantasies can be found there. Everything is happening as if our century has learned the lesson of the general masculine perversion that I mentioned above. We now know, and it is not surprising that psychoanalysis has no doubts about it, that everyone gets jouissance from his unconscious and his fantasies. Furthermore, we would like to be able to take this jouissance into account, both in words and practice. Look, for example, at sexology, and all the effort to talk about sexuality and to induce people to talk about it! Now, as I have already had the occasion to say, people also claim sexual jouissance as a right. This new cynicism is intensified by the fact that the paradigms of love, elaborated in other ages, are no longer current. Neither the Greek *philia* nor the model of courtly love, nor the divine love of the mystics, nor classical passion captivates our jouissance any longer; now, we are left only with loves that have no models, loves that are constructed like the symptom; these chance unions are presided over only by the contingency of encounters and the *automatons* of the unconscious.

THE ETHIC OF THE BACHELOR

We must now ask a question: How much are the different symptomatic solutions, by which subjects resolve the absence of the relation between the sexes, worth? This question may be delicate, but it is also inevitable, since every clinical form—neurotic, psychotic, perverse, or more generally, the clinic of love—supposes, in each case, the subject's ethical option. Indeed, the term "defense," which was included in Freud's notion of the psycho-neurosis of defense, implied an ethic in the symptomatology. General perversion also cannot escape this question, for it too leaves a place for the various ethical choices that analytic discourse must bring to light.

In fact, what is in question is not a single ethic, but a plurality of them, and each discourse, as a type of social bond, has its own ethic. This is why Lacan speaks of "the racism of discourses in action": the discourses' reciprocal aversion for the way that other discourses arrange jouissance. What is inevitably lacking, however, is any point outside these discourses that would allow each person's specific symptoms to be placed in a hierarchy. Psychoanalysis itself can only "give a report"[10] about these matters, for it is no more than one discourse among others. It is not astonishing that psychoanalysts prefer the discourse that they have chosen, but that they sometimes set themselves up as rectifiers of mores is quite simply an abuse.

We are present today at the rise of what Lacan designated as the "ethic of the bachelor." Greek friendship, the ancient *philia*, illustrated this in the past; more recently, Henry de Montherlant incarnated it. Immanuel Kant, with his "practical reason," made a system out of it; in claiming to determine a will by excluding all motives and all the "pathological" objects of sensibility, the categorical imperative of the moral law excludes, beyond all particular interests, woman herself. This ethic is also "beyondsex" for it short-circuits the Other[11] to the profit of the same.

In this option, the subject takes "refuge"[12] from Alterity by confining himself in the phallic One. It is a strategy of eradicating the Other, an exclusion that intensifies the Other's structural foreclosure and is not necessarily incompatible with a fascination with a woman's supplementary jouissance.

SUBSCRIBERS TO THE HOMOSEXUAL UNCONSCIOUS

Let us ascribe this bachelor's ethic not only to Montherlant's kind of homosexuality (there are others), but to all those who, by

---

10. The expression is Lacan's.

11. What is in question here is not the Other as a place, but precisely what can be called the absolute Other, because it is not inscribed in this place of the Other.

12. See "L'étourdit," p. 24.

other paths, succeed in avoiding any approach to the Other, all those who could be called abstainers or strikers against the Other, among whom are the confirmed masturbators, and also, more paradoxically, certain hysterical women who are completely devoted to the One. We also must not forget the new indifference of the sexless, whom I will mention later.

I call all of them subscribers to the homosexual unconscious, to echo Lacan's description of Joyce as someone who had canceled his subscription to the unconscious. I use this label in order to note that the unconscious, as homosexual, is not what chooses between homosexuality or heterosexuality. In each case, the decision goes back to the contingency of the responses of jouissance in one's approach to the erotic. We do not see what would allow us to say that one of these responses is worth more than another, but we can survey their various subjective implications.

In this respect, we see in any case that feminine homosexuality is a completely different option: its ethic makes room for the Other of sex, without eliminating a secret link with man. This is why, as I recalled above, Lacan, in 1958, could make an argument that was the opposite of Freud's: the Eros of this homosexuality, as illustrated by the *Précieuses*, works against social entropy by the information that it conveys.[13] He could also emphasize, in 1973, that everyone—whether man or woman— who loves women is heterosexual, for if there is no relation between the sexes, a sexed love is, however, quite possible.

I will call "hetero-ethic" (I am not saying "heterosexual") the ethic that inaugurates the Other of sex in the place of the symptom. This ethic is obviously not to be confused with a promotion of the values of the *conjugo*, for the latter has nothing to do with an ethics, at least if we define an ethic as the relation to the real. It constitutes another response to what is impossible in the relation, a response that maintains the interest in the Other. Furthermore, it gives existence to the latter, although this existence has no benefit for the sexual relation, since the missed encounter remains irreducible. As a result, the "macho" seducer, the pet hate of any egalitarian ideology, takes on a certain merit. With his conquering arrogance, he cannot do less than to raise in his con-

---

13. Lacan, "Guiding Remarks for a Congress on Feminine Sexuality," p. 98.

sideration precisely what he claims to be lowering with his contempt: the feminine Other.

In this respect, we cannot fail to question ourselves about the pressure exercised by contemporary discourse. At the end of this century, in terms of what can be adjusted in the relations between the sexes, the whole of our discourse is in obvious complicity, by which I mean in sympathy of taste, with the bachelor's ethic. I would like to say what paths this sympathy takes; I believe that they are diverse, but that one of them is that of human rights.

NO SEXUAL CONTRACT

I have referred to the liberalism of mores. This, inevitably, carries with it the question of limits. We have no other limit to oppose to the possible excesses of the drive than that of human rights, with their requirements of equality and respect. As far as sexuality is concerned, I could formulate their anti-Sadian maxim in the following way: no one has the right to have the body of the Other at one's disposal without a mutual agreement. The paradox of this statement is inescapable: whatever the pacts of love may be, no contractual relation is possible with the Other of jouissance! There have been cultures in which abduction was raised to a rite, but in which very real mutual agreements presided over marriage, and which required commitments on the part of many people other than just the husband and wife. Such commitments, however, were covered over by the ritualized violence of a fictive kidnapping of the bride, as if to symbolize the non-contractual part of the sexed relation between a man and a woman. In our culture, one can go to court to expose as an abuse any sexual initiative that dispenses with explicit mutual consent! Thus we have all the new trials for sexual harassment, or for looking at women in a certain way, or even better, for date rape! Now, the respect due to any subject is extended to the most intimate space; human rights are trying to submit general perversion to contractual ideology, which, today, is no less general. This is certainly good, for to incriminate the extremely fragile barrier of human rights would be a very extreme action.

It is clear, however, in regard to analytic experience, that with this laudable intention of justice, we forget a bit quickly that the ego's consentings or refusals disavow most often not only those of the unconscious, but those of the responses of jouissance. This division is manifested at its acme precisely in the space of the relation to the sex. How can we be unaware that the choices of love, like the responses of the body, are generally surprising to the ego's aspirations? It is therefore to be feared that a legislation that claims to subject the partner to the norms of this ego will give inordinate powers to the faithlessness of the hysterical intrigue. The rights of man have finally been extended to women, and this can only be applauded, but they will never include the rights of the absolute Other! A woman herself, inasmuch as she is a subject, and subjected therefore to the agreements necessary if one is to live as an equal with any other subject, would be quite incapable of negotiating with the Other that she also is for herself.

INTENSIFIED FORECLOSURE

A question therefore forces itself upon us: How much of the Other can come into being in the age of the contract? Isn't it destined to be gagged, and isn't the Other, by definition, incompatible with any legalization?

The Other that I am referring to is obviously not the Other of language, the one who does not exist, but the living Other who, on the contrary, ex-sists to language. The two go together, in fact, for the first, which we would like to use to stifle the real so that we can organize the coexistence of jouissances, makes everything that escapes its grip arise as Other. This is how Lacan uses the term when he speaks of woman as the absolute Other, who could also be called the real Other, inasmuch as she is excluded from discourse. More generally, this Other takes on existence with each appearance of configurations of jouissance that exceed phallic limits, configurations that go beyond the normative regulations of a discourse; we see this Other whenever something of the drive imposes itself beyond the limits fixed by the pleasure principle. In this sense, the female sex is not alone in being Other, and we can even say that each of us is Other, since we all incur the element of jouissance that is foreclosed from phallic jouissance. We are "Other like everyone," as Lacan said in 1980.

The epiphanies of the Other are also varied: they appear between cultures (racism) and within a single culture as well, as a symptom of a discourse's failure to unify jouissance, for it is insofar as there are failures of the One that something of the Other is ejected as a castoff.

Today, it seems to me that the values of equality, combined with the growing homogenization of lifestyles for both sexes, work to reduce, as much as to fail to understand, the *dit-mension* of heterogeneity. Indeed, women themselves participate in the process, since they are now more devoted to contractual and egalitarian ideology than to mysticism! Not content to rival men at the level of phallic achievements, for which we know now that they are not at all handicapped—anatomy is not destiny—they are the ones who have introduced contractual ideology into sexuality itself, as the trials I mentioned earlier show, and that sometimes push things to absurd lengths. From this, it is only a step to thinking that by cultivating the same too much, we are programming the bad surprises that *heteros* can reserve for us!

In this context, what option does analytic discourse represent? The discourse that allowed us to elaborate the unconscious as a knowledge cannot be unaware that the unconscious knows nothing of the Other, that it only knows the One—the ones that repeat, or the "One-saying ("*l'Un-dire*")[14] of the enunciation. It is at this point that we can say that the subject of the unconscious itself is, in its essence, a bachelor. Yet psychoanalysis is not the unconscious and the analytic process, because it attempts to explore the other of language[15] in its inconsistency, also pushes us to the Other, if I can use this expression by analogy with the "push to woman." The psychoanalyst herself takes part, incidentally, in the logic of the not-whole, the structure of which is not that of the set but of the series, a phallic series in which the Other appears only on the edges, as in the margin, unless it is covered over by the object as semblance. Psychoanalysis must therefore be acquainted with the Other; it is a name of the real, a real with which it is concerned and which is its own. Although this real is "extimate" and impossible to say, it is not unincarnated, and is therefore animated by a palpitation of jouissance.

---

14. Lacan, "Ou pire," p. 9.

15. Jacques Lacan, "Compte rendu du Séminaire sur l'Acte psychanalytique," *Ornicar?* 29, p. 20.

THE ETHIC OF DIFFERENCE

I will therefore conclude that psychoanalysis, unlike the dominant discourse, excludes any complicity with the growing ethic of the bachelor. If Lacan was able to situate the desire of the psychoanalyst as "a desire to obtain absolute difference,"[16] analysis makes something pass into saying-well (*bien-dire*): the singularity of the mode of jouissance that, for each subject, makes up for the sexual gap, in other words, the difference of his/her symptom, if we use the largest definition for this term. In this sense, psychoanalysis loses its way each time that it militates for whatever conservatism of the norm that may be in vogue at the moment, and we have known many of them: genital oblativity, heterosexuality, maternity for women, marriage for all, and so on. The unconscious conditions all symptoms, from the most autistic to the most unifying, whether they preside over solitary pleasure or over the couple, whether they are psychotic or a part of general perversion. No fault is to be found with any of them. To analyze someone is not to "straighten him/her out"—an operation that, incidentally, is impossible. Nevertheless, an ethic of difference is a choice that can only be antipathetic to the taste of all the ethic of the same, which presides over the segregation of what is Other.

Lacan perceived the rejection of the Other at the very heart of psychoanalysis, and stigmatized it as the "scandal of analytic discourse."[17] I started with this point,[18] and it can be imputed to Freud himself. Let us recognize in this elision something like an insurance against the real, a determination to know nothing about it; such a determination cannot be without an effect, and it allows us to anticipate the rise of some returns of the real as the result of the mechanism of foreclosure.

No one, however, can subscribe to the Other, since it is not listed in the directory of the unconscious. We can raise the question of what this hetero-ethic can make of the Other, this Other with whom there is no logical relation (*rapport*), and perhaps not even any relation (*re-*

---

16. Jacques Lacan, *The Four Fundamental Concepts of Psycho-analysis*, trans. Alan Sheridan (New York: W. W. Norton & Company, 1978), p. 276.

17. Lacan, "L'étourdit," p. 19.

18. See above.

lation) at all. This ethic will do no more than to knot this Other to the unconscious, which also means to the phallic order. Love is one of the names of this knotting: the one that makes it that, for a man, a woman can be a symptom and that a woman can consent to it. Perhaps there is no better usage of this Other: to let it exist, while knotting it to the One.

Must we then make predictions and say that the less a civilization succeeds in sustaining this knot of the One and the real Other, the more it will have to bear the proliferation of other occurrences of the real, a real unbound from the phallic order, and that it will no doubt discover that as far as the Other goes, woman was surely not the worst?

13

"Social Impact of Feminine Sexuality"

In 1958, Lacan asked two questions that served as theses: Why does "the social instance of . . . woman remain transcendent to the order of the contract propagated by work?" and Is it not "an effect of this that the status of marriage is holding out in the decline of paternalism?"[1] Forty years have passed since that time, but the question of the social effects of feminine desire—whether homosexual or heterosexual—is still being asked. This gives us a more than adequate reason to update the thesis.

AGAIN, WHY GET MARRIED?

We would perhaps hesitate today to recognize in marriage the final "residue" of the fracturing (*morcellement*) of social groups. Certainly, people are still getting married, but they are also getting divorced; they

---

1. "Guiding Remarks for a Congress on Feminine Sexuality," p. 98.

are living together more, and it is being announced to us that the family—which had already been reduced to the couple and their offspring—has taken on a new, single-parent form in more than forty percent of cases. This is probably still only the beginning.

More essentially, haven't the elementary structures of kinship changed? Lacan liked to recall, by referring to Lévi-Strauss, the law that reigns unknown even to those who occupy the places that it ordains, and in which women—whether they like it or not, he said—circulate as objects of exchange and alliance between the male line. How could this still be the case when the egalitarian ideal has passed into the real? Have we perceived this passage? It has passed into the real at least to the extent that it has swept away all the hierarchies of symbolically instituted places. We have not witnessed, however, the advent of the reign of equality, as we know; the leveling of symbolic differences now only allows such disparities to subsist de facto among us—which changes everything. We fight against the latter, of course, in the name of distributive justice, which is never accomplished perfectly in the distributing either of goods or of positive rights, but by now only children and some of the mentally ill are still deprived by law of the right to free self-determination.

Each of us doubtless continues, despite the law, to experience the touch of the coercions of the unconscious, but the real circulation of bodies, from one country to another, from one house to another, from one bed to another, is now controlled by other constraints, which are both more circumstantial and more real than those that organized the symbolic. Only the contingencies of life have replaced the ordered *automatons* of the symbolic—the circumstances of birth, the singularity of tastes, the accidents of politics, the avatars of the labor market —which, when combined, preside over the chances of our encounters.

Thus we are all pilgrims of chance! The new religion already has its priests, its confessors, and its merchants, all the conjurers of the gospel of "perhaps tomorrow," of the absolution of "tough luck," of the managing of the probabilities that can offer everything: a mother, a father, and even a whole family for the orphan, a child of any color you would like, "a little fiancé" from the East, a partner for life or for the moment, and so on. One can doubtless suppose that the regime of perfervid individualism, which is triumphing today by fragmenting the old social bonds, is going to generate its own regulations and perhaps, as the optimists would like, new solidarities.

Whatever the situation may be, the union of marriage has now been reduced to the dimensions of the sexual couple. It no longer, as was once the case, combines two families—with their goods, their fortunes, their history—but two individuals, brought together by the contingencies of taste. As a result, marriage has become subject to the hazards of love: it aspires to last forever, but we know that this is only an aspiration and that it will probably cease to be written. We know this so well that we can now prepare our divorce contract simultaneously with our marriage, as is already being done in the United States. Show-business celebrities give us examples of all this, with the chronicle of their repeated unions and divorces, which contributes, through the media, to making the idea of the provisional couple seem more ordinary. More generally, don't the transitory and multiple unions of our age indicate the fragility of the famous symbolic pact—the seductive "you are my wife"—of the love speech, which seems to have had, for a long time, an impact on civilization when it comes to founding lasting bonds?

It is not by chance that psychoanalysis has come, with Lacan, to demonstrate that there is "no sexual relation"—the hole situated at the heart of everything that is woven of the social bond—at the very moment when modern civilization has carried individualism to its culmination. This simultaneity itself indicates something real. What it brings out is that the traditional couple—the one that was united for life by marriage, and that found itself inscribed in the unconscious, as Lacan says, in the form of the two who have taken the trip of life, together—was soldered together by something other than the knots of love alone. What can be expected of such knots? In any case, one can raise the question of whether they are in accordance with the practice of marriage.

Love may make the couple, but which form of love? Is it the love that, making up for the failure of the sexual relation, presides over the bringing-together of the sexes? The "couple's non-relation"[2] introduces, indeed, the question of knowing what can knot together for life the two bodies that sex does not succeed in making partners.

---

2. Jacques Lacan, *RSI*, session of April 15, 1975.

If we take the question at the level of jouissance, we must start with this: Between the sexual relation, which does not exist, and the sexual act, which does, what provides for the coupling of bodies? This question is asked in *Encore*, and the text gives an answer. What is capable of responding by the "jouissance of the Other's body"[3]—which, moreover, does not exist, and is always only the jouissance of a fragment of the body—comes neither from love nor from a woman's sexual organs, nor from the secondary sexual characteristics, but from *significance* itself.

In other words, the mystery of the sexed body-to-body connection of beings who have been made "speakingbeings" is resolved only by the unconscious itself: nothing presides over the copulation of bodies if not the copulation of signifiers, which is what the unconscious consists of. The cause of the non-relation, *significance* is also the cause of the a-sexed body-to-body connection. As Lacan says, man makes love with his unconscious.[4] This is the thesis formulated in 1973, one that reverberates throughout the following seminars, especially in the famous formula from the session of January 21, 1975, according to which, for a man, "a woman is a symptom."[5] In other words, a body lends itself to the partner, in order that the latter can, via his unconscious, deduct his surplus jouissance from it.

But then a question arises: Does this symptomatic physical connection, which is the sexual act, and which is ensured by the unconscious, work to give the couple a long life, when such a couple has no reason to be exclusive? The symptom is certainly constant, but is not, for that reason, faithful. Or better, let us say that it is only faithful to the letter of the unconscious, since the partners who lend themselves to it can be enumerated in a series. It is therefore necessary, if the duo of bodies is to acquire a bit of permanence, that love be added, and love is a relation of subject to subject. In other words, the two couples, bodies and subjects, must succeed in knotting themselves together.

But what can be expected from love itself? Is it "*velle bonum aliqui*," as Saint Augustine says? A little, doubtless, but only a little, for true

3. Lacan, *Encore*, p. 4.

4. Jacques Lacan, Seminar, *Le sinthome*, session of March 16, 1976.

5. Jacques Lacan, "Seminar of 21 January 1975," trans. Jacqueline Rose. *Feminine Sexuality*, p. 168.

love is also "*hainamoration*,"[6] which insists on what is quite the contrary of the other's well-being. Between this little bit and this limit, all the avatars of modern marriage find their logic.

It is probably by this little bit, by the concern with the other's well-being, that love can slip into friendship, *philia*, with "all that it implies of devotion to the economy, to the law of the home."[7] Plutarch's *Dialogue on Love*, which Michel Foucault comments on in the third volume of his *History of Sexuality*, remains instructive. The effort to construct a new erotics that exalted in the union of marriage the complete and accomplished form of *Eros*, the only one in which desire and the appetites (*aphrodisia*) are knotted with friendship (*philia*) by the mediation of grace (*charis*), participated in a sublimation. All of this is doubtless a dream, which Christianity has handed down to us, and which our century, as much as psychoanalysis, has undone.

The union between *philia* and *aphrodisia* is never one of harmony, and the gap and tension between them are irreducible. The first favors a companionship of bodies, and with the shared habitat, the habits and agreeableness of its homeostases. The other is not inclined to share, is possessive and touchy, and is full of all the tragicomedies with which we are familiar. Perhaps the conjugal bond only survives by circumventing them, by placing itself beside *philia* and the well-ordered furrows of cohabitation that it makes possible. Thus Lacan's strong affirmation in *Television*, which places the *conjugo* and habit in a state of equality insofar as they do not concern ethics. Ethics itself is a function of the proximity of the act and of thought with what is most real—what is in play in the drives—and when it is the ethics of the well-spoken, it is without any regard for whether or not love is long-lasting. What, then, works to make it continue?

We can observe, first of all, that the symbolic value of marriage is not yet completely outdated. One proof of this is that many subjects still oppose it fiercely for ideological motives. Remember Georges Brassens's song, with its slightly anarchist protest, "I have the honor not to ask for your hand." This theme, however, is already dated. The era in which people declare their hatred for the family has passed. We

---

6. *Encore*, p. 90.
7. Lacan, *Television*, p. 39. (Translation altered).

can certainly observe, even today, arguments for living together made by those who want all the qualities of life in common—including the social advantages—except for the contract and the commitments that it includes. They claim that they only need to count on the always renewed currency of the knot of love, as if the pact of marriage were opposed to the authenticity of the feeling. Yet they still call for social recognition.

Beyond the rationalizations of the pros and the cons, we must wonder whether what in love militates for the *conjugo* comes more from women than from men. I will therefore come back to the question of Lacan's that I mentioned at the beginning, and to some elements of a differential clinic.

Men, it is believed, are generally more subject to a quasi-generic polygamy. What, then, pushes them to a married union, which love alone does not impose upon them, and which only rarely serves jouissance? The father-symptom, the father-version (*version père*) of man's general perversion, if it implies that a man makes a woman his own, does not necessarily imply that his symptomatic choice must be molded into the form of marriage. Yet there is something else that is quite favorable to the *conjugo*: the contamination, as Lacan says, of woman by the mother, which puts her in charge of maternal presence and care. She takes care of the body, which cannot be reduced to the erotic body, although it sometimes includes it, and she takes care, as well, of narcissism. I have emphasized that Freud's reduction of woman to the mother may have owed something to the status of marriage in his age. This is confirmed here, in the other direction: marriage owes something to this reduction. Freud is inexhaustible here. In other words, the love for the mother that presides over the debasements of the love life is the best ally of marriage. We can see immediately that on women's side, the homologous doubling of the object, which puts the man in a series with the father's love and protection, and which therefore reduces a woman to the child that she was, could perhaps play an identical role. Is this all?

This is still not the answer to the question that I started with: Is there something in feminine desire as such that sustains the institution of marriage?

In truth, in our age, which is called that of the emancipation of women, contradictory facts can be observed. On the one hand, women's

social as well as professional autonomy contributes to the easier rupture of marriages and allows those who are allergic to life in common
to act on this position more easily. Yet on the other hand, each woman's
aspiration to find *her* man, the man of her life, as many people say, does
not really seem to be diminishing. On the contrary, between these two
types of data, we cannot doubt that a culture of nostalgic dissatisfac-
tion tinted with depression is progressing!

Let us postulate, against Freud, that a woman aspires to marriage
not only because she needs protection, or, as she sometimes believes,
because she wants children, but rather, and more fundamentally, as a
consequence of being not-whole. I will come back to this. The latter
generates the call to love a name, the quest for a saying (*dire*) that in
naming her being as symptom—the symptom that she is for the Other
—delivers her from the solitude of her jouissance and knots what cannot be identified—the Other that she is for herself—to the One of elec-
tion. This does not promise happiness, for it is at the joint between this
jouissance and this requirement that, on the contrary, we can see the
development of everything subsumed under the term "ravage." This is
the occasion to verify, however, that ravage can also serve as a bond.
For the moment, it is the function, at once subjective and social, of love
in the sexes that must be examined.

THE CLAIMANTS OF LOVE

Freud, as is well-known, posits that women are asocial. He supposes
that there is, in feminine desire and sexuality, something that does not
favor the bonds of community. His thesis, which he stated in various
forms, is that something in femininity rebels against the sublimations
of culture. I sometimes say to myself, indeed, that when we see where
the sublimations of culture have led us, it would not be useless to re-
evaluate them and to question the desire that has engendered them.
This feminine asociality would be seen in a better light if we were to
do so! In any case, this is Freud's thesis. The feminine libido, if this term
can be employed, is supposed to be too centrifugal, too disposed to fold
in upon itself, too inclined to invest only the objects in its proximity:
the child, the husband, close friends and relatives. They subtract themselves from the great values—the homeland, the nation, common work,

the collective, and so on, which are expected to supplant individual interests. The achievements of culture would thus rest on the sublimation of the single homosexual male libido, in which Freud sees the true cement that bonds the community together. Thus, again, we see the complementary idea that the unsublimated part of masculine homosexuality, which passes into repression, also goes in the direction of social entropy.

Lacan, as I have said, challenges these theses of Freud's, in terms of both female homosexuality and heterosexuality.

Concerning the social effects of female homosexuality, he discusses the movement of the *Précieuses* in the seventeenth century, who, instead of working toward the loss or reduction of the social bond, went in the opposite direction, by conveying information that sustains the social bond. Lacan, who in *Encore*, deplores that women do not say more about their sexuality, pays homage to the *Précieuses* for what they were able, on the contrary, to bring into the culture and the language (*langue*).

This solid thesis is clearly anti-Freudian: the effect of women's homosexual Eros goes against social entropy, and, on the other hand, the ideal heterosexual love—courtly love—had antisocial effects. Moreover, in 1973, Lacan persists and signals, in "L'étourdit," where speaking of the women's liberation and the feminine homosexual movements of the 1970s, he gives them a little compliment, the significance of which goes beyond its immediate circumstances; he recognizes in what they asserted the testimony of something real. This is truly worth reflecting on, and we see that it does not go in the direction of what is generally repeated, even sometimes among psychoanalysts.

As to the desire of heterosexual women, it also does not go toward social entropy, if we can attribute to it the maintenance of the family in a time when social bonds are in decline. Lacan lends it a positive social significance, one that is contrary to fragmentation (*morcellement*) and which, at least, stops the latter before it reaches the final residue— the individual—by sustaining the family unit. It is here that a critique of Freud that will situate him in relation to history becomes vital.

Today, the contractual and egalitarian ideology is dominant. The latter does not work any better for the marriage union than does the capitalist discourse, with which it is in solidarity, and which only favors consumers, whether they are taken one by one or as a mass. It can doubtless interfere in the space of the couple, and this is precisely what happens whenever the feminine object places herself, or is placed by legislation, as a subject to be respected. There is nothing to criticize in this, and it is obvious that we have all more or less been shaped by this point of view, but it is certain that it does not really militate for Eros. Indeed, this egalitarian claim makes the partners homogeneous and erases the dissymmetry between them, whereas what is expected from Eros is that it will unite the differences without reducing them. This elision of the Other will doubtless come back to us with a few surprises of its own.

We can now better understand Lacan's objection to Freud concerning what women require. In Freud's time, the father reigned more than he does now, and when the father reigns as the principle that unifies the social bond, his position carries certain consequences: the requirements of love—a term that is always singular—object to the sublimations made for the collective and hamper the collectivizing aggregations of the libido. This is why, in one of the little remarks he knew so well how to make, Lacan imputes the disappearance of courtly love to its social character.

Yet when the fragmentation of the social bonds carries the day, and when, moreover, as is the case today, this fragmentation is combined with the imperatives of the schizophrenic Superego, which I mentioned before, then don't love and its requirements take on another value? When the collectivizing One binds the sets together, love objects by its taste for the particular and the intimate. Yet when the social bonds crumble and fragment to the extreme, in a movement that seems inexorable, we can wonder whether the requirement of love, which sets a limit on this fragmentation, doesn't take on another value. This, if my reading is correct, is Lacan's hypothesis in 1958, in the passage that I mentioned. And, indeed, when the bonds are undone, don't the requirements of love, which is imputed especially to women, alone remain to represent Eros, the principle that unites, that unites not the crowds in this case but one to one: one man to one woman, and reciprocally, or in homosexual marriages, one man to one man or one woman to one woman?

Thus, according to the conjuncture of civilization, one can accent in the call of love either an excessive taste for the intimate, which goes against the collective, or its aspiration to a minimum cohesion between two—or more, if it presides over the family. I think that, today, the

emphasis should carry the day over the claim that there is too
.... of a taste for intimacy in love; this taste is perhaps all that remains to us to set a limit to contemporary forms of solitude, as well as
to the false universal of the ever-more-numerous cults of our age. This
is how I understand Lacan's objection to Freud, and I accentuate it
because of the new context, almost forty years later.

I will come back now to women. How do they reconcile their
claims for parity with their requirements as sexed speakingbeing, as
Other?

That a woman is Other in the sexual encounter implies that she
is also always divided, indeed is "shared" (partagée),[8] between the subject that she is as speaking being (être parlant), and then the Other that
she also is as a "speakingbeing (parlêtre)." She is also shared out between
phallic jouissance, which is homogeneous with the register of the subject, and the other jouissance, which is not. Would it be too much to
say that what happens in each woman is what happens in civilization,
if civilization's principle is that of taking the helm of the drives in order
to make them homogeneous, and thus to make them compatible and
allow them to co-exist? All society is, in this sense, an enterprise for
support the Other. Now, for women, for each woman in particular, the
struggle is played out internally between what she is as subject and what
she is as Other, and the question is always to know on which side the
scales will tip.

In the configurations of today's discourse, it is certain that modern women are far from being mystics dreaming of abolishing themselves in the divine Other; they serve, instead, the egalitarian ideology
that infiltrates all our minds. As a result, the "male chauvinists" are
obliged to mask themselves and swallow their sarcastic remarks. In any
case, it is clear that women today are adepts of the contractual ideology, activists for equality, and not only at the level of social life. They
go further: it is women and not men who claim to impose the sexual
contract, if I can make an ironic reference to Rousseau. I will take as
proof what I mentioned a moment ago: the various harassment trials.
The pivot of the speech for the defense is mutual agreement. This brings
us to what, from my point of view, seems a kind of craziness that is also

---

8. The term is borrowed from Gennie Lemoine, in her title *Partage des femmes*
(Paris: Editions du Seuil, 1976).

rather typically American: a young woman, having accepted an invitation to a party, having accepted going into a bedroom, having accepted certain maneuverings on the part of the man she has accompanied there, then, at the last moment, claims to withdraw her lovely, freely given consent. This scenario obviously does not take the drive into consideration at all. Then she takes the man to court.

I have already mentioned the problem, which is not only that there is no possible contract with the drive, but that especially, there is no possible contract with the Other, which, by definition, is outside contracts. We will perhaps say this is one more reason to consider women to be deceitful—an old song; along with the lure of the phallic masquerade to which discourse condemns her, there is added the impossibility of any guarantee concerning the Other that she is. Yet this would be to count without the artifices specific to discourse itself and to its function as screen. In the perspective of psychoanalysis, the opposite evaluation is no less credible.

We know that in the 1970s, Lacan gave women a supplementary credit. To the one I mentioned above, he added another: their relation with the real is quite superior to man's. The real is to be understood here in the double sense of the impossibility of writing the sexual relation and of the ex-sistence of a jouissance that is not ciphered by the Other of language.

It is by virtue of this real that the claimants of sex, aspiring to jouissance, are, in fact, converted into aspirants of love. This is completely different: it is an attempt to give a partner—human or divine—to this real. To this partner, the real of the jouissance without an Other could, as it were, be dedicated, at the price, possibly, of making herself his symptom. Its social significance is, indeed, obvious: it secures the jouissance that is too real to the snare of an elective bond. And if the social bond is in peril, isn't it also becoming the final recourse against segregating fragmentation? At least, it is the final recourse that can stand against the postures of the collectivizing One.

VI

THE CURSE

14

Love That Isn't Mad

*"All love is supported by a certain relation
between two unconscious knowledges."*
Jacques Lacan, Encore, p. 131.

MALE-DICTION

People are happy to repeat, following Lacan's traces, that psychoanalysis promises to bring something new to the field of love. It is still necessary to say what that is, since, for a century, it has never ceased attesting to "a curse on sex."[1] Since Freud, psychoanalysis has never stopped claiming to elaborate a knowledge about "the love life," and it is true that what his analysands said (*les dits analysants*) gave him some unique insights on these questions, insights refused to other discourses. As we know, the message was not rosy: Freud's itinerary led him from the "nervous" symptoms of that age to the affirmation of discontents for everyone and the irreducible disharmony between the sexes.

The malediction in question comes from no other God than the unconscious itself, which because it is language (*langage*), wants and

---

1. Jacques Lacan, *Television*, p. 30.

can know only something of the one, whether this one is differential or not. As a result, it says badly (*il dit mal*), and even not at all, the Other of sex—and there is only one step from this to speaking ill (*dire du mal*) of it. Love aspires to the two in order to inscribe the relation of fusion or effusion between the partners, but the unconscious condemns the subject to separation from the Sex. Between man and woman, there is the wall, the wall of language, as Lacan said, which has forged its "*amur*"[2] in order to mark out the impasse where woman manifests herself.

It is not by chance that we had to reach the twentieth century before what has always been intuited could be formulated in terms of a method. If Man is made of language (*langage*), and is thus a "speaking-being," he is also made of the other *dit-mension* that Lacan named discourse: this is an organization of *mores*, of "habits and customs," as people used to say, offering to each historical community a regulation of the *jouissances* that were permitted—that is, possible—and were suitable for ensuring a stable and livable configuration of the social bond. There was no other remedy to the misfortunes of existence and of sex than these discourses. The remedy was itself quite awkward, for if discourses are plural, as the history of societies shows, "Man," in the singular, with its claim to universality, has to take a hammering; this is not, however, the question I am going to ask today.

In any case, Freud was not wrong when he believed that he could impute to the voice of the fiercely sacrificial civilization of modern capitalism the impasse of irreducible "discontents." As we know, other cultures succeeded, in the course of centuries, in lessening this impasse and in blotting out the structural aporias of sex by inventing either figures of love or, on the contrary, practices of detachment; on this subject, Lacan evokes the Tao. Yet we no longer have access to these solutions except by paths that are dislocated by erudition, which is quite unable to give them life. Perhaps psychoanalysis has only revealed what it has been allowed to discover by the civilization of science; this civilization is prescribed by the globalization of free-market capitalism, which has almost been accomplished. It is certain that the existence of analytic discourse, as well as the revelations that it brings to light,

---

2. "*Amur*" is a pun that condenses *amour*, love, and *mur*, wall. (Translator's note.)

owes much to this conjuncture, and now, after a century of Freudianism, we must ask what effects it has had on the phenomena that we have witnessed. An updated diagnosis of what our age offers in this place is also imperative.

FIGURES OF LOVE

I am saying "figures of love" since love invents itself, between the symbolic and the imaginary, by discourse, which sets up the semblances that can captivate us. Its historical forms are a product of art, and are cultivated by various sublimations, especially religious and literary. From civilization to civilization, from century to century, we can follow their successive changes and adjustments, as Denis de Rougement did for the West.[3] Very little, even nothing at all, of what he described survives today—apart, perhaps, from nostalgia, which is still flourishing. And how can an age in which science has ended up bringing down all the traditional semblances—that of the Father with a capital "F," but also that of Woman—become the epoch of a new love?

Since the subject of science, in the sense in which Lacan understands it, emerges in the seventeenth century, I will take that period as my point of departure. Love, as it was exhibited on the classical stage, at the French court, where people had no doubt that they were incarnating the universal form of civilized man, can serve as a point of comparison; it gives us a very different model and may signal the end of a world.

Glory

François Regnault's fine analyses in *La doctrine inouïe* (*The Extraordinary Doctrine*) will serve as my guide. I will take a look, first, at his chapter on glory, the glory about which Corneille and Racine's heroes speak, and with which they identify their being. The signification of love and politics in their distinguished forms are conjoined here. Private and public destiny, intimacy of feeling and membership in the

---

3. Denis de Rougement, *Love in the Western World.* (New York: Pantheon, 1956).

community are united here, in order for the classical hero to attain them. He never gains or loses one without the other, since this theater makes them "equivalent." There is

> A subjective knot where a subject is knotted to a woman (or a woman to a man) and, at the same time, to the figure that he will cut or will leave in this world, or in the beyond. This means that a man, or a woman, does not fulfill her/his existence if s/he is not loved.[4]

Such is the major signification that founds all of this theater's tragic motivating forces, and that confers a rare unity on its heroes, one that preserves them from being torn apart and from the alternative, which is nothing less than our petty modern vanities. In this theater, the rights of love, narcissism, and the collective are harmonized.

Confession

A second remarkable trait intensifies this effect: love goes hand-in-hand with a confession that it exists. It is always declared, and it can even lead to an arrangement. This is not an implied love, as it is evoked metonymically by the baroque theater, nor the love that the *Précieuses* always postponed by adding new detours, but love as confessed, where its declaration "determines the undecidable love"[5] in a moment of concluding that is always evaded. This is a major characteristic, and it introduces into this theater a unity that is far more important than the famous three unities. This unity quilts this discourse together through the prevalent notion of glory, in which the combined satisfactions of Eros, self-affirmation, and membership in the community converge and are knotted together, in a single knot of "*joui-sens*."

The Quilting Point

It is not by chance that, at the moment of inventing the notion of the quilting point as the place where signifier and signified are knotted together, and thus before he added to them the satisfaction that

---

4. François Regnault, *La doctrine inouïe*. Hatier, 1996, p. 58.
5. *Ibid.*, p. 31.

solders them together, Lacan sought his first illustration in this same classical theater. He went back to the first scene of Racine's *Athaliah*, and to the signifier, the "fear of God," the same signifier, curiously, that Descartes, many years before his cogito, had placed at the head of one of his manuscripts[6] entitled *Preambles*; Lacan knew this text, since he cites it, attributing it, by a slip of memory, to a Letter to Beckman. Such an illustration goes back to the signifier of exception, which conditions all the quiltings of discourse, the very quiltings that the pure subject of science, as isolated by Descartes, was going to disrupt.

Disjunction

We can measure the extent to which this knot of glory has been lost to us. The loss occurred well before our century, as the romantic theater of the nineteenth century already attests. Love and politics are present in it, but are disjoined; rather than being knotted, they are simply braided in alternating peripeteias, whether of failure or success. If they sometimes become conjoined, it is the fruit of a fortunate and rather ephemeral chance, rather than of a reciprocal implication. Think about *Lorenzaccio*, *Hernani*, and *Chatterton*: they all illustrate the same division, the same separation of private and public objectives—let us say those of love and ambition.[7] When Freud emerges at the end of the century, he obviously inherits this disjunction, which he takes up himself when he states the two poles at which neurosis fails: love and work. The same division can be found in the words of today's analysand, when s/he deplores a failure in one or the other, and sometimes in both!

"LOFTY DEEDS" OF LOVE AND NEWS IN BRIEF

Will anyone object that the theater cannot be compared with reality, and a theatrical success can be likened even less to a failure in reality? Yet why not, since both theater and reality are products of discourse

---

6. The complete title in Latin was *Praembula. Initium sapientiae timor domini.*

7. These three texts are romantic tragedies by Alfred de Musset, Victor Hugo, and Alfred de Vigny, respectively. (Translator's note.)

and both attest to the facts produced by discourse? One would, of course, not say the same about the real, but anything related to love is played out so much on a stage that whatever it includes of the real is problematic. This is Lacan's thesis in *Television*. The stage where the "lofty deeds"[8] of love are exhibited is so much the stage of fantasy that one wonders— without any need of a psychoanalyst—whether life is not a dream. Nothing assures us of this, Lacan adds, except the fact that one kills! I translate this statement as saying that from the lofty deeds of love to what is called today the "news in brief" of crimes of passion, there is but one step, and perhaps this is the one that approaches the real most closely. Nothing of this kind is needed to make a love believable! The love that leads to death is not a modern theme: Tristan and Iseult, a legendary couple inscribed in the Western unconscious (Denis de Rougement again), already marked the place of an impossibility. Yet it is a hell of a change that the death spoken of here has now passed from myth to the news in brief! Doesn't this change go from the glimpsing of a necessity of discourse, in the first case, to a mere striking contingency in the second?

Here again, the nineteenth century testifies to this, whenever a novel is inspired precisely by this kind of news in brief; the novel takes from such incidents something of the virulence of passion, as the sign of the real. We know that for *The Red and the Black* Julien Sorel's crime had its precursors in two bloody events: the execution of a seminary student who was guillotined in 1828 and the murder of an unfaithful mistress. Contemporaries reacted to what they thought of as a blow against good taste, and Mérimée himself commented on the subject: "The wounds of the heart are too messy to be shown uncovered"! They preferred *The Charterhouse of Parma*, which was softer and more Apollonian. Likewise Madame Bovary, who was going to become a paradigm, was preceded in the annals by someone named Delphine Delamare.

ANTICIPATIONS

I am mentioning Stendhal and Flaubert as two markers of developments in discourse.

---

8. See *Television*, p. 38.

The first of them, when he writes not his novel of passion but his study *On Love*, produces an apologia for Werther, who loves, as opposed to Don Juan, who possesses, and thus allows us to read, by anticipation, the symptomatic debasement of love life that Freud would study; to this, Stendhal adds only a highly romantic exaltation of feeling.

It seems to me Flaubert introduces something else, and does so more subtly in his *Sentimental Education*. His Frédéric Moreau is no longer the hero of passion and is not yet the pathetic hero of the twentieth century, but he is already disenchanted. He has lively feelings, sensitivity, and even a fineness of emotion, but nothing of a definite desire. Spineless and irresolute, he never concludes or decides, allowing himself to be led by circumstances, encounters, or the chance of the event, in love as in politics. At the end, however, once he has received his sentimental education, when he has lost all his idols—those of love as well as those of meaning—this endlessly drifting waverer nevertheless reaches a conclusion about one thing: in his final words, he tells us what was most worthwhile in his life. Seeing again his old friend, Deslauriers, who has himself left behind his political hopes, they mention their friends, summarize their lives, talk about their schoolboy memories. They go back to the famous day when they had wanted to go visit a house of prostitution and mention how Frédéric had run away; he had become frightened as soon as he heard the prostitutes laughing and glimpsed a group of them together, and there was quite a to-do about all of this. . . . In the warmth of memory, he concludes, "That was the best time that we had!"[9] Deslauriers, the failed politician, approves, but hesitantly and not without raising an eyebrow, with an interrogative "perhaps": "Yes, well perhaps. That was the best time that we had."

This is what nostalgia is: the choice of the dream rather than life, of hopes from the past instead of acquired experience, and the delectation of disenchantment. This choice needs to be interpreted. Isn't this, finally, a confession that, after all the disappointments of love and life, what still shines in their memory is the period when they were part of a pack of boys, a period that is also the time before their encounter with

---

9. Gustave Flaubert, *Sentimental Education*, trans. Robert Baldick (Harmondsworth: Penguin Books, 1964), p. 419.

women. The episode of their failed trip to the house of prostitution is
there to remind us of this fact, in case we should forget it. Thus, when
the heartfelt cry that quilts the entire novel is heard, a cry that stops
the countability of jouissances, it is . . . the homosexual libido that gives
us the key to the conclusion.[10] Freud is not far off—this is in 1863.

GOING ASTRAY

I will remain in the field of theater or literature in order to define
what is specific to our century. We know that our age brings something
quite different onto the stage: the Ubus, the Roquentins, the Godots,
all the insomniacs from all the journals of disquiet, lost and laughable,
pathetic or grotesque, without any plans or any future, outside the social bond. For them, there is not even any alternative: it is neither love,
nor ambition, nor glory, nor even vanity, except perhaps for the new
narcissism of despairing apathy. Heroes of inconstancy, they count the
hours and the days, stagnating in an inert, a-signifying temporality,
which is unaware of the function of haste and the moment of concluding. Nothing here is capable of quilting discourse. The logical consequence of all this is that this same century, with its "avant-garde"
literature, has played more on the letter than on meaning (sens). Either it has made significations float by attacking punctuation, and has
gone to the point of suppressing it with Apollinaire, who was preceded
a bit, it is true, by Mallarmé; or it has played, in surrealist literature,
with the automatism of language and has worked against the author's
intention; or finally, with Joyce, it has cultivated a-semantic enigmas.

People will say that all of these figures are postmodern. Indeed, or
then, we have Claudel, a great figure, but from earlier, and it is as if he
were outside the century—and thus a lost cause. I don't forget Brecht,
who was also a great one, with his epics of the mechanical march forward, but I am afraid that the course of history has already placed him

---

10. It is enough to go back to the *Memoirs of a Madman*, which Flaubert wrote
when he was fifteen, some thirty years earlier, to see that a possible homosexual counterpoint to the misfortunes of love was already explicit for him, since he mentions its
sublimated forms, in connection with various remarks about women. See the Pléiade
edition, p. 466.

in the cemetery. What comes afterwards? In philosophy, morals, we see what is appearing: wherever there are no religious fundamentalisms, we, no longer knowing which saint to devote ourselves to, put our hopes in social agreement, and call upon the trio debate/consensus/contract. See Habermas, Rawls, and many others. There is nothing there that is not respectable, and they would be worth turning our attention to, but they have nothing to do with what would nourish a theater of love's passions! Perhaps, on the contrary, as I said above, marriage could find something to renew it in such a theater. There is a need for this, since it is founded now only on the choice of love, which is what is most contingent and ephemeral, and it is therefore threatened with the same risks of contingency and ephemerality.

INVENTORY

I will come back to our reality, which is unfavorable to myths of love; the consumer superego, the new status of semblances, and the new consensual practices that respond to it, constitute a triple objection to it.

Schizophrenization

There is, first of all, what Lacan named the "going off the track" of our jouissance,[11] which is now commanded by the imperatives of a market that devours people, that tells each of us what we need, what we are still missing. Unisex uniformization goes along with a supplementary effect, one that is less apparent but that has perhaps greater impact: the prosperous consumer's standard superego leaves each of us married to the surplus jouissance that short-circuits the social bond. Such jouissance is fixed on semblances that we can get off on but that are not mediated by the counterpart. This autistic fragmentation (*morcellement*) has something homologous to the schizophrenic symptom: it is outside transference and without an Other.

The paradox is that this phenomenon is accompanied by a discourse of rights that wants to compensate for it, but that intensifies its

---

11. Lacan, *Television*, p. 32.

effect, by preaching what I would call an abstract universal. We can see that this discourse would like to proscribe the traditional lifeblood of the *polis*: segregation and racism. It preaches respect for difference— and who would not agree with this?—but as soon as such a difference asserts itself in an Other jouissance (the problem of female circumcision, the Islamic veil, etc.), this discourse is constrained to condemn it in the name of the abstract Human. Yet the latter is realized only at the level of the market and the universalization of anonymous market imperatives, which command us to obtain jouissance in the forms of the supply (*offre*).

Consequently, it is not astonishing that this pseudo-schizophrenization, combined with the generalized cynicism of the right to jouissance, which our century has promoted, keeps a lack of satisfaction alive, a lack that is also quite general, and for which we can turn again to psychoanalysis.

Pulverulence of the Semblances

On the one hand, in the changes wrought by this century, love is lacking in semblances. It is not that they have disappeared; quite to the contrary. Multiplied along with the objects and forms by which we can get off, they cannot escape the constraints of trade, and they find themselves in the grip of an unstable and schizophrenic pulverization, which, far from unifying them, parallels the growing fragmentation of social bonds. From X-rated films to the standards of fashion, we continue to fabricate our standardized dream-traps. Today's supermodel, for example, is just an image, and not even a semblance, for the latter would want to speak. Let us say that she is the Hollywood *femme fatale* when there is no longer anything fatal about her but her silhouette—a silhouette that, furthermore, is so often tailored to the frenetic taste of the male homosexual, whose predilections in turn are sometimes altered with hormones in order to make them more marketable! The *femme fatale* was still a figure of the Sex, a place-holder for the Other, an Other that was completely other, invested with a mystery that was irresistible and dire. The model is reduced to her surface, the image of the body, which is almost the same as that of a thousand others, which could always be substituted for it; she is at best a bait for lust, and with her, the Other fades away. This brings about, however, a return effect, for the foreclosure of differences produced by the consumer's realized universal supports, in turn, the rise of configurations of dissident jouissances. The Other arises at the heart of the same, especially in the form of drives that are outside discourse.

Numerous examples reveal this logic. Can't we see, for example, that just as much as the Don Juan of the fantasy, with his thousand-and-three women, the modern serial killer, who worries the crowds and who is studied now as a rare monster, also counts women, but for another use, one that is outside any social bond? Last December,[12] the Australian press played up a news story that it thought could put the Internet on trial: that of a woman who had used the Internet to provoke contingency by launching the bidding for her future murderer, whom she did indeed find. Is this a pathology? Doubtless. One that has always existed? Perhaps. Such a practice is being spoken about and multiplied as a new response to the modern insufficiency of our mode of jouissance; uniformity, if it drives out the Other jouissance, also stimulates it. I am mentioning these rare and extreme cases—there are more ordinary ones—only to situate the problems of love in the right place.

Exclusion of the Other

The era of democratic dialogue is no more favorable to love than is the inconsistency of the semblances. We dream of the passion of love, which has had its great models, its mythic couples, its historic bards, but don't we see that the union that is painted in glowing colors owes nothing to any contract and is even heterogeneous to any democratic ideal of distributive justice, which would give equal rights to all subjects? Such justice has certainly become our only symbolic recourse for maintaining and regulating a social bond that is ever more compromised by the ravages of capitalism, which is now universal, but it implies the exclusion of the Other. In a contract, in spite of any disparity, the same talks to the same. The pact of full speech, the famous "you are my wife," itself makes this clear: beyond the act of adoption that it appears to signify, it is only uttered in order to reduce the other's alterity. That this

---

12. This allusion was made in 1997.

Other can consent to it is another matter. As for Sacher-Masoch's masochism, against all appearances, it does not really challenge the reduction of Otherness. It certainly claims to establish a possible contract with the Other, but this is only feigned, since it is at the price of "I ask you to ask me," which wards off any surprise. True perversion is something else.

And what, again, is to be said of the fact that today men marry each other and women marry each other? Certainly this leads us to take note of the malediction, and of a disjunction between love and heterosexuality which is confirmed by all of our experience of the unconscious. Antiquity already recognized it and the Christian Middle Ages allowed it[13]; since then, it has been proscribed, but that is an abuse. We can only rejoice in the new equity of our time, but it is nevertheless a sign of a neutralization of the alterity of the sex, and of the way in which it has been covered over by the contractual aspect of the socialized union that is the *conjugo*. There are various manifestations of this. Several weeks ago, one of the American weeklies,[14] from which a large part of our messages concerning our civilization's symptoms come, announced something new from the land of the Rising Sun: a surprising generation of "sexless" young people. A television serial, playing on this new asceticism, has been a great hit—as popular as the hard-core pornographic shows—and at the same time, families had already been expressing their worries on the subject to psychiatrists, at least one of whom echoed their sense of astonishment at these young men, who testify to a calm indifference: not at all toward the company of a woman, but toward the sexual. Let us insist on their youth, to indicate that it is not a question of lassitude due to age. Let us also add, in dividing the world into the "haves" and the "have-nots," that the first, those who have not renounced the "realm of the senses," are condemned to refine the erotic imagination ever more fully in order to maintain its spell over them.

I am not discussing the exactness of such descriptions, but I suppose that they are partly true, for this splitting sticks too closely to structure for it to be a journalistic fabrication. For those who have read Freud, such a splitting does not fail, indeed, to evoke something like a debase-

---

13. See John Boswell, *Same-Sex Unions* (New York: Villard, 1994).
14. *Newsweek.*

ment made real, one in which the splitting has passed into the real. We do not know anything about the subjective forces motivating these calm, sexless young people, who are apparently not sacrificing anything to any dark god, who are perhaps simply disheartened by the sense that "that isn't it," which characterizes phallic jouissance. Short-circuiting, however, the powers of the Sex, they signal the beginnings of an especially fanatical eradication of the Other, since this eradication operates on the bastion of the sexed couple itself, which we would imagine to be what can least be reduced to the contemporary reign of the unisex one.[15]

What is important is that they do not make a symptom of it—this is what is emphasized—and there is especially no question about which sex they belong to. They are "sexless" but not "genderless." Neither homosexual nor heterosexual, they designate for us the line of fracture, discussed above, that passes between belonging to a sex and choosing a partner. They are also not "homeless"! This is the completed reduction of love to *philia*. This may not be bad, but who would confuse "home" with the storms—whether of anxiety or delight—of the encounter with the Other?

THE OTHER WHO *DOES* EXIST

It may still be necessary to clarify what justifies us, with Lacan, in speaking of the Other with a capital "O," as if it existed, whereas for at least two centuries the entire Western world has been deploring its end. What allows us to do so is that the structure is incarnated. The not-all certainly forbids any universal predication, for in dealing with the multiple, it only makes a series out of it, because of the lack of an exception that would constitute it as a set; it is inhabited, however, by the Other jouissance that femininity conceals, a jouissance that does itself exist, and even makes itself ex-sist in a real way, on the margins. This, at least, is the thesis of *Encore*, and which is also present in "L'étourdit." This is why Lacan could say that women are Other but also that they are real. For in general, the Other takes on existence each

---

15. This, at least, is the hypothesis I made concerning "The Hysteric in the Discourse of Science."

time a drive makes itself felt outside the limits and forms circumscribed by a discourse. We must also see that the correlate of the formula "the Other doesn't exist" is that each person, and especially "others," can exist. If there is no longer an Other, we are all Others, to the extent that each of us presents some foreclosed jouissance. Thus we feel a sense of disquiet, which is becoming ever more general. If there is no Other with a capital letter, the speakingbeing has no other compass for orienting himself in his vital choices than the "fixion" specific to his jouissance; this fixion alone operates as the hidden principle of every decision and evaluation. We can approach this fixation through the fiction of the fantasy, and can say, as Lacan does in "L'étourdit," that "judgment, up to the last one, is only fantasy." We can also give it, on the contrary, the name "symptom," and say that each person exists only by it, for this symptom is what is most real. The modalities of the Other are diverse, but as far as the Other of Sex is concerned, the question today is to know how it can be lodged in current discourse, and whether love is still a good way of giving it shelter.

FUNCTION OF LOVE

I mentioned above the expression Lacan used to designate the female sex: the "claimants of sex." How can this voice make itself heard now? Feminism cannot incarnate it when it can only reflect the problems mentioned above, split as it is between claiming an equality of the same or an incommensurable femininity, which is set up as a fiction. If we think that this voice will never cease to make itself heard in love—its almost natural place—we may worry about what I mentioned earlier, something to which many women in analysis testify: once the euphoria of conquest has passed, the "holders of desire" hide from their call. They are quite happy to seduce and to show other people that they have a mistress, but they do not come anywhere near the Other!

It would be necessary, in this context, to examine once again the social importance of the feminine requirement for love, since its specificity is not absorbed by unisex, which is always progressing, or by contractual egalitarianism. Lacan's suggestions, as I read them, go in the direction of affirming both its irreducibility to the same and its positive function in the social bond. We speak of love in general, but there is only love in the singular—or, rather, loves. There are various types of it.

On this point, Freud opened the way, with his famous text, "Group Psychology and the Analysis of the Ego." He certainly discusses a socializing love in this text, but it is not that of the couple, and still less that of women, although Freud places the love for the leader, hypnosis, and transference love in a series. This is the basis of the compactness of crowds, with all that this implies of blind, infantile submission to the place of the substitute for the father-object.

Freud's schema is very simple: he makes love the basis of the group, since love calls upon an ego ideal—a master signifier—which, by being what the different egos that make up the group hold in common, allows them to identify with each other and constitutes them as a set. Lacan explicitly takes up this schema of the group in the "Remarks on Daniel Lagache's Report."

> Freud showed us how an object reduced to its most stupid reality, but set up as a common denominator by a certain number of subjects—which confirms what we will say about its function as a badge (insigne)—is capable of precipitating the identification with the ideal ego to the point of this stupid power of the mis-chief (pouvoir débile de méchef) that it reveals itself fundamentally to be. Must we recall, to make the importance of the question heard, the figure of the Führer and the collective phenomena that have given to this text its significance as a clairvoyant look into the heart of civilization?[16]

This "stupid power of the mis-chief" is a good way of designating something that is not emphasized often enough: the coalescence of the signifier, which is always stupid, and the stupid contingency of an object.

We can distinguish the levels of this structure. From the leader to his groupies, the ideal trait, the "unary trait" (UT),[17] founds a bond that can be called vertical, which is not one of identity, but rather of

---

16. Lacan, *Ecrits* (French Edition), p. 677.

17. In French, the expression *trait unaire* gives rise to the acronym "TU," which is also the familiar form of the second-person pronoun. (Translator's note.)

disparity. On the other hand, among the members of the crowd, it founds a reciprocal, horizontal identification, which creates a union:

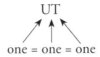

$$\text{one} = \text{one} = \text{one}$$

This union—it should even be written, with a few slight changes, in two words, with a hyphen (*trait d'union*)—this uni-one,[18] for it is what conditions precisely the unison within the group of all the ones (*on*), the ones who are all the same when they make up part of the united crowd. This does not, indeed, make them into a unity (*l'unien*), quite to the contrary, and this is what the great theme of the lonely crowd means. This union is precisely what becomes manifest in the uniform. The pun that is possible in both French and English allows us to link what is uniform to the uniform as a piece of clothing, which is what, at the level of visible form, of the envelop, makes present the homogenization of the egos; it shows us the uniformity that makes them all the same. Freud had noted that the power of identification in a group is so strong that it can even efface the difference between the sexes. It is not by chance that it is in our age—that of the boom in science and mass techniques—that unisex has emerged in clothing.

What Freud sets in opposition to this love of the One, which generates the same, is women's love. What he designates as feminine asociality is thus nothing other than what he perceives as women's resistance to *massenpsychology*. If this is the case, who will say today that they should be reproached for it? In psychoanalysis, let us not forget what we never stop repeating: that the phallic all does not exhaust what is effective about the master signifier (see the discussion of "using" the father) and it is also not the ideal of the social bond. Hasn't the century paid dearly to learn this?

The risk of an unbridled Other on woman's side, with which people sometimes play at frightening themselves, is not the exclusive alternative, as a tireless misogyny, which would like to scare us, would have it. There remains the more frequent choice of a singular love, which is will-

---

18. In French, "*on*" is a third-person-singular pronoun, comparable to the English pronoun "one." "One" is thus used here as a pronoun, rather than a number. (Translator's note.)

ing to make any concession, and where a limit is incarnated; this love gets its jouissance from the bond with a partner who is also singular, and it allows us to conclude, as Lacan does, that the women whom people are pleased to call "all mad" are "not mad from the all."[19]

The failure of the great forms of totalitarianism of the last century does not make these conclusions lose their validity. The defect in the ideal Unifying One may change something in the universalizing social quality of the mass, but the homogenization and coexistence of standardized jouissances loses none of its power from this; on the contrary, they are now supported by the fierce market imperatives that have been substituted for the one of the master. Thus the "not-all" triumphs in an unexpected way, but without any benefits for the Eros of the social bond, and difference does not gain anything from it. What remains, then, for whoever wants to distinguish him/herself from the common lot? Performance, the exploit, the record, all the things that are now commercialized in the different fields of sports, art, and politics. Or again, there is the barbarism of the drive. How can we fail to understand the horrified fascination inspired—on the reverse side of humanitarian ideals—by whoever goes to extremes. The collective atrocities that continue to mark the century after the *Shoa*—the serial killer who acts as a bookkeeper, the new forms of terrorism, and others—give us a new perspective on crimes of "passion," which begin to seem almost trifling.

DOING THE ACCOUNTS

We see how psychoanalysis plays a compelling role here, for it founds a bond of one to one, in which "transference" love plays a crucial part. The new love that Lacan talks about in 1973 in *Television* is not, as one could imagine, a promise that has to be postponed until the end, if not of history, at least of analysis. It is already there, but in a form so unexpected that we hardly perceive its "subversion,"[20] for in

---

19. See *Television* again. (This reference to the *pas-tout* makes use of an idiomatic expression, *pas folles du tout*, which could also be translated as "not mad at all.") (Translator's note.)

20. Jacques Lacan, "Introduction à l'édition allemande des *Ecrits*," *Scilicet* 5, Paris: Le Seuil, 1975, p. 16.

transference, love "is addressed to knowledge"[21] and it is expected to produce a knowledge; this is not just any knowledge, for in it, a real specific to the experience is demonstrated. This effect is as new as it is extraordinary. The mysteries of love are not concealed here, as they are elsewhere. It is not that psychoanalysis has to deliver any message, either for or against, but rather that it has to do the accounts.

The Incapacity of Love

The experience of an analysis, by attesting to the sexual impasse, appears to reduce the powers of love radically. It seems sometimes even to be the prosecutor who has put the mirages of love on trial; it reveals them to be illusory, lying, deceptive. Illusory, for it does not keep its promises of uniting "those whom sex is not sufficient to render partners,"[22] an insufficiency that challenges jouissance; lying, for it is narcissistic, concealing self-love under the mask of love for the other; deceptive, finally, for it wants only its own good under the cover of the other's good. In sum, it is the twin of hatred. Freud had already enumerated the forms of the statement "I do not love him," for psychosis.[23] Lacan generalizes this "hainamoration." Yet these are still only truths, truths that get off on themselves, and that therefore simply intensify the curse, whereas they should demonstrate the real.

Loves Without a Model

We no longer have any ideal love, but we still have loves. There were ages in which the Other was consistent enough to cover over, through its myths, the gap of the non-relation; in this way, it could knot jouissance, the partner of the solitary drive, to a relation between two beings who are subject to sex. Now, however, the Other no longer nourishes these knots of love—neither the homosexual love of antiquity, nor the courtly love of the middle ages, with its variant in the age of the *Précieuses*, nor the glorious love of the classical age, nor divine love.

---

21. *Ibid.*

22. Lacan, *Television*, p. 25.

23. Sigmund Freud, "Psychoanalytic Notes on an Autobiographical Account of a Case of Paranoia (Dementia Paranoides), trans. Alix and James Strachey. *SE* 12:59.

Once these typical figures of the past have been lost, what remains are our loves, which have no model. This is the characteristic of our own century. Contemporary love has been orphaned by its myths, and has been reduced to only the contingency of encounters. From now on, chance alone appears to weave them together, whereas the Other, when it existed, had offered us a unifying standard. We love love, however, more than ever and perhaps more desperately than before, in this age in which, when we love, we say prosaically that we have a "relationship" or an "affair," doubtless because we know that here is where the shoe pinches us.

Love as Symptom

Psychoanalysis adds a supplementary grain of salt here—which brings me back to the question of the effects that a century of Freudianism has had on the phenomena of love.

The question confirms this love without a model—which we are happy to believe fell from the heavens—and reveals, in the same movement, that it is not without constraints, and these are very precise. These are the restraints of the unconscious itself, which, through its own constraints, which are singular for each subject, presides over the contingency of encounters. The fact that it has no model does not mean that it is free. Love, as contingent as it may be, has the structure of the symptom, which goes along perfectly with its repetitive and compulsive character.

The symptom designates for a subject the organization of his/her jouissance as a speakingbeing, an organization that binds not one person to the other, but only one person to his/her jouissance. Love is the symptom that succeeds in knotting this first relation—which does not form a social bond, and is thus autistic—to a bond with the sexed counterpart. Thus we get Lacan's final thesis, that a woman is a symptom for a man. We could add that she is one type of symptom, for there are others.

You are my symptom: this may be, at the end of an analysis, what is the most solid of what can be said. This eye-opening love, which, unlike the mad love of the surrealists, exalts neither the Lady nor Man, which takes the wind out of the self-enjoying (*auto-jouis*) prattling of love, is perhaps the best that we can expect in this age.

15

Because of Jouissances

Thus my expression "speakingbeing," a substitute
for Freud's Ucs (the unconscious, as we read it):
move away from there so I can move in.

Jacques Lacan[1]

Does jouissance command? Yes, certainly, if, as I am going to show, it induces differentiated subjective effects, and if its characteristics on the man's and woman's sides have repercussions, especially at the level of the differential clinic of love.

This thesis can be surprising since we often impute a structuralist approach to Lacan. If I had said that the signifier and its presubjective combinatories command, we would be on familiar ground. We could even take it as established, in reference to the later developments in his teaching, that the subject of desire is commanded by the object-cause—the lost object, as Freud would say. This is the jouissance subtracted by the castrating operation of language, in conjunctures specific to each subject, which impels the dynamisms of desire.

Yet the question here concerns neither the signifier nor the subject, but the effects of the living body's positive jouissance, especially

---

1. Jacques Lacan, "Joyce le symptôme II," *Joyce avec Lacan*, ed. Jacques Aubert (Paris: Navarin, 1987), p. 32.

the jouissance that occupies the field of the sexual relation. Doesn't this also determine specific effects? I have emphasized above that one of them is linked, in part, with identity. There is no other identity than that of the mode of jouissance as completely or not-completely phallic, a mode that determines the unsubstantial subject of the signifier and makes him/her the *speakingbeing*, the being specified by a jouissance that, in all cases, holds to "the being of *signifiance*."[2]

THE HYPOTHESIS OF THE SPEAKINGBEING

These are the questions opened up by the seminar *Encore*. They rest on an hypothesis that Lacan makes explicit in its final chapter.

> I do not enter there [the unconscious], no more than did Newton, without a hypothesis. My hypothesis is that the individual who is affected by the unconscious is the same individual who constitutes what I call the subject of a signifier. . . . Qua formal medium (*support*), the signifier hits something other (*atteint un autre*) than what it is quite crudely as signifier, an other that it affects and that is made into a subject of the signifier.[3]

Lacan calls this hypothesis his own with good reason, since it is unique not only in psychoanalysis but also in contemporary culture. Contrary to what the reference to the signifier could make us think, this hypothesis is as much a rupture with the linguistic approach as it is with everything that has been formulated, in the course of the century, as philosophy of language: from the first steps of logical positivism, which foreclosed the unconscious in principle, to research in pragmatics, which vainly struggles to reach the real. The individual mentioned here, which is other than the signifier, is defined, following Aristotle, as a body and even as a living body. This living being affected by language is poles apart from the hypothesis of the language-organ. It is the hypothesis of language as an operator that transforms this organism, even denatures it in a real way.

---

2. Lacan, *Encore*, p. 77. Translation altered.
3. *Ibid.*, p. 142.

In other words, the unconscious is incarnated, is made flesh, and the individual becomes the speakingbeing. The hypothesis posits not only that the drive "is the echo in the body of the fact that there is a saying (*dire*),"[4] a thesis that is already old, for it dates from the time of the distinction between need and demand as the condition for the appearance of the void of the subject: it posits that the unconscious-language regulates the jouissance of the living body, which is subject to sexed reproduction. The step that has been taken can be measured when we read a strange sentence, which seems to mess up all the dichotomies: "The real, I will say, is the mystery of the speaking body, the mystery of the unconscious."[5] We are very far here from a thought that proceeds by successive binary oppositions, and this hypothesis opens up new developments. It marks an advance, in fact, in the questions of the economy of jouissance and of love within a couple, and opens the way to the new definitions of the symptom that we find in the seminar of 1974–1975, *RSI*.

This, therefore, is the question: What do the various kinds of jouissance—phallic jouissance or supplementary jouissance—possibly prescribe in the space of the symptom, and what repercussions do they have in the space of the subject?

THE SYMPTOM GENERALIZED

Obviously, the question itself cannot be understood if we do not take into account the extraordinary displacement in the definition of the symptom to which the psychoanalysis oriented by Lacan leads. If there is no relation between the sexual jouissances—I have mentioned general perversion—the subject has no relation to jouissance except as symptomatic: ordered in a singular way on the basis of the unconscious-language. This is the symptom for everyone, which is thus disjoined from any pathological connotation. This is not to say that one symptom is just as good as any other in terms of the comfort of

---

4. Jacques Lacan, *Le sinthome*. Session of November 18, 1975. *Joyce avec Lacan*, p. 42.

5. *Encore*, p. 131.

the subject who is affected by it or of that of society itself. Symptoms, nevertheless—in other words, "events of the body," to be distinguished from events of the subject—can include all the various fixations, the various modalities of access to jouissance that each person has at his/her disposal, whether they conform or not to the specific norms of the age.

Thus Lacan comes to redefine the symptom as a function of jouissance. The change in direction is immediately obvious if we remember that in "The Instance of the Letter in the Unconscious," Lacan had made the symptom a metaphor—a function of the signifier—that has the structure of a chain. That thesis was in harmony with the symptom's ability to be deciphered and to release meaning, but in fact, it could already be observed that the relativity of the signifier—its nonidentity to itself—did not go well with the fixity of the symptom, and this fixity is what differentiates it from the other unconscious formations in speech or conduct: forgettings, slips, bungled actions, all of which are characterized by their ephemeral quality. Thus it becomes necessary to call upon a transformation of the signifier to account for what it becomes in the jouissance-symptom. It is here that the distinction between the signifier and the letter becomes valuable. The letter is the only linguistic element marked by an identity to itself and is thus an asemantic element that stands outside the chain; it ex-sists to the laws of the composition of the signifier as articulated in a chain and is a part of the symptom as a jouissance-function.

The symptom, thus redefined as a knotting between language and jouissance in the form of an enjoyed letter (*lettre jouie*), is excepted from the "unconscious formations," although it derives from them, and acts as a "fixion" of jouissance. It thus accentuates what Freud emphasized from the beginning: that the symptom is, first of all, much more a way of getting off than of speaking. In a certain way, as I said in the past, in Lacan's teaching, such formulations are the outcome of a "second return"[6] to Freud, which began as early as 1964, in *The Four Fundamental Concepts of Psycho-analysis*. It allowed him to renew the symptomatology and to promote a new clinic in terms of the modalities of knotting or unknotting between living jouissance, language, and the

---

6. Colette Soler, "The Second Return to Freud," March 1986, Publicaciones del Circulo psicoanalítico de Galicia.

representations of the counterpart. Formulated in terms of the knotting between real, symbolic, and imaginary, this new clinic can be called borromean, as I have done earlier.[7] From this starting-point, we come to all the new statements concerning the father as symptom, the symptom-woman, the Joyce *sinthome*, and also "mentality illness," which I have illustrated with Fernando Pessoa.[8]

THE FATHER AS SYMPTOM

For the first and perhaps the only time in his teaching, Lacan, if I am not mistaken, defines a father who is worthy of this name: he is a symptom. To speak of the father as symptom is to define him by a mode of jouissance. It will be acknowledged that this position is a complete reversal of what he had said, at the beginning of his teaching, about the Name-of-the-Father as dead father. In this respect, the session of January 21, 1975 of *RSI* is worth our particular attention, for Lacan puts forward here, with his new formalism of the symptom, two other new definitions, which stand together in their logic: those, precisely, of the father as symptom and the symptom-woman.

A father, he says, "only has a right to respect, if not love . . ."—already marking by this simple conjunctive phrase, "if not," that love is not necessarily required, that it is even almost superfluous, and that, in any case, it is not the index of the function.[9] On this point, we have the inverted proof of Joyce: he did not respect his father at all, but nevertheless seemed to have loved him.

To continue: the father has a right to respect only if he is "perversely [*père-versement*] orientated."[10] This father is thus included in the whole of man's general perversion. It is necessary, however, that he not be "just anyone," on pain of *Verwerfung*, although it is necessary that

---

7. Colette Soler, "A Borromean Clinic," November 1996, Buenos Aires, in "Satisfacciones del síntoma," August 1997.

8. See Colette Soler, "Pessoa, le sphinx," in *L'adventure littéraire, ou la psychose inspirée: Rousseau, Joyce, Pessoa* (Paris: Editions du Champ lacanien, 2001), pp. 103–142.

9. Lacan, "Seminar of 21 January 1975," p. 167.

10. *Ibid.*

anyone "must be able to be an exception for the function of the exception to become a model."[11] This is what is most complex, for there is a double use of the term "anyone," which must be unpacked.

Anyone, that is to say, any of the set of all men, can attain the function. The possibility is for all: $(\forall(x))$. Yet in this all, only the fathers who are worthy of this name, and therefore not all of them, are models of the function. Thus, the set of all men is divided into two subsets: that of the fathers who are not just anyone, not just any man, for they have the father-symptom—and in this case it does not matter whether they have other symptoms—and the subset of those who do not have the father-symptom.

There are thus at least two versions of man's "general perversion": the father version—the paternal *père-version*—and the other, the version (or perhaps versions) that could be called non-paternal. This yields at least two types: the Fathers and the others. The term "Fathers" is not used here, of course, in the sense of progenitors, but in that of having the Father-symptom, and this is why I have written it with a capital F. The others are no less *père-vers*, but are so in other ways than by this symptom, which does not prevent them, when the opportunity presents itself, from being progenitors.

It is clear that the question raised is that of the difference between Father and Man—the universal of Man, defined by the phallic One.

Lacan proposes this new definition of the father in two stages. He does so first by a rather outrageous remark, which states that the Father is the one who makes of a woman "an *objet a* who causes his desire."[12] We would not believe our ears, Lacan warns us. Isn't this, at least apparently, the definition of all heterosexual men, a definition that leaves outside its field only the supporters of the Beyondsex [*hors sexe*] ethic of the bachelor,[13] who do not make a woman into an object-cause? Whenever it is a case of the "all men" $(\forall x \, \Phi(x))$ of generalized perversion [*père-version*], the Father is on the side of the subset of the heterosexual.

---

11. *Ibid.*, p. 166.

12. *Ibid.*, p. 167.

13. I am using this term in its Lacanian sense, which does not designate the absence of a wife, but the various libidinal positions in which a woman is not the object.

$\forall x.\Phi(x)$ = anyone

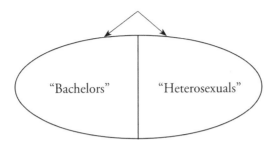

This, however, is not everything. Clarifications on this point will follow. Lacan adds that, concerning the woman-cause, it is still necessary that she be "secured to him in order to bear him children, and that, of these children, whether he wishes to or not, he takes paternal care."[14] This is not generally the case.

The clinic shows, indeed, that to choose a woman and to secure her for himself (in the double sense of the expression, i.e., a woman who becomes his own and who consents to being so) is not within the grasp of every man. I am not speaking of homosexuals, for whom this is obvious, but of heterosexual men; for many of them, as we know, women succeed each other in a countable series. To distinguish one of them, however, as having been elected, and to choose her as their own, remains out of their reach—by this I mean outside the reach of their symptom. Thus the set of heterosexual men is divided, in turn, between the Fathers and the others, the non-Fathers.

$\forall x.\Phi(x)$

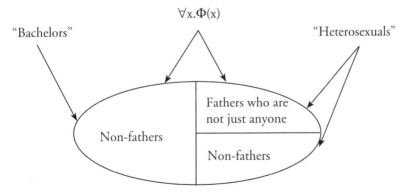

14. "Seminar of 21 January 1975," p. 167.

This demonstrates that a Father is not "just anyone." He is so far from being "just anyone" that he is a model—but a model of the father-function. This model is not common, and it does not require him to be a model father—far from it. Normality is not what defines him; his own symptoms, like his abilities, his talents, or anything that could be exemplary about his person, do not matter much. His function has nothing to do with a consideration of his ideal attributes, which Lacan had made fun of from the beginning, waxing ironic about the research that tracked the paternal deficiency "between the thundering father, the easy-going father, the all-powerful father . . . the stay-at-home father, and the father on the loose"[15]; such research goes astray in a phenomenology of the father, a phenomenology that is still more or less normative. Whether he is mediocre or eminent is not the question; the Father as such is only a model of the function, for which there are no degrees, and no "more or less": it is either satisfied or not.

DESIRE FOR PATERNITY?

More than a Name, the Father is a matter of desire, suspended as he is in one of the modalities of the cause of male desire. The paternal metaphor made the desire of the mother the prerequisite and the necessary mediation for the function of the Name. With the new formulations, we are far away from the theses of "On a Question Prior to Any Possible Treatment of Psychosis," although we already find in this text a discreet and discrete remark about paternal subjectivity as such. In an inverted, although not a contradictory, perspective, the support of the function is placed here on the side of the One father taken as subject, or better, as speakingbeing, so that the formula of his symptom could be given as: to make his wife, or the chosen woman, into a mother.

We see that this is not just any desire of man, for many men, who do not recoil before the Sex, or even before the choice of an elected woman, recoil nevertheless—and this is well-known—before the transmitting of life. Instead, they maintain the formula: a woman, yes; a mother, no.

---

15. Jacques Lacan, "On a Question Prior to Any Possible Treatment of Psychosis," p. 207.

To make a mother of his woman is also to be distinguished from what is the more general case on the man's side: that "the Mother remains the contaminator of woman,"[16] as Lacan says, with the consequence that Freud perceived: the temptation, which is always open for a man, to make himself his wife's child. This means, very concretely, to expect maternal care from her in his everyday life, a care that would extend to solicitude for his narcissism, and sometimes also, more widely, to the erotic plane. This configuration of the child-man is not only distinct from the paternal position, but creates an obstacle to it; because of this "contamination," a man will be led to refuse a paternity that would subtract from him a part of his wife's maternal care, and that would thus place him in a position of fraternal rivalry with his own children. To accept himself as Father supposes, on the contrary, the effect of separation that allows a man to leave her a little to others— at least to the others who are the children.

The Father-symptom therefore provides us with the example of a knotting between love for a woman, sexed desire, and consent to the reproduction of life. Perhaps it is even more than consent, if I were to go by the connotation of a purpose in the expression "secured to him *in order to* bear him children." A desire for paternity is mentioned here in plain language, one that is distinct from any pedagogical desire, as is indicated by the statement "whether he wishes to or not," through which Lacan splits paternal care from any educational vocation. This theme has been present in Lacan's teaching from the beginning, and was already strongly affirmed in his "Question Prior": there is nothing worse than a father who identifies with a *magister*. One is even surprised to find him writing the expression "paternal care." What is this care?

Care is more usually thought of as the mother's privilege. She devotes herself to giving sustenance to the body, and she employs herself in mediating language and its various effects, both castrating and erotogenic for the child; all of her concern serves as a first manifestation of her maternal love. For the father, it cannot simply be a matter of duplicating this maternal care. Let us, instead, place him in charge— along with the separating function of his presence, which is affirmed in whatever way in relation to the mother—of symbolic care. This is

---

16. Lacan, *Television*, p. 30.

nothing other than the transmission of the Name, which is always crucial, for it inscribes the child in the chain of generations and in a desire that is not anonymous. On this point again, the clinic allows an inventory to be taken of the symptomatic refusals of transmission. They have many degrees, but, at the extreme, we can find biological fathers who are miserly with their names. By a curious paradox, they sometimes go so far as to consent to sharing maternal care, and even to paying for childcare, while refusing fiercely to recognize the child and to inscribe him/her in a family line.

The Father-symptom is not just any symptom. It is the standard symptom of what could continue to be called the paternal function, on the condition that the latter is redefined, as Lacan did, in terms of a borromean knotting of the three consistencies of the imaginary, the symbolic, and the real. In the paternal metaphor, elaborated twenty years earlier,[17] the Name-of-the-Father metaphorized the signifier of the desire of the mother to give it a phallic signified, and thus knotted the symbolic of the signifier and the imaginary of the signified, with the real remaining apart from them. The final elaborations, which use the borromean knot, are in harmony with the taking into account of living jouissance as real, which is itself disjoined from the two other consistencies.

The enlarged paternal function has the effect of knotting together the sexes (the male-female couple), the generations (the parents–children couple), and also of bringing together these two couples of sex and generations; it does so at the very time when contemporary civilization is working to disjoin them more and more. We thus see its importance in socialization—and this was a constant thesis in Lacan—and the whole question is to know whether this symptom is regressing, whether it can be maintained beyond the "decline of paternalism," and whether something can make up for its failure. Lacan obviously did not envision homosexual parenting.

This question can be placed in the dossier of the debate over the new forms of the family. It is not easy to evaluate fairly the political significance of Lacan's theses. On the one hand, they seem to reinforce the couple of the classical heterosexual family, and could be qualified

---

17. See "The Instance of the Letter in the Unconscious."

as conservative. Yet in other respects, Lacan has brought out a double disjunction: between, on the one hand, the anatomy that gives us our legal status as either man or woman and our actual sexual identity, and on the other, between this sexed identity of jouissance and the choice of the sexed partner. As a result, hetero-sexuality and homo-sexuality seem to be allowed equally as figures of the general perversion that I spoke of above. This is a liberal position, for in the name of what could they be made into a hierarchy? In the name of their consequences, some will say. To confuse one's voice, however, with that of the oracle of the good that is to come has nothing to do with deciphering the constraints of the unconscious. As for the unconscious itself, it says nothing about the use of the liberties that it allows us, and remains mute in matters of ethics. This, indeed, is the reason that psychoanalysis cannot position itself as an expert in mores.[18]

A WOMAN, SYMPTOM

This thesis is announced in the same session that redefines the father as a function of the symptom. "[M]aking the leap, for whoever is encumbered with the phallus, what is a woman? A woman is a symptom."[19]

The dissymmetry between the two formulas is massive: a father has—with the verb "to have"—the father-symptom, whereas a woman is a symptom—with the verb "to be." What is at work here is the same play with verbs that was already used for the phallus, as I mentioned above. Indeed, a woman can be called a symptom of a man and not only of a father; this distinction confirms the disjunction Lacan had already affirmed, in opposition to Freud, between a woman and a mother. This disjunction marks the gap between the father and the heterosexual norm, for the latter is not in itself paternal.

In this year, 1975, Lacan came to the point of renaming with the term "symptom" all the elements that had first been situated as the object *a*, the cause of desire. This is the case for woman, who is mentioned in the same session as object *a* and then as symptom, but it is

---

18. See Elisabeth Roudinesco, *La famille en désordre*. Paris: Fayard, 2002.
19. "Seminar of 21 January 1975," p. 168.

also so for the analyst. In the formula for the analytic discourse, the analyst makes the object present, but Lacan ends up saying that s/he is a symptom.[20] If this new denomination served only to suggest that the object is chosen by nothing other than the unconscious, it would be nothing new. We would find once again the problem of the unconscious conditions for object-choice, which Freud had already explored, and we would say only that because the speakingbeing lacks any programmed partner, the unconscious serves as a compensation. It makes itself the instigator of the encounters of the love life. To use the term "symptom," however, is to evoke more than the bonds of love and desire; it is to mention jouissance itself. Yes, but which one?

The jouissance of the sexed couple's body-to-body connection creates a question since it does not create a relation (*rapport*). Lacan makes this explicit: the statement that "there is no jouissance of the Other as such" tells us that a woman is a symptom. This had already been included in *Encore*, in order to conclude precisely that the jouissance of the body-to-body connection, as paradoxical as it may seem, gets through by means of the jouissance of the unconscious. Furthermore, it even ensures that a subject will get off on his/her unconscious. If the symptom is "the way in which each person gets jouissance from the unconscious,"[21] when the person in question is a woman, it follows that she lends her body so that the man, by getting off on her, in fact obtains jouissance from his own unconscious. Conversely, it is through getting off on the unconscious that he has access to body-to-body jouissance, which is not the jouissance of the Other but phallic jouissance.

GETTING JOUISSANCE FROM THE UNCONSCIOUS

We remember that, after having affirmed in the first session that the jouissance of the Other's body is not the sign of love, *Encore* asked: Where does what responds through the jouissance of the Other's body come from, if not from love? It then went on to enumerate the negative responses. It comes neither from woman's sexual organs nor from

---

20. See the session of the seminar, *Le sinthome*, April 13, 1976.
21. *RSI*, session of February 18, 1975, *Ornicar?* 4: 106.

the secondary sexual characteristics; it is not, furthermore, the jouissance of the Other, for jouissance does not go toward the Other, and
copulation induces only the fallacy of a false finality. Lacan finally responds that body-to-body jouissance has its cause in the signifier itself,
the signifier that is situated at the level of "enjoying substance (*la substance jouissante*)"![22]

Such is the response, which was new in 1973, that Lacan developed
on two pages that deserve to be more famous than they are—pages 24
and 25 of *Encore*—where he developed the four modalities of the signifier as cause; the latter term should be understood not as cause of a loss
of jouissance, which was the classical thesis, but as the positive cause of
the jouissance of the body. I have occasionally said that the semblances,
the norms of constituted discourses, stop at the foot of the bed; well, this
is not the case for *signifiance*, which reigns even in bed, giving life to the
space of the sexual relation. The signifier is erotogenic.

For man, it also presides over the ejaculation, over this foreign
jouissance outside the body which is phallic jouissance. What is at work
is not an erection pill! Since we are in the age of Viagra, it is amusing
to note the insistence with which doctors emphasize that it does not
make up for the vigor of the libido, or, as we would say, for causation
by the signifier. Thus we have the striking formula of the seminar on
Joyce: "Man makes love with his unconscious"—and the "with" should
be taken in the double sense of the instrument and the partner. Thus
also, for women, the affirmation that their being lies in a jouissance that
is not-whole is no less a part of their being of *signifiance*. I will return
to this point.

In the words of the session of March 11, 1975, "only signifiers
copulate in the unconscious, but the pathematic subjects that result
from them in the form of bodies are led to do as much—fuck, as they
call it."[23]

This statement is one of the consequences of the theses advanced
in *Encore*. He had claimed that the speakingbeing, here named the
pathematic subject—the body whose jouissance is commanded by
the signifier—couples only by the angle of language. In other words,

---

22. *Encore*, p. 23.
23. *RSI*, session of March 11, 1975, *Ornicar?* 5: 28.

the One jouissance clings to the "body signified as Other,"[24] only to couple this body to the signifier of unconscious knowledge.

A woman-symptom is first of all a body to enjoy, and to enjoy by the angle of the unconscious, but with the result that the jouissance borne by this Other body is, for man, only an enjoyment of the unconscious. This also means that the phallic One, which is repetitive and does not cease to write itself, has no other company, even in love, than the ones of language, with the fate of solitude at the end of it all, which brings about so many sighs. This leads us, however, to the other side of the symptom.

THE MADNESS OF LOVE

If in the act that the English language calls that of lovemaking, in embracing an Other body, man remains nevertheless alone with his unconscious, we can understand the reference to the ellipsis of the symptom. The three dots write that the phallic One, coupled with the One of the symptom, lacks an Other.

I indicate this by a parenthesis: One(Σ) . . . (A). The dots represent, as Lacan specifies, so many question marks concerning the nonrelation: One(Σ) . . . =? The One continues to question the lack of the Other that would create the two of sex. It is here that the dimension of believing in the symptom is introduced. It is obviously heterogeneous to its dit-mension of jouissance, but it is commanded by it. Thus we have the title of this paper, which addresses the subjective effects of the characteristics of jouissance.

Belief in the symptom, even the invention of the Other, is one of them. It is not by chance that Lacan introduces it in Encore. "Man believes that he creates—he believes-believes-believes, he creates-creates-creates. He creates-creates-creates woman."[25] This rattle-effect will not escape its various resonances of irritation and vanity. This theme reappears in RSI, where it is generalized: ". . . what constitutes the symptom . . . is that one believes in it."[26] In other words, one believes that it can

---

24. Ibid.
25. Encore, p. 131.
26. "Seminar of 21 January 1975," p. 168.

say something. Isn't making the symptom speak the very principle of psychoanalysis, since "believing in" it is the postulate of any deciphering?

Nevertheless, when the symptom is this other speakingbeing—a woman—a woman who also speaks, beyond believing in her, there begins a turning toward the madness of "believing her." The distance from one to the other is the same as what separates transference from true credulity: the first goes toward latent knowledge, and the second subjects one to the text of the Other; transference supposes and seeks the concealed enunciation, whereas credulity succumbs under the subjection to the manifest statement. From "believing in" to "believing her," there is the same distance as between neurosis and psychosis. It is the point of homology that makes love into a kind of madness, since one "believes her" as much as the psychotic subject, who, more than believing in his voices, believes them. In this way, according to Lacan, love, what he calls "major love," is a comic sentiment ballasted by "that well-known comedy, the comedy of psychosis."[27]

Thus, the solitary jouissance of the phallic One, leaving the Other inaccessible, commands effects that push love to madness. Yet it also creates a limit to it on the side of jouissance. Indeed, as we know, it is rather in women that this madness of love takes on its full dimension, since in man it is always only sketchy and hesitant.

It is not that he does not love; it is rather that for him love can go without saying, as Lacan notes in the session of February 12, 1974, of the seminar *Les non dupes errent*. It goes without saying, for he can be contented with his jouissance, in the double sense of the expression: the jouissance that does not have its cause in the saying (*le dire*), but in the discrete signifiers of the unconscious, is enough for him; it also satisfies him, making his identity as man substantial, far from being opposed to it.

MAN RAVAGES

This is not at all the case for women, and this is why Lacan has sought an expression that creates a dissymmetry between the partners of each of the two sexes.

---

27. *Ibid.*, p. 170.

Whereas he spoke of a woman-symptom for man, on woman's side he found nothing better than ravage or affliction, the man-ravage. These two terms connote both the throes of pain and annihilating destruction.

It is remarkable, furthermore, that Lacan uses again this term "ravage," which he had first employed to characterize a girl's relation to her mother. He seems to take over the Freudian thesis that the man inherits the girl's relation to the mother—more precisely, the reproaches made to the mother—and becomes, after her, the target of her requirement that she be given the phallus.

I do not believe, however, that this is Lacan's thesis, for ravage is not such a claim for the phallus; it sometimes includes such a claim, but it cannot be reduced to it, and in the last analysis it is of another order, since it does not belong to the phallic register.

Its true nature can be grasped only from the characteristics of feminine jouissance, for it is a consequence of the latter. The orgasm, like the symptom, is an emergence of jouissance in the space of the subject, as Lacan said in the session of April 27, 1966.[28] Its value lies precisely in its being a vanishing-point of the subject as divided; in other words, it is a point that subtracts this subject from its causation by the object to the profit of a jouissance closed upon itself. The result is that between the orgasmic jouissance and the subject properly speaking, there is a mutual exclusion: the presence of one brings about the absence of the other.

The clinical consequence for a woman is that, at the very time when the orgasmic experience is most affirmed, even most fulfilling, it never fails to destabilize the subject. Dislodging the subject from the foundations provided by her identifications as much as from the support that she finds in the object that divides her, this experience kidnaps her to itself, especially if it happens to be experienced in joy.

Such is the nucleus of ravage: it is the other jouissance that ravages the subject, in the strong sense of annihilating her in the space of a moment. The subjective effects of this eclipse are never missing. They go from the slightest disorientation to profound anxiety, and pass through all the degrees of aberration and avoidance. This context can throw light on certain kinds of frigidity. One grasps, furthermore, what

---

28. Seminar of 1965–1966, *L'objet de la psychanalyse*, unpublished.

imposed the reference to the mystics upon Lacan: What precisely is the mystical aspiration, as all the texts proclaim, other than the abolition of oneself in the Other, the abolition of oneself as subject of any creaturely project?

No such condition exists on man's side, for phallic jouissance, far from being in opposition to the foundations of the subject's identity, constitutes it. This is so true that if he is ever confronted with some proof of impotence or failure, a man very often resorts to exercising his organ; whether it is with a woman or a man or by masturbating, this exercise always serves as a reassurance. A man often resorts to it in order to plug up the effect of castration in an analysis. Such is the secret of many performances within transference. For a woman, on the contrary, when she is overwhelmed by failure, the most frequent recourse is to seduction, which is always phallicizing, and sometimes also to competition in having the phallus. She turns much more rarely to sexual jouissance properly speaking, which brings her back to a state of annihilation.

MAKING LOVE ABSOLUTE

The major subjective consequence of the other jouissance, even beyond its affective effects, is to be sought on the side of a woman's position in relation to love. I formulate it thus: her jouissance commits her to a logic of the absolutizing of love, a logic that pushes her toward an insatiable quest for the Other.

This quest, however, has two sides. On the more visible side, where the S(A) of jouissance has demolished the identifications, love restores a phallic identification. In this sense, when she asks the man for the sexual act to be enveloped in love, and even a unique love, a woman is in fact asking to be assured as subject of her phallic ballasting. The other, less visible side, is, in my view, what is essential. What I decipher here is this formula: to abolish herself, yes, but in the Other. From this comes women's sometimes frantic efforts to elevate their men to the dignity of the Other, so that they will lend themselves a little to a confusion with God, as Lacan says in *Encore*.[29] Light is thus thrown

---

29. Lacan, *Encore*, p. 89.

upon a fact that is clinically obvious: for women, "love does not go without saying (*sans dire*),"[30] and they complain of nothing so much as masculine silence. To say that this silence "aphlicts" them is to say too little. The little comic dramas of everyday life come from this "aphliction": her complaint that "he doesn't say anything to me," to which he replies, "but what does she want me to say to her?" They doubtless expect this saying to give substance to the *agalmatic* object, but more essentially, they aspire for it to fill up the S(A). In other words, they require a man to want to take the trouble, and even tire himself out, I could say, to give more than his presence as desiring alone: they require his efforts to make himself a bit into the Other.

Thus, ravage, properly speaking, seems to me quite distinct from the simple requirement to have the phallus. It does not exclude the latter and it may become combined with it, but it is different from it. It is remarkable, as I have said, that Lacan uses the same term, "ravage," to qualify the mother–daughter relation. Freud had recognized the stream of reproaches that a daughter can make to her mother, which seemed so enigmatic to him before he subsumed them all, finally, under the single notion of penis envy. Is there not, however, beyond the dimension of the requirement, a soliciting of the mother to reveal the final secret? This secret is not only that of the feminine *agalma*, which is always phallic, but also that of the jouissance that ex-sists, although unknown to the Other, and for which therefore a woman appeals to the Other.

It is true that penis envy can take ravaging forms. The feeling of a lack-in-having (*manque-à-avoir*) culminates, in certain feminine subjects, in a deleterious conviction that she is of little value; this conviction is often intensified by a frenzied rage in relation to all phallicized figures. Thus one sees women who become as furious with their rivals as with the supposed ease of masculine jouissance.

This element of the clinic has been widely explored in psychoanalytic literature, but it fell to Lacan to have completed it with the term "ravage," which in the main designates phenomena of another type: nothing other than the pathematic effects that the other jouissance induces in the subject, and that are split and divided between the subjective abolition to which I have referred and the correlative absolutizing of the Other.

30. Seminar *Les non dupes errent*, session of February 1, 1974, unpublished.

VII

ANALYSIS

16

Separation Symptom

When a psychoanalysis reaches its terminal point, can it really claim to produce a new subject? This question is less concerned with the terminal point of the analytic sequence than with the subject that results from it. More than once, Lacan, in speaking of the transformation of the subject by analysis, did not hesitate to use a very strong word: "metamorphosis." Freud, whom we think of as having retreated a bit in terms of the ambitions assigned to any finished treatment, also did not avoid the question.

In his text "Analysis Terminable and Interminable," when asking himself about the possible result of an analysis, he mentions the transformation that the subject must undergo if we are to use the past participle and call him/her "analyzed": "Is it not precisely the claim of our theory that analysis produces a state which never does arise spontaneously in the ego and that this newly created state constitutes the essential difference between a person who has been analyzed and a person who has not?"[1]

---

1. Sigmund Freud, "Analysis Terminable and Interminable," trans. Joan Riviere. SE XXIII (1937–1939) (London: Hogarth Press, 1964), p. 227. References to all further citations will appear in the text.

There is a wide divergence between Freud's and Lacan's statements, and they can sometimes seem antinomical. Whereas Freud emphasizes, at the beginning of the same Chapter III, that his intention is "radically to exhaust the possibilities of illness" in his patients (p. 224), Lacan announces the production of what is incurable and comes out with the expression "the final identification with the symptom," which is quite strange in terms of the therapeutic effects with which analysis deserves to be credited. Yet if we do not treat the formulas as the trees that keep us from seeing the forest, and restore their logic to each of their procedures, this divergence can be greatly reduced.

FREUD'S REVISED POSITION

When he published "Analysis Terminable and Interminable" in 1937, Freud, aged and ill, knew that he was going to die. In this text, he assesses some fifty years of experience, giving us a theoretical testament in which the tasks for the future are sketched out. He brings back to life the figures from the past who torment him: Fliess and his sexual theories, Adler and his seemingly forgotten "masculine protest." Then, and especially, there is Ferenczi, whose living reproach—although at this date, he was already dead—concerned his own unfinished analysis. These responses were Freud's final ones, and they still interest us.

The question that Freud asks deals not so much with the episodes of analysis, its inertia, and even its possible stumbling blocks, as with its result, with the possibility or impossibility of producing a subject who could no longer generate new symptoms.

Freud's principal thesis, which is in harmony with the origin of his discovery, is that the repression of the drives conditions their return in the symptom. Freud works with two terms here: the drive as a requirement of specific jouissance, and the *Ich* as the principle of defense and rejection in regard to this irreconcilable requirement. The question is thus that of the fate of repression both in and after analysis. When he speaks of becoming conscious or explaining unintelligible material (p. 219), he accents the epistemic aspect of the process, the gain in knowledge that is to be expected from an analysis: an "I know." Yet when he mentions, in parallel, the possibility of "a revision of these old repressions," of reaching a "subsequent correction of the original processes of repression," something very different is in question (p. 227). We are no longer on the axis of what analysis reveals, but on that of how it operates and the changes that it can produce at the level of the defense against the drives—at the level of the subject's statements "I want" or "I don't want."

Freud distinguishes two sorts of possible transformations: among the repressions, "a few are demolished"—and thus, the drive is admitted—"while others are recognized but constructed afresh out of more solid material," and the consequence is a strengthened rejection (p. 227). As we see, Freud does not dream of a subject who would have ceased to defend him/herself against all the real of the jouissance of the drives; such a being, incidentally, could not be assimilated to any social bond. Instead, he is concerned with a defense that, in cases in which jouissance remains unacceptable for the subject, would stop generating repression and the return of the symptom that accompanies it.

The two obstacles to the possible treatment of the drive by psychoanalysis are thus indicated clearly: on the one hand, the famous "quantitative factor" and the ever-present threat of a possible "instinctual strength," and on the other, the incomplete "transformation in the defensive mechanism" of the *Ich* (p. 230).

The result, says Freud, is that "analysis, in claiming to cure neuroses by ensuring control over instinct, is always right in theory but not always right in practice" (p. 229). This conclusion succeeds in creating the remarkable alliance between a conceptual requirement that affirms its goal categorically and a pragmatic realism that is concerned with the contours of experience.

In this text, Freud never envisions that analysis will modify the requirement of the drives in itself. The term "sublimation," which always designates in his work a process of transforming the drive, and which can even be a socializing transformation, is not present in this essay. What analysis modifies, on the contrary, according to this text, is what can be called the treatment of the drive by repression—we would say the relation to the real. It remains then, for the subject, once s/he has been enlightened by the deciphering that occurs in analysis, to make a new choice. Thus Freud, who is accused so often of acting as a master, gives an important place to a renewed decision by the subject.

This same trait can be found elsewhere, very explicitly, in regard to the famous impasse that Freud introduces in his final chapter: castration as a "bedrock" (p. 252). In situating it as "transference-resistances" (p. 252), he tells us that this impasse cannot be reduced to the fear of bodily mutilation, and that the images that proliferate there and that he has catalogued are only translations into the imaginary of a different process, which is not itself imaginary: the effect of loss implied by the relation to the Other. The threat of this appears in a new version at each approach to this Other—here a transferential approach.

We know Freud's last word on this point:

> It would be hard to say whether and when we have succeeded in mastering this factor in an analytic treatment. We can only console ourselves with the certainty that we have given the person analysed every possible encouragement to re-examine and alter his attitude to it. [pp. 252–253]

A funny Master—one who allows a choice! People could say that this is a liberalism of powerlessness—which, indeed, is what the reference to consolation connotes—but it remains no less true that the last word and the final outcome are returned here to the subject, or rather to "the unfathomable decision of being."[2]

In short, therefore, the subject transformed by analysis will be defined by a new relation to both castration and the drive.

IDENTIFYING WITH THE SYMPTOM?

This is the same thesis to which Lacan returns starting in 1964, although he formulates it differently, and through which he completes the accent, which he had maintained for ten years, on the linguistic formation of the subject's experience. From the affirmation, in Seminar XI, *The Four Fundamental Concepts of Psycho-analysis*, of a subject for whom, at the end, the fantasy is reduced to the drive, to the later references to a final identification with the symptom, the same ques-

---

2. Jacques Lacan, "Propos sur la causalité psychique," *Ecrits*, p. 177.

tion is being asked: whether or not there is a new relation to the drive, and more generally, whether it is possible to treat jouissance on the basis of the unconscious as language (*langage*).

Lacan surprised people when he said that, at the end of an analysis, identifying with one's symptom is the best that the subject can do. That people were surprised shows that his thought had not been followed well up to that point. Everything depends, obviously, on how "symptom" is defined; its definition is only implicit here and makes this affirmation seem almost like a coded statement. It is even possible to think that this statement is pregnant with some ironic provocation. The analysand, indeed, addresses himself in analysis in the name of his suffering, because he *has* a symptom. The psychoanalyst will go on to promise him that in the end, he will be able to say: "I *am* my symptom!" The symptom's passage from having to being is an odd therapy! Obviously, it must be supposed that the same symptom is not in question in both cases, and that in this gap, the therapeutic effect will be able to find its place, but it is still necessary to elucidate what identification with the symptom means, and what problem the expression gives an answer to.

It seems curious to speak of identifying with the symptom. After all, identification borrows from the Other, whereas the symptom inscribes a singular jouissance.

As psychoanalysts of all persuasions would acknowledge, identification is a mark on the subject of the influences of the Other, and even of others without a capital "O"—the counterparts. It takes from this Other, with or without this capital letter, an element, the unary trait, which will mark the subject, orient him, determine him at least partially, and which signals that he can be educated and is open to influence. For every identification, we can ask whom the subject borrows it from, and which trait is taken. The identified subject is always an influenced subject, whether he knows it or not. Most often, he is not aware of it—unless psychoanalysis reveals it to him—and he sometimes even believes that he is autonomous! This is why, from the beginning of his teaching, Lacan could state, "I is another." We also remember that Freud, in "Group Psychology and the Analysis of the Ego," makes identification the motivating force of each person's relation with his counterparts as well as with the figure of the exception.

The symptom is the complete opposite. If identification creates the same, the symptom creates difference. Always singular, rebelling against universalization, it is the principle of dissidence, to employ a term with a political resonance, one that Lacan applies to the drive. This dissidence of the symptom is so manifest that the history of societies recorded, not so long ago, in the East, a definition of symptomatology that included political divergences. This is not at all by chance, and it has its logic, for the symptom never marches in step; even when it is inoffensive, it rebels against the commandments of the master signifier. Impossible to make homogeneous, it has something real about it: it would not be excessive to speak of the symptom's autism, since it objects to all dialogue. It is true that the hysterical symptom seems to be distinguished on this point. It is borrowed, indeed, from the Other (see Dora's cough) and seems thus to make a collectivizing use of the symptom. This, nevertheless, is only a false objection, since her trait is taken from the Other's own symptom.

Thus, in a first approximation, identification and the symptom are opposed to each other, as the principle of homogenization on the one hand, and the source of gaps on the other. Thus the expression "identification with the symptom" is paradoxical. It can only designate a change in the way that the subject is related to his/her symptom, and this change must be defined.

TWO IDENTIFICATIONS OF THE END

The ego psychologists—especially the Americans, but also the entire English school, and by osmosis, the whole of the IPA—exalted, in order to reduce the deviancy of the symptom, the ideal that analysis ends in an identification with the analyst. Lacan, in an ironic echo, proposes that the subject identifies, instead, with his/her symptomatic singularity. This response is not a simple act of defiance. It has its logic and even allows us to grasp the necessity obeyed by those who argued for the identification with the analyst.

The function of identification for the speaking being can be grasped only on the basis of the status of the subject as Lacan constructed it: as an effect of language. This subject, whose existence is supposed in relation to every articulation of signifiers, has no other essence than its difference from the chain that represents it by hiding it. Its presence is affirmed only by a dynamic of displacement and cutting: it is a moving void. The subject is a kind of ghost, and this may be why there are ghosts in its imaginary. It haunts the house of language with its presence as a formless enigma, to which it is impossible to assign a residence. Identification is precisely what gives it a face and a place.

Identification is the principle that arrests and fixes being. This obviously happens at the price of an eclipsing, for from then on, the mask takes over the stage, and the affirmation "I am," where the subject is installed, is paid for with the words that complete the statement: "not thinking." The latter may not prevent our subject from being an intellectual; s/he will think of everything except of what s/he is as subject of the unconscious. Whatever their compensations and their level of diversity may be, identifications—including the "final identification"[3] with the signifier of the lack of the Other, the phallus—dress up the void of the subject, ensuring a determination of its being.

Thus the subject's normal state—I am not saying "the normal subject"—is an "I am" that does not think about what it is. The "healthy man" whom Freud mentions in his text of 1937 on the end of analysis, the one who would have no need of analysis, is nothing other than this: an *Ich*, which is the subject itself, but set up as an Ego by identification.

The subject addresses himself to analysis, with a few exceptions, only on the basis of a symptomatic manifestation of his division, which undoes his unity. This is true of the Rat Man when he calls upon Freud. He is a subject who can no longer identify with the ideals of uprightness and military bravura, ideals that had made him want to teach the career officers a thing or two! Unfortunately, this good officer has fallen prey to strange phenomena: an inhibition in working, which disturbs his studies, and then finally the rat obsession and the panic that it inspires in him. Here is something that he cannot identify with, a symptom that inspires in him what Freud calls horror, and here lies the question: Can one identify with the horrible thing? Of course, the division of the subject at the beginning does not always manifest itself in the form of such a consistent symptom. The hysteric, on the contrary,

---

3. "The Direction of the Treatment," p. 251.

can choose to give it the form of an experience of inconsistency, which leaves the subject in a painful uncertainty about what she thinks, what she wants, or her very place.

Analysis, in introducing the subject to free association, which must not think, calculate, or judge, commits him/her to a questioning of being. It does so in the double sense of the term, "questioning": it wants to produce an answer at the end, but it also suspends his/her assurances. Thus it first introduces a waiting period, a state in which questions are left open methodologically. Once, however, one has gone past the suspension that is necessary for elaboration—in which what divided the subject under the grimace of the symptom will be revealed to him/her— analysis must bring the subject back to another type of "I am." On this point, and despite very opposed formulations, the whole of the analytic movement converges. What both the master signifier of identification and the symptom have in common is their inertia, which fixes and determines being.

As a result, we can grasp a first level of the logic implicit in ego psychology: since a-symptomatic normality was thought of in terms of identification, this is what was to be restored to the subject. His "true" being has been disturbed by the symptom, so what is to be re-estab- lished, in the end, is an improved identification-effect. Where can this better identification be found, if not in the analyst taken as a model? What is sketched out for us is an analysis that would go from the fail- ure of a normalizing identification to its success in the end, by identi- fication with the analyst. The objection jumps immediately to our eyes: in this case, analysis becomes a second education, which rectifies and reinforces the marks of identification left by the Other. There was no need to invent psychoanalysis for this; ego psychology confuses the dis- course of the master with analytic discourse.

WITHOUT THE OTHER

The notion of identification with the symptom is coherent with the necessity, at the end of an analysis, of renewing the being-effect: to obtain a subject who is newly determined concerning what s/he wants and what s/he is; this determination, however, does not follow the path of identification with the Other. This had been Lacan's thesis from the beginning. As early as his "Mirror Stage," he mentioned a termination in which the subject would reach the ecstatic limit of a "Thou art that."[4] The word "ecstatic" is there to say that what is expected is the response of what cannot be represented in being, for an extremely simple reason: identification can only perpetuate the reign of the Other. The being that it seems to ensure is only that of masquerade and lies, and the analyst cannot make him/herself its accomplice. The identification with the symptom, at the other extreme of Lacan's teaching, designates the first aim of analysis, which is to reach an "I am" that is not that of the semblance. It indicates the effort, by the technique of speech, to attain whatever, in the subject, is not of the symbolic register but of the real. The real makes fun of what we think and judge, and even *that* we think and judge: "we" is nothing other here than a name of the Other, of the subject supposed to know. The symptom represents precisely such a real.

Although the parallel formulas of identification with the master signifier or the symptom aim at an homologous function, they designate two totally heterogeneous processes: the first fixes the void of the subject, whereas the second fixes jouissance.

The correlate of identification is the mortifying effect of the signifier: the castration of jouissance. It is not enough to say that it gives artificially, to the subject who is lacking an identity, its representatives and its figures, enveloping what is unrepresentable in clothing cut according to the Other's fashions. It must also be emphasized that this void of the subject is not simply a defect of representation. It is a void that is not inert, but dynamic, and whose activity is named—in memory of Freud—desire. This desire is also a defense against jouissance.

The symptom, on the contrary, is, in its Freudian definition, a way of getting jouissance. All of the successive elaborations that Lacan offered of it in the course of his teaching aimed at conceiving how two elements are articulated: that of language—a term that must necessarily be supposed in order to account for the fact that the symptom can

---

4. Jacques Lacan, "The Mirror Stage As Formative of the *I* Function As Revealed in Psychoanalytic Experience," *Ecrits: A Selection*, p. 9.

be deciphered and yields to deciphering—and jouissance, which pushes itself forward despite the subject's own disparagement of it. The first definition of the symptom as a function of the signifier, structured as a metaphor, already implied that there is jouissance in the combinatory of signifiers; it referred to the "enigmatic signifier of sexual trauma"[5] as a memorial of the intrusive encounter with jouissance. In the same vein, Lacan could distinguish "the formal envelope" of the symptom from its kernel of jouissance.

The final definition of 1975, in *Seminar XXII, RSI*, as a function of the letter, responds to the same necessity but introduces something new. To say that the symptom is jouissance of the letter is not to say simply that the letter represents jouissance as a memorial. It is to say that it is itself an object and that, therefore, jouissance infiltrates the field of language entirely, blurring the border that is habitually traced between mortifying language and jouissance. Yet in this field of language that is enjoyed—there is a jouissance of deciphering and also a "*joui-sens*"[6]—the symptom is distinguished as a fixity that "does not cease to be written"; the letter is defined by its identity with itself whereas the signifier always includes difference. The unconscious as language works, as Freud said. Lacan added that it was an ideal worker, one that never goes on strike. Well, the symptom is something of the unconscious that has passed into the real: it is a striker.

In conclusion, beyond their homologous function of fixation, ending analysis by identifying with the analyst and with the symptom are opposites: the first accentuates the defense against the real; the second, on the contrary, supposes that this singular real is confronted. What is prior to this is the fall of identifications with the signifiers of the Other; this fall has a separation-effect that uncovers the void that constitutes the subject. This is still only a necessary but insufficient condition. Lacan's option consists of valorizing the identification with the symptom. This is what he does, although very discreetly, when he says that it is *the best the subject can do*.[7] This expression indicates that there is a possible alternative.

---

5. "The Instance of the Letter in the Unconscious," p. 158.

6. *Television*, p. 10. The English translation of *Television* prefers to translate *jouis-sens* as "enjoy-meant." (Translator's note.)

7. Our emphasis.

THE FUNCTION OF THE SYMPTOM

This option is in harmony with the new insight into the function of the symptom, which I spoke of, and which generalizes it and reduces its pathological connotation. It is not enough to say simply, as Freud did, that the symptom is the anomalous substitute for a sexual satisfaction. If the sexual relation cannot be inscribed in the structure of language (*langage*), as Freud's elaborations demonstrate, without, however, saying so explicitly, it is always the symptom in its singularity that ensures the subject's copulation with his/her jouissance. The symptom is therefore what makes up, in every case, for the absence of a sexual relation that can be written. It follows that there is no subject without a symptom, and that the partner him/herself comes in this place. This fact obviously obliges us to distinguish, on the one hand, the various states of the symptom, and on the other, the subject's varied relations with it, and to ask what state of the symptom it is possible to identify with, and in what sense.

The variations of the symptom appear at the level of phenomena, for it is obvious that such phenomena can be either more or less uncomfortable. Some are intolerable because of the deleterious jouissance that they include; others are only too well tolerated—whether we think, for example, of drugs, or even of a woman as symptom: they are not always so disagreeable, and occasionally are not disagreeable enough! Certain symptoms are partially misunderstood—since the subject remains the captive of forms of behavior that are filled with a jouissance that is not perceived as such; they are not subjectivized until analysis makes him/her take their measure. And then, there is the therapeutic effect that reduces one or another of its forms, which erases phobias or somatizations, such as the Rat Man's obsession, which disappears. Yet whatever the extent of this effect may be, it always leaves something behind: a remainder of the symptom, which no finite analysis can reduce, in which the jouissance that makes up for the failure of the sexual relation is fixed for each person.

Experience also shows that two scenarios can already be distinguished, according to whether the placements of jouissance that remain at the end are tolerable or intolerable for the subject. As we know, analysis will not be able, in every case, to reduce the painful fixations of neurosis and reconcile the subject with the drives. There is sometimes a negative therapeutic reaction, as Freud brought to light, in which suffering rises like a phoenix from the treatment and wins out over every therapeutic benefit, in a choice of pain. In this case, analysis can only be prolonged, and when it finally comes to its end, it is nothing more than a renunciation. In such cases, one will be tempted to confuse identification with the symptom with a simple acceptance; the war-weary analysand recognizes and admits what remains, in the end, impossible to transform. This loose definition of the end would not, however, allow us to distinguish it from resignation alone. If identification with the symptom had to consist only of "making do" with what is unavoidable—is this the means of escaping it?—the expression would not merit so much attention. Bearing things through clenched teeth may have its advantages, but it is only a merit in Stoic ethics. For psychoanalysis, this will not be seen as progress if it is not connected with a more radical change. Freud spoke of a revised position. Now, between the refused symptom of the entry into analysis and the accepted symptom at the end, there is a third state of the symptom, which defines its insertion into transference.

A SYMPTOM IN TRANSFERENCE

The symptom, which as such ex-sists to the unconscious, and is found outside meaning, can be brought into question and interrogated about its meaning and its cause. This may be an unmotivated act (*acte gratuit*), but it is always possible. If Lacan uses the term "letter" to designate the element that is enjoyed (*se jouit*), it is precisely to include in his definition the always possible juncture with the unconscious as chain. The letter, having become an object that is identical with itself, is not just any "one": it remains capable of being connected, and it can always move from its place outside meaning to the unconscious, in a trajectory that goes from the real to the symbolic. Thus the symptom, which goes on strike against meaning, is always ready to start back to work in analysis.

The subject who comes to analysis *believes* in his symptom. This is very different from identifying with it. He believes that what encumbers him, what he experiences as constraint and affect, "is capable of saying something."[8] To believe in the symptom is to add "ellipses"[9] to it, as Lacan said; it is the announcement, "to be continued," by which the nonrelation is interrogated. It is to believe that the "one" of the letter can return to the "two" of the chain, trusting in the substitution of signs by which the symptom takes on meaning. In other words, it is to believe in the idea that "it speaks."

From this, we can give a more precise definition of identification with the symptom, which is not reduced simply to taking upon oneself—whether willingly or reluctantly, it doesn't matter—what remains of the symptomatic inertia at the end of an analysis and recognizing in it the subject's central, privileged mode of jouissance. According to Lacan, the expression does not designate an analysis that ends in a given subject's specific incapacity. It designates, rather, an ending compatible with the impossibility that the subject has ascertained in analysis by the work of the symbolic. This impossibility can be stated in this way: it is impossible not to articulate something in language that implies castration. Consequently, to identify with the symptom supposes that the subject has ceased to expect that the complementary term will arise from translating the ellipses. S/he can then cancel her/his subscription to the unconscious, like Joyce. And since we are speaking of the fall of identifications in the course of analysis, let us speak also of a fall of belief. It is another type of fall at the end of analysis, which returns to what is outside meaning. After the great unfolding, the great quest for meaning that analysis was, it erases at the end the ellipses of the symptom and places silence at the place of the final period.

Here is what marks out the distance that has been traveled: at the entry, there is a belief in the symptom, which connects it with the signifying chain of the unconscious—this is transference. At the exit, there is unbelief, which disconnects it from the unconscious chain—the unconscious closes. There is thus a return to the statement "I am not thinking," which is not that of the identification with the analyst, and which is, instead, what Lacan designated as an effect of "counterpsychoanalysis." The identification with the symptom is, with the act, the second guise of an atheism of the end of analysis, one that has no

---

8. "Seminar of 21 January 1975," p. 169.
9. *Ibid.*, p. 168. Translation modified.

profession of faith. The act does not believe in the unconscious, and this is why I once spoke of "actheism": although the analyst must make him/herself the dupe of the structure of language, the identification with the symptom no longer believes in it. These are the two fault-points in transference to which analysis can lead, and they are points of silence.

BELIEVING IN IT

One can, however, question both the belief of the entry and its fall by asking about their true motive forces and the jouissance that they bring into play.

What authorizes us to suppose that in the unconscious, there are signifiers that can respond from what is outside meaning in the symptom? It must be said that we believe it freely, before verifying it, and without any guarantee. It is an act of faith.

That, in psychoanalysis, faith precedes proof is certainly an inconvenience from the point of view of the requirements of science. However, contrary to what is believed, this is not peculiar to psychoanalysis; in spite of appearances, it is the same in science. The problem is that in psychoanalysis, this faith could become an obstacle to the production of proof.

Despite the growing fame of psychoanalysis, common opinion is suspicious about both its rational foundation and analytic communities, which are often considered to be cults, gatherings that share only beliefs. A partial foundation, and not a justification for this suspicion lies in the fact that one enters only on condition of transference: by believing that the symptom is going to be docile and by supposing that there is a knowledge that will respond to it. This is the entry postulate, which is present implicitly as soon as someone considers that what does not work for her is a symptom: from this moment she believes that it is decipherable and that it says something about her. She only suspects that believing is always more than believing.

We can certainly formulate, as Lacan did, the recourse to analysis in terms of a question that is seeking its answer. The subject, overwhelmed by the jouissance of her symptom, shows it as an enigma, and calls to the subject supposed to know, from whom she expects the answer through interpretation: she believes in her symptom, and at the

same time, hopes that the response from the symbolic is going to operate on the real. Yet at the very place where the subject believes and
apparently hopes for an answer, where she thinks thus that she is in a
purely epistemic register, one that is empty of jouissance, she has already bartered one jouissance for another. For to enter into free association is to convert jouissance by making a metonymy of the
enjoyment that was fixed in the letter of the symptom, splitting it at
the same time between a jouissance that comes from deciphering and
a jouissance that comes from meaning. Lacan formulates this in 1975
in "La troisième," as "I think, therefore enjoyment happens (se jouit)."[10]

At the end, the subject, having identified with his symptom, stops
believing and breaks with this mode. This is a reconversion of
jouissance. In interminable analysis, the temporizings of the end have
the meaning of a choice of jouissance. They last as long as one is cap-
tivated by the jouissance that comes from the staging of the desire that
insists in the demand. Desire and demand are certainly equivalent to a
lack in jouissance (manque à jouir), but there is also a jouissance within
this lack in jouissance; there is a satisfaction taken in perpetuating the
defense. We understand that if there is an alternative to the identification with the symptom, it is to be found on this side, and that this
defense must have been crossed in order for the final identification with
the symptom to come into being. Yet the symptom with which the subject possibly identifies at the end is a transformed symptom, beyond the
traversing of the fantasy. Having given up what it had, it is divested of
the lie of the signifier—"Proton pseudos,"[11] as Freud said, and "falsus,"[12]
as Lacan took it up. This symptom is not a compromise formation, for
it has ceased to include the (–1) of the defense. Consequently, the letter of the symptom resolves the void of the subject; this resolution puts
an end to the question of being and the lucubration of knowledge that
is related to it: one no longer talks about it.

Analysis will thus produce a subject who could be said to be married to his/her symptom. Yet what place, not to say what chance, does

---

10. Jacques Lacan, "La troisième," Lettres de l'École freudienne 16, p. 179.
11. Sigmund Freud, "Project for a Scientific Psychology," trans. James Strachey.
SE I (London: Hogarth Press and the Institute of Psycho-analysis, 1966), p. 352.
12. Jacques Lacan, "Radiophonie," Scilicet 2/3 (Paris: Editions du Seuil, 1970),
p. 80.

this configuration leave to the social bond, and particularly to the singular symptom of love? I will take up this question from man's side, the only one where we can predicate for all, and this side is not without consequences for women. What does "identifying with his symptom" become when the symptom is a woman?

LOVING ONE'S SYMPTOM?

The Bible placed woman among the goods, between the ass and the ox. We can now see what places her in a series with obsession, phobia, the fetish, and even, to complete the series of clinical structures, the voices of mental automatism.

We can grasp the logic that leads to this apparently strange affirmation: language certainly couples man and woman as signifiers, and discourse prescribes to them the norms for their conduct, but at the moment of truth of the copulation of bodies, when it is no longer the semblance, but real jouissance, that responds, there is nothing in the unconscious to inscribe a relation between sexed jouissances. Thus we have the eternal mystery of the couple in love, which psychoanalysis since Freud has claimed to explain by means of the rational path of the deciphering of the unconscious.

There is no double inscription of jouissances in the unconscious, but for each subject, there is an inscription—the representative of the representation, as Freud said—which is the mark of the first encounter with jouissance, a mark that is to be repeated. Thus the object-investment is doubly determined. Castration is its first condition, for it is the minus jouissance inherent in the subject and is also what allows a jouissance-value[13] to be transferred onto the object; by this jouissance-value the partner comes to represent, almost to metaphorize the jouissance of the subject himself. Yet, through the chance of love, this object must still necessarily come to bear, by means of an encounter, the mark that has come from the subject's unconscious. That she is a symptom, and not only an anonymous and interchangeable object, means that the "one" in question always carries some enigmatic signs,

---

13. See the developments of the seminar *La logique du fantasme*.

which are unknown to her and most often to the subject himself; such signs create an affinity between her and his unconscious. If this were not the case, how could we conceive of the imperatively chosen character of love, a love by which a man imagines that he can say to *one* woman: "You are *my* wife"? Is this a lie that time will take it upon itself to expose? Perhaps, but it is not the subject's lie. It is "the real which, capable only of lying to the partner, is marked as neurosis, perversion, or psychosis."[14] Thus the whole (*tout*) of love comes to take sustenance from the word, whether this is in the seducer's speech—the function of which is less to seduce than to constitute his object—or in the love missive that substitutes the letter for the partner—beware of a lover who is too devoted to his letters—or in the symptom that makes the word real.

This means that a woman, like an obsession, a phobia, or even a voice, allows the subject to get off on his unconscious, from a term taken from his unconscious. That this is the case says nothing about whether this will please her or not. Whether she gets off on it—then there would be reciprocity—or not is a completely different problem, the problem of her own objects or symptoms. Lacan once noted this astonishing thing: one judges a man by his wife, but the reciprocal is not true! Is this prejudice, belief, an oracle, or the wisdom of experience? It is, instead, unanswerably logical: if *a* woman is a symptom for a man, and a symptom is the making real of the unconscious, then, in her, we see something of his unconscious appear as externalized; we see the unconscious on the surface.

In fact, she sometimes resembles something very close to an obsession; between the Rat Man's rat and a woman, there can be very large analogies! This appears as soon as the phenomena of love do, and can be seen, first of all, in the fact that love, not a vague feeling but true love, is a forcing; it is unexpected, is sensitive to the encounter, and is often in contradiction with the subject's options. Furthermore, a woman can obsess a man in a ravaging way. According to an idiomatic expression, "He's got her under his skin." It can be observed that very often, a man, instead, has "one" of them in his head and cannot get her out of his mind. This is sometimes accompanied by a phobia: he cannot approach her, and can even approach every woman (*toutes*) except for

---

14. Lacan, *Television*, p. 10.

her, to mention the formula, "all (*tous*), but not that one," which Lacan applies to Socrates's wife. It also does not exclude fetishization: that one and no one else, the absolute, vital condition without which the subject believes that he is on the verge of death.

Believing in her (*Y croire*), in this woman-symptom, puts the subject in an awkward position for it is outside meaning; *believing in her*, as in an obsession, a phobia, or any other symptom, consists in thinking that the choice of a person whom one loves can be deciphered. This is what Freud did in considering that what seems to rebel most against reason—passion in love—can nevertheless be deciphered rationally and provide us with a key to itself, just like the symptom. As soon as he writes on the psychology of the love life, he takes the option of believing in it, by postulating that the unconscious can be made to answer the question "Why her?" This is also what the analysand does in analysis.

Long ago, a remark of Lacan's astonished me. In his seminar on the *Non dupes errent*, in developing the idea that in order not to wander (*errer*), the psychoanalyst must make him/herself the dupe of the unconscious, he makes a remark about a quotation from Chamfort: "One is never quite duped by a woman inasmuch as she is not yours."[15] In saying "yours," does he mean that she is your woman or that she is your dupe? This is a question. We can see here how there is a sliding from the unconscious to a woman.

AN ATHEISTIC LOVE

That the subject interrogates the unconscious about his loves is one thing, and that the response comes to him from the "one" in question is another. This is no longer to believe in her (*y croire*) but to "believe her" (*la croire*). This, Lacan says, is the risk of love. Here is where it differs from obsession, phobia, and so on: a woman speaks without our asking her to. To believe her is not only to suppose that she has been elected by the unconscious; it is also to confuse her speech with

---

15. Jacques Lacan, *Les non-dupes errent*, unpublished seminar, session of November 13, 1973.

the truth of this unconscious, to recognize in it the statement, "you are . . ." that interpretation delivers to us. It is to put what she says (*ses dits*) in the place of the ellipses of the symptom, where the deciphering should come. The clinical reality of this fact is quite certain. There is thus an amusing variant of the biblical imperative: love the woman who is as close to you as the voice of your unconscious!

We know the weight in experience of the "*Magister dixit.*" In analysis, "my wife says that . . ." has to be taken into account. This can throw light on many clinical facts, and especially those in which a woman can sometimes take on a quasi-persecuting role, as a deafening voice. "She says that . . . I don't measure up, am not brave, don't behave well with the children, am not the father who's needed. . . ." This is not conducive to harmony in everyday life, since women, on the contrary, like to be talked to and, most often, try to show men how to do so. We can also notice that, because he cannot reduce her to silence, a man's solution is sometimes to listen to several of them, to have them play a symphony, because when he has only one to believe, the result, as people say, is madness.

In hallucinations, the subject is identified by the message that is heard, which is why Lacan can say that such a figure believes his voices. Well, believing one's wife isn't very different. Yet there is a nuance here: as with the voices, it does not mean submitting to them! Look at Schreber, who receives from the other a message that could be formulated as "you are not a man!" and he believes his voices, but he protests and struggles to the point of finding a compromise. "My wife says that . . ." has the structure of persecution, and it is not as a jest that Lacan posits that what is comic about love is what is comic about psychosis: one believes her, like a voice. With this difference, however, that if paranoia "identif[ies] jouissance in the place of the Other,"[16] what love places there first of all is the message of truth.

Thus we find the very masculine wish, "Let her shut up," which is also expressed as "Be beautiful and be quiet!" It must not be imagined that aesthetic criteria are dominant here. The weight is on "be quiet." It is as if one were saying to her, "Don't come where my

---

16. Jacques Lacan, "Presentation of the *Memoirs* of President Schreber in French Translation," trans. Andrew J. Lewis. *Analysis* 7 (1996):2.

unconscious is." In analysis, "where it was, I must come into being,"[17] but when, in love, "where it was, her speech comes into being," one is in a structure that is discretely paranoiac, a structure that creates a large part of a couple's tragicomedy. With truth, which is the place where she is found, there is only a single certain relation: castration.

I have come to know the case of a man who, for thirty years, wrote in his notebooks what the woman in his life said, as if his being were in play there! There are also less extreme cases of conjugal surveillance exercised by men over a woman who is not necessarily their wife, but who is the "one" in question. We are aware of women who have been consigned to staying at home because the danger must at least be circumscribed—it is a mechanism equivalent to what is produced in phobia. In the latter, the threat is located in a signifier, and one can be calm wherever that signifier does not happen to be. Well, in certain cases, when the lady is in the house, the man can calmly go about his business outside. Yet if she moves around and says something in public, the situation can become more dangerous. There is also another type: the male inquisitor, who wants her to say what is deepest in herself! Why not also mention the phenomenon of beaten women? This phenomenon is doubtless overdetermined, but I will mention a particular case: a woman is struck not as soon as she opens her mouth to talk about something in general, but when she wants to say something about the two of them; then the blows start falling.

To account for this structure would involve rethinking a subject whose existence Freud recognized: the debasements of love life.

Since Freud, we have been commenting on this splitting between love and desire, the ambivalence toward the beloved woman, this mixture of idealization, bad aggressiveness, a propensity to torment the object, and we have been right to approach such actions in terms of the implication of castration in love. Indeed, if to love is to confess one's lack and to provide the beloved with what one does not have, it can be conceived that love can provoke, especially in men, something like a defense, a kind of masculine protest against love. It must not be imagined that the play between the rich and the poor woman is only car-

---

17. "[L]à où c'était, je dois advenir." The author is alluding to Lacan's rewriting of Freud's maxim, "Where Id was shall Ego be." (Translator's note.)

ried out on the level of the purse or wallet, for love can be the metonymic equivalent of castration. There is a sort of necessity, if she is to
be desired, for her to become poor again. Debasement remedies the
problem, for to debase the object is to give it the meaning of castration. This is a strategy of the male subject to make imaginary castration *oscillate*—the term is Lacan's in "Subversion of the Subject and
Dialectic of Desire"—from one term of the couple to the other.[18]

This first development can be completed by observing that "believing her" is not situated at the level of having but at that of being:
believing one's wife is believing that what she says does not speak only
about her, but also about you. Of course, there is the speech of love,
which a woman is believed to be able to handle exquisitely, and which
makes the one to whom it is addressed more attractive. Yet there is also
the speech of truth, which is what concerns us here, and which is always something else.

The speech of truth is never a speech of love—which does not
mean that love is not true—it can be—but when the subject says the
truth, it appears that love has lied. Isn't this one of the many reasons
why women are accused so often of lying? They prefer to handle the
speech of love, and when that of truth comes out, the deception becomes blatant. Our language (*La langue*) bears the traces of the fact that
truth and love are not a harmonious couple: "to tell someone some
home truths" ("*dire à quelqu'un ses quatre vérités*") is very closely related
to a message of castration. It resembles very closely what Schreber heard
from his voices: "You are not a man—not enough of one!" The result
is that to believe a woman is not only to set her up in the place of a
fierce superego, but is also to place her in competition with the articulation of the unconscious. Many things can be deduced from this: first
of all, that a woman, if one believes her, is not a symptom that can easily
be analyzed, for believing her exempts one so easily from transference-
work. It can also be deduced that the surveillance exercised by certain
women over their man's analysis has its own logic; this is just like the
strange silences sometimes observed in the testimony of men taking part
in the pass (*passants*) concerning a woman who is obviously important
for them, but about whom nothing is said until the end.

---

18. Lacan, "Subversion of the Subject," p. 311.

What, then, can be said about identification with the symptom when the symptom is a woman? The question of the impact of a finished analysis on the male/female couple is in play here. It would be too simple to authorize oneself with the statement, "there is no sexual relation" and to make a destiny for oneself with the vague proposition, "it never works." Analysis, on the other hand, seeks to say not only the "why" that applies to everyone but also the "how" of what is specific to each person.

To identify with the symptom is, in this case as in every other, to cease to believe in it, and after having reduced it to what cannot be deciphered, to leave the question that it raises definitively unanswered. If the symptom is a woman, this will be to cease to ask oneself, "Why her?" We see the benefit of this in relation to neurotic doubt. It does not necessarily rule out such doubt completely, but it does make the subject's choice move into certainty and silence. Who loses in this? Love will doubtless give up its ellipses and will become less talkative, but not necessarily less real. On the other hand, there is no doubt that the lover's discourse will come off worse.

Perhaps this is an atheistic love, separate from speech. For as far as believing her is concerned, it is certain that the work of analysis makes it fall. This work can only set in operation a separation from the oracle of the Other speech. It is well known that people are worried about these effects. Yet does this mean that in ceasing to take her for the Other, the subject will assume, instead, a casual and ironic "Just keep on talking" ("*cause toujours*")? This can happen, but it will not necessarily be for the worse, for isn't it necessary to be separated from the speech of the Other in order to hear difference?

17

Ends . . . of Love

The question of what analysis promises has been asked for a long time. What is the difference, especially concerning love, between an analysand and someone who has been analyzed? If the analysand, as we know, is the lover, should we suppose that the person who has been analyzed has been cured of love?

We know that the strategy of transference is not the whole of the analytic action. As early as his "Beyond the Reality Principle,"[1] Lacan distinguished a double level, which he designated by the opposition between "intellectual elucidation" and the "affective maneuver." This first approximate binary opposition is retranslated into the distinction between the two axes of transference: that of the subject supposed to know, where the analytic revelation is expected, and that of the "enactment of the sexual reality of the unconscious," where libidinal change is in question. In order to be conceptually distinct,

---

1. *Ecrits*. (French edition), pp. 73–92.

these two axes must, however, be articulated in experience, thanks to the analyst.

The first step of the analyst's strategy is precisely to proffer the semblance of the subject supposed to know for the analysand to love—in other words, to produce an analytic enamouring. The latter may be as true as any other, but it has its own specificity. The love at the entry into analysis is not such a great mystery. We know that simply welcoming the complaint is enough to produce love for anyone who offers to listen—advisor, therapist, priest, and so on—for in itself, listening signifies implicitly to the subject that s/he is worthy of this interest. In analysis, the bid of free association intensifies this first effect. It indicates to the subject that beyond the possibility of saying everything, whatever s/he says—stupidities, improprieties, absurdities, nonsense—will be worth something, or that at least s/he will get something worthwhile out of it. It takes no more than this to credit the analysand with some mysterious *agalma*, which constitutes him/her as the beloved, *eromenos*, to use the terms from Plato's "Symposium," which Lacan commented on at length in his seminar *Transference*. The *agalma* of the unconscious is supposed to proceed from his/her mouth—Lacan calls this an act of charity—and is destined to be revealed by the bid of interpretation. Yet in another deal of the cards, free association also transforms this first effect: mobilizing the lack in being (*manque à être*) that is inherent in speech, it leads to an appeal to the Other, and engenders the strange love-metaphor that makes the beloved into the one who loves, the *eromenos* into the *erastes*, the object into a subject. This conversion of the analysand obviously has repercussions on the analyst, who is raised to the dignity of the object of love. Thus the entry into analysis corresponds to the almost automatic production, and without any repetition getting mixed up in it, of the analysand as the one who is in love.

This entry-strategy, which should be called one of seduction, is not without analogies with that of the hysteric. It is not by chance that Lacan finds in the conduct of Socrates—the perfect hysteric—the anticipation of the transferential bid, since he succeeds in trapping Alcibiades, the man of jouissance, in the seduction of love.

The question of the analyst's use of love can thus be raised. This question has been there from the beginning of psychoanalysis with the principle of abstention, and we know that it raged in someone like

Ferenczi. It is a totally new use, in fact, which knots love to knowledge. The common, spontaneous use of love aims, as I have said, at producing a being-effect. This effect certainly has its disadvantages and its limits, which produce the dramas of love life, but however uncertain, alienating, and obscurantist it may be, it is still genuine. The analyst is the only one who makes what I could call a disinterested use of love. He does not expect his being from transference—and in order for him not to do so, it is better for him to have stopped being ill from his lack in being; he doesn't give a damn about distributive justice, and he knows that he is destined to de-being. He attempts, in fact, to make love serve not being but knowledge; it serves to produce a bit of knowledge.

THE BATTLE OF TRANSFERENCE

The result is that transference is a battlefield; a secret struggle inhabits it. This is not the "you or me" of our everyday loves, which language leaves traces of by translating the most effusive feats of love into the warlike vocabulary of possession, conquest, victory, submission, forcing someone to beg for mercy, and so on. It is a struggle in which what is manifested is the disparity between the two transference-strategies in play in an analysis.

The analysand's is inhabited by a wish for appropriation. "The pitfalls of transference-love have the end only of *obtaining* . . . ," as Lacan says in the *Proposition of 1967*: obtaining what the analyst is supposed to *hold*—let's say the keys to one's being—whatever name we give to it, including phallus, *agalma*, surplus jouissance. The analysand seeks to obtain it in the particular or typical forms that characterize subjects and structures, for example, by the obsessional siege or the hysteric's attempt to make herself absent.

The analyst himself develops a strategy that cannot simply be called one of refusal. He refuses love, but he also gives it: by interpretation and by his presence. Or rather, it is his retention—this is Lacan's term—sustained retention, methodical and instrumental. It intensifies the frustration specific to free association and has, as its end and horizon, the programming of mourning. We can see the misunderstanding of those who, in the history of psychoanalysis, believed that it was necessary to gratify the transference-demand rather than the question of knowledge. The analytic method programs love and the analyst programs mourning—which could be called unhappy love. It would certainly be a deception to disappoint the first hope, to arouse love and frustrate it methodically if the mourning that is to be produced were a sorrow of love like any other—a simple repetition of the original mourning. For the subject in analysis has already encountered mourning. This is even what the "oedipal" period describes: the mourning for the primordial object; a large part of infantile neurosis tells of the loss of jouissance and the incapacity of love to make up for it. We understand from this fact that the more one tries to give a therapy to this open sore by gratifying love in the present, the more one reduces transference to a repetition from which there is no way out.

This war continues through several phases. Lacan mentions three of them in "The Direction of the Treatment": primary love, regression, and the satisfaction specific to transference neurosis, which, he adds, is so difficult to resolve.

There is a paradox to being enamored, which is only one of the states of love. Lack, without which no form of love is thinkable, is experienced not as a painful insufficiency, but, on the contrary, as an elation of completeness, rapture, and even quasi-certainty. One should take a look at all of Freud's and Lacan's explanations of this fact. I will simply note that it indicates how much the state of being enamored is in itself jouissance, and thereby, how little it favors analytic work—Freud noted this as early as 1914. In analysis, it is a matter, rather, of containing it, keeping it unsatisfied, without also reducing the transference-love that conditions the subject's ability to maintain the method.

The fall of the state of being enamored in transference, or at least its reduction, obviously aims at the beggarly side of love. Yet more must be said: the analyst, refusing to reciprocate the analysand's love, introduces, between silence and interpretation, the void where the subject is going to locate repetition itself. It is certain that transference is not repetition. We insist rightly on this point. This is even the condition by which transference allows us to operate at the level of repetition. Transference is not repetition, but leads to it. Lacan makes this clear at several points in *Seminar XI*, after having introduced the distinction between the two concepts, but the thesis was already present in "The Direction of the Treatment." This, indeed, is what classical theory perceives with the notion of analytic regression, in the often emphasized analogy between transference neurosis and infantile neurosis. There is more: in "our practice of the saying (*dire*)," repetition "is not left to itself"; our practice "conditions it."[2]

The phenomenology of analytic experience allows us to see at its plainest that the analyst's abstention generates and maintains the demand. Thus it brings the dramas of the past back into the analysand's memory, and brings to new life in the space of analysis what does not cease to be written: the *ananké*, the great necessity. This is not for nothing. In analysis, disappointed love is what allows a questioning of the first mourning, its imaginary and symbolic coordinates, its long-term effects on choices in love, its marks at the level of conduct, and the fantasmatic solutions that have made it bearable. Thus analysis, as soon as it organizes and restores their logic to the debris of memory, constructs the infantile neurosis in the strong sense, rather than simply making it appear. In doing this, it reveals that love itself is repetitive, and always repeats the same disappointment.

This was Freud's discovery: in all love, that between men and women, but also between the analyst and the analysand, the shadow of the primordial objects stands out. This is also what the subject sometimes perceives when he feels that, by the chance of the most improbable encounters, what is verified repetitively for him is the diabolical constraint that is called fate; he observes that the diversity of circumstances is crossed by something that is the same, by the appearance of something that is both a surprise and is also what has always been anticipated. In what the subject can only sense, analysis demonstrates that necessity is at work. Freud said that the first love is always the second, but there is more: at the end of the masked ball, the man finds that he has been mistaken about the woman, and the woman the man, as Lacan loved to repeat. We can see the consequence and the disadvantage of love. To say "I love him" is to lie to the partner and not only in psychosis, as Freud had posited.

It is certain that there are encounters, and there is even nothing other than them, but the speakingbeing is separated from the partner by the constancy of the singular mode of jouissance that responds for him to the universal of castration. The analyst, as I have said, programs

---

2. "L'étourdit," p. 43.

the disappointment of love. S/he is justified in doing so because disappointment itself turns out to be no accident, since it is programmed by repetition—the true repetition, since it concerns the jouissance that objects to love. Repetition supposes a unary trait that makes a trace of the first encounter, which, when it is repeated three times, engenders the repetition of loss. The first time fixes the trait as a memorial of the encounter. In the second time, the refinding of the trait completes the loss of the first jouissance. Therefore there is entropy. The third time is the loss of the second time, which is repeated *ad infinitum* as a missed encounter and allows jouissance to survive only as the series of these traits. The result is *re-petition*, which can be written in two parts, as Lacan does in " L'étourdit" in order to mark the repeating of the petition and of appetite, since the Latin verb *peto* resonates in both words. Analysis is the place of this repetition as the reiteration of the saying (*dire*) of the demand.[3]

SOLUTIONS FOR TRANSFERENCE LOVE?

Let us say what result analysis has for love. Such a result is not simple.

Analysis meddles with the repetitive aspects of love in a way that is indirect but logical. I take it for granted that an analysis "exposes" the subject's identifications. Now, "identifications are determined by desire."[4] To meddle with identifications is to allow the subject to perceive how, in relation to what desire and what ends, s/he was situated. I can therefore say that for an identified subject, there is an identified object—if identification of the object is the name that can be given to its traits. To disidentify the subject is also to liberate him/her in part from the restrictions that repetition imposed on his/her object-choices and to open him/her to a greater variety of encounters. This effect can be observed and recognized in analysis. It does not yet settle the question of knowing whether it extends to the mode of jouissance veiled by love.

Analysis does not only throw light on object-choices. It allows us to perceive that in the re-petition that resorts to the Other in order to

---

3. See "L'étourdit," pp. 22, 44, and 50.
4. "On Freud's *Trieb* and the Psychoanalyst's Desire," p. 419.

correct the lack—lack in being, lack in knowing, lack in jouissance (*manque à jouir*)—something is silently deducted from a satisfaction of the drive. The analysand certainly consumes phallic jouissance, which is the jouissance of the one implied in ciphering. S/he also consumes, correlatively, what remains impossible to cipher, which is incarnated by the analyst. This is why Lacan could also say that s/he "consumed" the analyst. Once the repetitive conditions of love have been lifted, what remains is what, in instituting the partner, proves to short-circuit the Other of language and operate directly by the drive. Love at first sight, even outside analysis, incarnates this possibility and already lets the cat out of the bag of the famous "object relation" by revealing what is most real in love. Beyond each person's lacks and through his/her tribulations, there is what Lacan designates in *Television* as the happiness of the subject: the satisfaction that asks nothing from anyone and always authorizes itself. Analysis reveals this to the subject and will perhaps make him/her give up deploring his/her lack. This would already resolve repetition inasmuch as it is addressed to the Other and produces an atheistic love.

Here is the main question: Analysis generates transference, but does it then succeed in resolving it as one would like if the analysand is not to remain in the subjection that love makes possible? On this point, how can we not see the extent to which the problems of the analytic institution are intrinsically linked with those of analytic discourse itself—whether or not analysts with clean hands, those who would prefer only to concern themselves with the latter, happen to like this?

This question is revived at each crisis of the analytic community, and we are quite happy to imagine that, in the moments when a choice is imposed upon us, the sufficient cause of the positions that each person takes is transference, which becomes the cause of everything. The result, incidentally, is amusing: without fail, those on one side of a conflict attribute the actions of those on the other side to transference, and vice versa.

It is easy to admit that analysands can be captured by their transference, but for analysts themselves, we are astonished and indignant: How is it possible for analysts, who are supposed to have been analyzed, to lose the compass of their intimate judgment? If the end of analysis consists in reaching and taking responsibility for absolute difference—that of the symptom—if the end thus registers the lack of the Other, how can we explain the outbursts of servile jouissance that are given free course in the analytic community? The question really should be asked, for the phenomenon that turns the analytic community into a cult is not new in history and it is too frequent to be completely contingent. The proof is the cult members around Wilhelm Reich and Jung, to take examples that are far away from us.

Yet is this the fault of transference?

We incriminate it since transference is love, and love makes us docile, for as long as it lasts. It leads to consent and sometimes to sacrifice. Freud accented this strongly in *Group Psychology and the Analysis of the Ego*. Lacan drew a nice, very stylish formula from this: love is a kind of suicide. The gradations of sacrifice go from the most benign to the most ravaging forms, but in all cases, sacrifice puts back onto the other the burden of thinking and deciding. Stupid blindness and irresponsible submission also place upon the Other the burden of desire and of surplus jouissance, which are what support thought and decision. In other words, the one who loves is pushed to sacrifice what is most real for him, which we call his symptom.

One can therefore be tempted to think that analytic cults have their motive force in unresolved transferences, which are open to the sacrificial slope of love.

Should we then set in opposition, on the one hand, those who have really been analyzed, who would resist the siren calls of influence, and on the other, those who are subjected to transference? Or should we say that analyses do not really end?

THE TWO LOVES

We forget in this question that not every love is transference love and that the latter is not just any love. It is Lacan who had this insight, since Freud did not have the slightest suspicion of it: discovering transference, he immediately identified it with the return of childhood loves and saw in it, in the final analysis, only a repetition of the old love for the father. I will note that if Freud were right, the transforming effects of psychoanalysis would be impossible, for the latter would only repeat the infantile position *ad infinitum*. If there is nothing beyond the father, then there is nothing beyond the child.

Lacan challenges this position and argues that transference is a new love. It is so new that it introduces "subversion" into this field. We know that Lacan does not misuse the term "subversion." That he applies it to transference after having applied it to the subject carries a certain weight, especially since he was never a great fan of love.

The whole argument turns on the following insight: transference love is not love for the father. Old love and new love are opposed as love of the S_1 and of the S_2, since we write knowledge as S_2; in the structure of language, it comes to guarantee the S_1, especially that of the father. These two loves are opposed to each other, although the second leads back to a consideration of the first.

The god of transference is not the god of any believer. The subject supposed to know may be God himself, but the god who does not exist, that of the philosophers, who is latent in any kind of theory, even mathematics; this god, then, is nothing other than the place that Lacan called that of the Other.

The god of faith, especially that of the prophets, is completely different. The tons of love and promises credited to him by Christianity can only mask the fact that this god is a god of the will, a god of fear and trembling, occasionally a god of sacred terror; this is the figure whom Lacan named the "dark god." This god, to the extent that he is opaque, pushes us toward a fascination with sacrifice. We write this god as S_1, the vengeful master and all his lay derivatives. Wherever the chord of sacrifice is vibrating, we can be sure that it is not the new love that reigns, but the old love of the old terrifying father. The latter is less a supposed knowledge than one who is supposed to want.

The Name-of-the-Father can be distinguished from him. Freud perceived this with his story of the two Moses, and Lacan took it over from him. We must therefore see what each of them promises and find out what is the final response that transference-work delivers to whoever has been analyzed, and what consequences can be expected outside analysis.

The dark god has no place to haunt an analysis. It is true that transference sometimes takes on a paranoid form. This can be explained by the fact that it leads the analysand to suppose the existence of the mysteries of an ungraspable subject, a supposition that recurs in all of his/her elaborations, and that is the ghostly minus-one of the analysis. It happens then that the subject's impasse drifts toward the instituting of this dark god. This is neither the most frequent nor the most favorable case, and it is commonly expected that the analyst will ward off this deviation, which leads the patient outside the pathways of transference love.

The elaboration of transference, beyond the fall of the subject supposed to know, goes in no other direction than in what I will call the clarifying of the exit-symptom, with which the subject can do no better than identify him/herself. Now, however, I must go back to what a symptom is and draw out the clinical consequences of Lacan's final elaborations on this subject, and see how they are connected with the problematic of the father.

THE NAME OF THE SYMPTOM

The unconscious is not only a subject; it is also jouissance. It is "knowledge without a subject," which gives form to the bodily jouissance that is in the symptom. Let us not forget that the symptom is not being defined here in psychiatric terms, as an anomaly, but that every partner is symptomatic: a partner is produced by the unconscious as a consequence of the fact that the relation between the sexes cannot be written, as I said above.

In the field of indefinitely cipherable jouissance, the symptom has the function of an exception. Every deciphered signifier ($\forall x$), every signifier of unconscious knowledge, carries castration (Φx)—the limited jouissance of the One—and what ensues from it: the infernal continuing induction, which only enlarges the swarm of the signs of the subject. This swarm can be written as $\forall x . \Phi x$.

Every signifier carries castration except one, for there exists one signifier—let's call it a letter or a sign—that does not represent the subject ($\exists \overline{\Phi x}$) but that fixes the jouissance of his body. There is one, therefore, that carries not castration but a solution to it; rather than being the metonymy of castrated jouissance, it fixes the jouissance that secures the subject. This is the one of the symptom, which Lacan calls a letter; it serves as an exception to the symbolic of the chain and makes the unconscious pass into the real (see the Seminar *RSI*).

In other, perhaps easier terms, this One of the symptom is also a signifier of the barred Other, a disconnected signifier, which has the same structure as the signifier in the real; the latter is the signifier which, as exception, does not belong to the chain of the Other, but which is the only one to quilt (*capitonner*) the variety of forms in which it manifests itself.

I have used formulations homologous to those of "L'étourdit" to mark that father and symptom are on the same plane. We must not forget, however, that this symptom is not the one that I have called "autistic," but one that is a social bond; it includes the *dit-mension* of desire and the fantasy. We have the proof of this with Joyce, and this kind of symptom changes something of the function of the father in psychoanalysis.

For the father himself—the Name-of-the-Father—is a symptom; this is the other part of the thesis. He is a symptom by his own version of the generalized *père-version*. This is not an S_1 but an S_2, just like the symptom. The Name-of-the-Father is a model, in the sense of an example, a solution to castration, one solution among other possible ones, but one that perhaps has the advantage of knotting together the sexes and the generations—the jouissance of sex and generations—in one livable configuration.

The first consequence of Lacan's renewed theses is that the famous distinction between the imaginary, symbolic, and real fathers becomes, if not null and void, at least of little significance. There is not the slightest symbolic father: the father who knots the three registers is real or he *is* not at all. The second consequence is that a symptom can do as well as the father; think of Joyce's symptom as artist. One can therefore do without (*se passer*) the father on condition of using (*se servir*) the symptom. The symptom can be used not only for jouissance, but also, and especially, as the single principle of consistency possible for a discourse and a social bond. The Other is missing, and the S_2 that would make it consistent is also missing, but the symptom that is specific to each person makes up for them. If there is no Other, every choice comes from the symptom and goes toward the symptom, even that, let us note, of having an analysis. Our compass is always the symptom, whether we know it or not.

Analysis has no other end, and this is an end by means of the real.

To attain this is a big change for the neurotic, a subject who has been made ill by the quilting point, and who, as Lacan said, has no name. This means that since he cannot recognize himself in his symptom-name, since he cannot take upon himself the jouissance that can alone cover over the fact that the Other is missing, he floats into inconsistency. In everyday language, we say that he does not know what he wants. Let us say that he is ill more because of the question than the conclusion—for there are also people made ill by the conclusion! We know the symptoms of this inconsistency: doubt, uncertainty, temporizing, avoidance, procrastination, the utopia of thought—these are its ordinary manifestations. Thus there is the side that, in spite of every intention, is irresolute and untrustworthy: the hysteric's faithlessness, the obsessional's about-face. Another way of formulating this would be to say that only his complaint is consistent, which is equivalent to getting jouissance from castration. In this sense, he is more subject than symptom.

Does analysis cure him/her? Yes. It generally allows him/her to choose (a woman, a man, a way of life, a profession, etc.); it makes him/her better able to decide, less inhibited, less ill at ease—in short, more decisive and more combative. What it reinforces is not his/her ego but what I will call the "symptom point," by an analogy with Lacan's "doxa point." It allows her/him to measure that s/he has already been oriented. To bring a neurotic subject back to the symptom is a great success that enables her to reach what is most real in herself, and is least similar to anyone else. This also allows us to understand that, at the end of analysis, when the subject has zeroed in on her symptom's absolute difference, there can arise, as Lacan says at the end of *Seminar XI*, not a limitless love—which is a misunderstanding—but "the signification of a limitless love"[5] which is quite different. The signification of a limitless love, as the end of the seminar presents it in its varieties, is precisely the absolute sacrifice. Identification with the symptom and the fascination with the dark god are mutually exclusive.

THE PROSTHESIS-SYMPTOM

But—and there is a but—and an after to analysis.

But is this subject—who has put a stop, through analysis, to the jouissance of the unconscious, who has been reconciled with his/her symptom—shielded from influence? Experience shows us the contrary,

---

5. *The Four Fundamental Concepts of Psycho-analysis*, p. 276.

and the motive force of this phenomenon must be grasped. It owes nothing to the subject supposed to know.

Its source is that not all symptoms are of equal merit as principles of orientation. Lacan mentioned the position of the unconscious. For my part, I would like to speak of the position of the symptom, to designate the affirmation of its jouissance-value. It is quite variable from one person to another.

I have used the expression "love your symptom," but not without some second thoughts. I can complete it by saying, "love your symptom rather than another—another symptom." One can identify with one's symptom, but against one's will, and this is often the case with the neurotic: rejecting the self, even hating the self exists, and not only in melancholia. Well, if he becomes a symptom that shimmers with a different jouissance and affirms it to the point of arrogant certainty, it is almost ensured that he will be captured by the consistency of this encounter.

In our discourse, which is without a compass, there is no longer anything but the symptom to orient subjects, but in a way that is more or less loose. As a result, subjects are looking for something like a back-up symptom that will bring them more of an orientation. This can go all the way from the symptom as a simple complement to a real prosthetic symptom. A symptom-prosthesis is a "godsend" for irresolute subjects, and the more irresolute they are, the better it is for them, for fitted out thus, they are often converted into inflexible and formidable cultists. Freud perceived this and said that collective formations could make up for neurotic formations. The support given by the symptom-prosthesis is *not* transference. On the contrary, it sutures transference.

There is certainly an erotics of the stupid power of the mis-chief, as Lacan says, but the erotics of knowledge is something different. Transference as love of knowledge is precious, for it alone can lead the subject to what is most real; it alone can lead her toward an end which, as Lacan said, "separates her from the herd." Here we can find again the difference of the Sex and suppose that women, by being not-whole, are more than just divided (*divisées*); they are divided up and shared out (*partagées*) between two modalities of jouissance. They therefore lend themselves less to the herd, which is the rule of homogenized jouissance. A woman does not "superegoize (*surmoite*) as easily as the universal conscience/consciousness (*conscience*)."[6] Freud reproached her for this, knowing full well that what he called, with an overvalued term, "civilization," was nothing more than a discursive machine for manufacturing the herd. Lacan himself gave her credit for this, at least when he posited, at the end of his teaching, that women have more of a relation to the real, in the sense of a living jouissance that is impossible to say.

---

6. Lacan, "L'étourdit," p. 25.

VIII

CONCLUSION

As a conclusion, I will return to the impact of the not-whole on the various modalities of the social bond. The *Che vuoi?* by which Freud questioned feminine desire and sexuality at the private level takes on a completely different social and collective dimension today. How could this be otherwise in an age that has loosened the age-old bridles that held women back? This is no longer a time in which they are wanted to know nothing and make no decisions. Reproduction, eroticism, family, profession—now all of these belong to them. Therefore we must ask what is being born in the desire that will inhabit these new powers and what this stronger relation with the real, which Lacan attributes to women, will produce. The question concerns not only the effects of feminine desire on the social level, in the ordinary sense of the term, but also its effects within the analytic bond itself.

SOCIAL EFFECTS

I have already mentioned the possible pushing-toward-love (*pousse-à-l'amour*), which is induced in the feminine subject by the heterity of her jouissance, a heterity that does not include an identification; this pushing works to resist the individualizing fragmentation of social bonds. This is the question of feminine Eros and its powers in what Lacan called the real—the same place that Freud, for lack of a better term, had called the "death drive," to designate what disrupts and fragments. We could credit women with this pushing-toward-love. Freud would not object to doing so, since this is precisely what he reproached them for; as for Lacan, he would approve of it, but he would not have put too much trust in this love. In any case, we will say, positively, that women would rather take upon themselves the bond of a singular love—whether in the couple, the family, or the new love of knowledge—than embrace the old love of the unifying leader. This leader, as we know today, is the principle of all forms of totalitarianism, and undoes all of these singular bonds to the profit of the mass.

On this point, however, hysteria as such appears to create a problem, even an objection. Isn't the hysteric, as all experience attests, inconsolable about the father? This does not settle the problem, however, for the hysteric's relation to the father and the group is complex.

Epidemics of hysteria, which are not uncommon in "hystory," could makes us think that the hysteric is a group animal. Freud presented the exemplary mechanism of her groups in Chapter VII of *Group Psychology and the Analysis of the Ego* with the example of the girls' school. Let us, however, make no mistake here: the contagion that acts there, while it is homologous to what engenders the love of the leader, also differs strongly from it, since what she spreads in her crises is nothing other than the identification with the lack that is in play in the misfortunes of love. Freud's example leaves us in no doubt that what the girls identify with is whatever disappointment the girl in love may have felt, and that they know nothing about the young man on the horizon. The paradigm of this identification is that the hysterical group is always secretly commanded by the avatars of a couple's relation; this relation is that of a woman in love with her Other, whether real or imaginary, an Other which, in earlier ages, included God or the Devil. This is not the case of the crowd in *Massenpsychologie*. On the contrary, such a crowd identifies vertically and directly with the single leader, who commands the horizontal identification between the brothers, the adorers of the One. If the vertical identification is undone, nothing will remain of the horizontal. Freud insisted that, in this mass structure,

when the voice of the leader becomes quiet, both panic and the rupture of the bonds ensue.

What is the difference between adoring the leader and "sustaining the desire of the father," the characteristic position of the hysterical subject, especially in transference? This is not a riddle, for the answer
is too obvious. The father who has to be bucked up is lacking in desire,
whether this be toward knowledge, a woman, or both at the same time.
The leader whose voice, as stupid as it may be, makes the law, inspires
and orients the libido. The hysteric's father has to be brought back to
life, for he is having difficulties. Far from being the fearsome god whose
will guides the crowds, he is the father who has fallen from any position of exception. Having been demoted to the rank of being castrated
like every man, he is loved more for his open sores than for his powers,
although the hysteric retains a nostalgia for an at-least-one who would
know. We know, furthermore, what happens when, by historical contingency, a subject supposed to know presents himself to the hysterical subject: submitting him to questioning, the hysteric will seek out
the point where he is impotent. From this, there is only one step—
which is quickly crossed—to reproaching the hysteric with loving the
Other less than his castration. This is a bit too simple, but is not in-
correct. Look at Anna O., with whom I opened this volume. She certainly failed in her transferential enterprise, for she was the victim, after
Freud's refusal, of Breuer's cowardice, but from this failure, she found a
vocation: that of devoting herself to all her sisters in misery throughout the world, all of whom were martyrs of men, as were also the young
schoolgirls whom Freud discussed.

I have just mentioned the clear fact that hysteria is subjected to
history and fluctuates according to its circumstances. Lacan introduced
something different: hysteria as a cause that is not without responsibility
for the evolution of civilizations. He thus attributes to the hysterical
position—upon which psychoanalysis, at the private level, throws
light—a major social role, particularly in the emergence of science and
of its unstoppable passion for knowledge. He recognizes the emblem-
atic figure of this operation in Socrates, the Socrates of Plato (there is
no other), who in questioning the ancient master, enjoins him to display his knowledge as master. Modern science, as founded by Galileo,
could well be a long-term repercussion of this challenge. We see how
Lacan locates the hysterical subject: she is the one who, as a vocation,

makes the other produce knowledge. The hysteric and the man of science are an attractive couple, one of whom stimulates while the other, who is not hysterical at all, works on knowledge. Thus we get the idea that the hysteric is looking for a man who would be impelled by the desire to know.

The hysteric's structural homology with science is to be found in a discourse in which it is the partner who is called upon, who is enjoined to answer. The two do not, however, have the same partner. Science is addressed to what has long been called the world or nature and it makes knowledge respond successfully in the real. This is to say, as Einstein did, that it deals with an unbarred Other, one that is complex but not deceptive, and who does not play dice. This is a methodological foreclosure, which excludes the whole register of the subject from its consideration, a register that always implies a singular truth of desire and jouissance.

It would therefore not be excessive to theorize the emergence of psychoanalysis as a return in the real of what science dismisses; science wants knowledge, only that and nothing more. It wants all knowledge, except for the unconscious knowledge that makes us "speakingbeings." In order to want the latter, there had to be hysteria. The hysteric had to carry her question to a place where science does not go and where Freud wanted to go: into the field of the sexual. Lacan rightly notes, in "Radiophonie," that a "sexual subversion" is always in solidarity with the incipient moments of science, and he recognizes here the same touch of hysteria. This subversion, which is manifest today, obviously does not promise happiness and especially not to the partner. When questioned about what remains mysterious in the couple, how could he answer if not with the signifiers of knowledge, which will never say what is impossible to say? The failure is assured.

I will conclude on this point: hysteria as such has contributed to the opening up of the "curse on sex." This is its virtue, but this says nothing about the powers of love and does not profit them; if one is to bandage the wounds, it is not enough to make a social bond, and that is the limit of hysteria. The distinction between the not-whole and hysteria does not differentiate one woman from another, but traverses each woman. It also reverberates on the level of love; there is a big difference between locating the basis of the couple in the partner's castration and his living jouissance.

IN PSYCHOANALYSIS

I arrive now at the field of psychoanalysis. Here it can be verified unequivocally that women are more attracted to the transferential bond than are the upholders of the One. This is logical: Isn't it always precisely on the basis of a bit of the real that we, as "pathematic subjects," can have recourse to the subject supposed to know? Consequently, it is not astonishing that for women, their stronger relation with the real goes along with more of a relation to the Other. Yet how can we evaluate the impact of this disposition, which certainly overdetermines the feminization of the psychoanalytic profession in relation to others such as medicine, teaching, the literary disciplines, and so on?

We can, first of all, credit women with it. We will say then, positively, that women go more willingly toward the new love of knowledge than toward the old love for the collectivizing leader. Hysteria, which is so frequent in women, operates in the same direction, and since its encounter with Freud, we have been aware of what psychoanalysis owes to it. The psychoanalyst views it as an advantage, for it opens up a possible analytic bond. This is not, however, a compliment.

The love of the One has already been critiqued, and we know that it instigates the mass, which removes the subject from his desire and his judgment. On the other hand, transference as love of knowledge does not merely have virtues. To love knowledge is not to desire it. The new love is no less illusory than the other; instead, it makes one prefer the dream to the real—the dream of meaning expected from interpretation. This is the thesis that Lacan stopped at in the 1970s. The knowledge in question here is obviously not just any knowledge, and in any case, it is not that of science, but of the unconscious in its relation to sexed jouissance. Now, the first promise of this knowledge is nothing other than castration. Who, consequently, could desire it? The love of knowledge certainly opens onto the possible elaboration of transference, but also creates an obstacle to the desire for knowledge. Thus Lacan falls back, although by a completely different path, onto Freud's thesis that transference is both the condition and the obstacle to the treatment.

Perhaps this is what makes Lacan say that women are the best analysts as well as the worst. They are the best, for they are freer in their interpretations, care less about every exactitude, and are more attentive to the truth, which is itself not-whole. They are the worst, because in loving this singular truth too much, they can forget structure, which is not singular. Lacan makes fun of the disproportion between the weight of their voice in psychoanalysis and the "slightness of the solutions" produced. Such an appreciation would be unjust to Melanie Klein, if he had not elsewhere rendered generous homage to her genius and highlighted her positive role.

I believe that, beyond this pointed remark, he designated a very real problem, on which I will conclude: there is a disparity between the sexes concerning the ends of analysis.

DISPARITY OF ENDS

This difference in ends echoes another difference: that of the entry into analysis. I emphasized this during the conference of the Freudian field on hysteria and obsession. Everyone agreed that it is easier to make hysterics enter analysis than obsessionals, but it is also more difficult to make them leave it. Now it cannot be doubted that the distinction between these two clinical structures can, as a whole, be superimposed onto that of the sexes.

The reason for this well-known clinical fact can only lie in what I have called the "commandments" of jouissance. I am positing that phallic jouissance is paradoxically more propitious to concluding an analysis. Already structured as the signifier, already molded by the one, it lends itself better to symptomatic fixation. Now there is no other conclusive quilting point for a given subject than his fundamental symptom in its function as Name-of-the-Father. This is obviously the case for both men and women, who are far from being outside phallic jouissance. Yet the letter of the symptom, which marries the sign and jouissance, does not secure supplementary jouissance, which always remains lacking in the Other, whether this Other is Man, God, or the Devil. In other words, there is some jouissance that does not pass into the letter. This, it seems to me, is why Lacan was led to refer to a schema for knotting heterity—the term is one he used to refer to what is heterogeneous—with the one, whatever this one may be.

A woman, each woman, can certainly always knot herself to One-saying (*Un dire*). There are several ways of doing so, according to whether this One-saying will fix her love, or on the contrary, her challenge, even her refusal, as in the case of feminine homosexuality. In every case, however, the solution is unequal to the challenge. I have mentioned that there is "no limit to the concessions made by any woman for a man: of her body, her soul, her possessions."[1] But "once you've gone too far, there's still the limit."[2] The solution by means of the One-saying of love is too much at the mercy of the contingencies of the encounter, and, especially, is too powerless to reduce the asymptotic character of the inextinguishable call to the One-saying, which remains manifestly different [autre encore]. The latter is not a matter of hysterical lack of satisfaction, and is even completely opposed to it, but it nevertheless often lends itself to being confused with it.

In other words, only a man, in identifying with his symptom, can stanch the recurrence of the call to the Other. The symptom's completely phallic jouissance, which would have not to be in order for there to be a relation, is enough to make . . . Man (L'homme). For whoever is not completely in this jouissance, the situation is not the same: there is something of the real in excess over the One, and no knotting will make woman suffice. None of it will reduce her sardonic expectation of the Other Man, which is maintained by the logic of the never closed series of possible ones. "Hence, the universal of what women desire is sheer madness: all women [toutes les femmes] are mad, they say."[3]

Between one man and Man, however, there is no excluded third term; there is a possible third term, the supposed knowledge offered by the analytic bond, and we can see how well it can sustain the asymptotic situation that I mentioned a moment ago. We can understand that, by preference, women place their hopes in analysis in order to lighten their burden of a supplementary real, but what does it promise them?

In general, analysts agree in recognizing that a treatment involves a mourning, even if their conceptions of it vary. There are, however, several kinds of mourning: a mourning, first of all, for the Other—the Other who does not exist—but which transference, at one time, made exist. As I have emphasized, it is at this point that the fundamental symptom subrogates, and allows each person to conclude according to her desire and her jouissance.

---

1. *Television*, p. 40.
2. *Ibid.*, p. 41.
3. *Ibid.*, p. 40.

Yet for whoever is affected by a jouissance that has no signifier, which makes what she says (*ses dits*) "be inconsistent, be undemonstrated, be undecided (*s'inconsister, s'indémontrer, s'indécider*),"[4] the conclusion by the symptom cannot be enough. A mourning, without any compensation, for a knowledge that would know everything, even the not-whole, is therefore on the agenda. When this mourning begins to emerge, it frequently has a different coloration depending upon whether the analyst is a man or a woman; in the first case, it leans toward nostalgic depression and in the second, virulent reproach. These, however, are only nuances of a single experience, in which the conclusion by means of an exit (*conclusion de sortie*) is, let us say, more difficult. Their consequences on the decision to exit, which is to be distinguished from the conclusion, are inevitable. They contrast, moreover, with each other, for the difficulty in concluding favors, in clinical terms, both prolonged analyses and those that come to a sudden end; it favors the retention of the act of separation and the perpetuating of the bond, as well as the passage to the act, which takes drastic action, without any real separation. Freud saw the first, but could not see any further than the tip of his nose because of his obsession with penis envy, which exists, but which is precisely not-all.

---

4. *Ibid.*, pp. 40–41.

IX

APPENDIX

THE DIFFERENCE BETWEEN THE SEXES IN ANALYSIS

What does analytic discourse allow us to formulate concerning the difference between the sexes? What can be put forward concerning men and women that does not come from public opinion or from a person's own wishes?

What is at stake in these questions is not so much the real relations (*relations*) between the sexes. These relations, as we know, function very well—or perhaps very badly, but that is their way—without our being able to say anything about them. What is at stake, instead, is the ethics of the treatment. Many questions about this subject have been left hanging, first of all, the following one: What is required, and is there something required, concerning sexed identifications, if an analysis is to be called finished? This is an old debate—the theme of access to genital oblativity once raged around it—but it is still open. One can also wonder whether the analyst operates as someone who is para-sexed (*para-sexué*), in which case it does not matter whether s/he is a man or a woman; the difference would only lie at the level of the analysand's representations. Finally, we can ask ourselves whether the treatment has the same effect on a man and a woman.

I am not going to answer these questions in the following remarks, but I am mentioning them in order to make us perceive what, in analytic experience, seems to me to be in play in Lacan's sexuation formulas: Concerning sexual difference, does analysis, which operates only by speech, allow a certain real to be reached?

Men and women, Lacan remarks, are real. No idealism has gone to the point of arguing that the division between the sexes is only a representation. Nothing, however, can be said of this real—the real of the sexed living body. Nothing can be said of it because of the "wall" of language; the real is outside the symbolic, but we deal with it, nevertheless, in the very precise form of jouissance. I will quote Lacan's statement that the unconscious is

> a knowledge that is articulated from *lalangue*, the body that speaks there being knotted only by the real from which it gets off on itself (*se jouit*). Yet the body is to be understood in its natural state (*au naturel*) as unknotted from this real, which, even if it exists on the basis of having its jouissance, does not remain less opaque. It is the less noted abyss of what *lalangue* is, the *lalangue* that civilizes this jouissance, if I dare to say so. By this, I mean that it carries it to its developed effect.[1]

If, therefore, the real from which a body gets off on itself is inaccessible, the only real that is accessible to the speakingbeing, the real that Lacan defines in terms of the impossible, remains to be delimited. For a "semblance of being," a being commanded by discourse, what is most real is what discourse forbids in the strong sense: what is impossible in the logic belonging to discourse, what therefore is not transgressed. It will thus be a matter of seeking "what of the real makes a function in the knowledge that is added to it [to the real]."

How, in the experience of analytic speech, can one approach this real, which is grasped at the limits of what can be articulated, through

---

1. Jacques Lacan, "La troisième," *Lettres de l'École freudienne*, November 16, 1975, p. 189.

the impasses of formalization, this real as impossible? How is the difference between the sexes involved in it?

Let us start with the obvious: first of all, there is what the analysand says (*les dits analysants*), which is impulsive, risky, and groping, and which cannot be taken back. It certainly aims at the subject's singular truth, but in pursuing the latter, it sketches out the movement specific to the treatment, by which speech turns around on itself, reducing all truth to the truth of speech, the truth that Lacan stated but that every analysand demonstrates: the subject is divided. In order for it (*ça*) to pass into the saying (*dire*), it is enough for the analysand to speak. The saying is to be distinguished from what is said, for the former is not of the dimension of truth. It is the moment of enunciation and its content is not what is stated in what is said (*les dits*), but what is inferred from all that is said; it is what is demonstrated by means of what is said. On this point, the analytic method touches the real of speech.

The neurotic devotes himself in his life to avoiding castration, but if he speaks, there are many things that he will not be able to avoid. First of all, the equivocation of the signifier, if the analyst sends it back to him, dispossesses him of the intentionality of what he says (*ses dits*) and fixes him to what has possibly been said (*s'est dit*), without him: without his "me-I [*moi-je*]." The equivocation of signifiers therefore makes him the subject, who is subjected, of an enunciation that could almost be said to be without an enunciator. Furthermore, he is the subject of an enunciation whose meaning—a meaning or meanings—is impossible for him to stop. This meaning thus remains impossible to articulate although it is articulated. Anyone who has dreamed of synthesizing his statements (*énoncés*), of grasping the final word of what has programmed his history, discovers that he is the subject of the unconscious. This is the failure of any synthesis. One could say that synthesis is forbidden to whoever speaks as such, and this is the division of the subject. In drifting in this way through his speech, could he hope at least to moor himself to the synchrony of his last signifiers? Not even that, for there is primal repression. We can conclude, from his inability to bring together what would be the battery of his fundamental signifiers, that there is a logical impossibility, which Lacan designated as S(Ⱥ). The linguistic notion of synchrony is revealed to be an illusion here, as the analysand discovers, and Lacan gives the reason for this. What cannot be done is to take all the signifiers at the same time. We cannot make a set of them for there is always at least one missing—the signifier of the subject. It is this impossibility, he says, that illustrates best what castration is.

We can therefore say that analysis puts castration to work in speech. In this sense, it is the experience of the logic specific to speech, a speech which, let us not forget, is incarnated, and which, no matter what dualism says, makes the speaking body. Like logic, therefore, analysis is the "production of a necessity of discourse," with the paradox that this definition implies. Indeed, if necessity is produced, it must be thought not to have existed before, but as necessitated, it must be supposed already to have been there before it has been produced. Many of the particularities of experience are caught in the same paradox: for example, the castration that Lacan calls symbolic. On the one hand, we recognize it as a fact of structure that is not accidental—in other words, there is no way of cutting it—but on the other hand, we speak of assuming responsibility for castration, for the access to symbolic castration. We therefore speak of it both as something that is, that has always been there, is necessary, and as something that must come into being, must be produced. This is the same nuance that we find in Freud's sentence, "Where it was, I must come into being."

What is this coming into being in analysis other than a coming into existence through speech and the saying (*dire*) borne by it? This is not at all, however, something that one becomes aware of (*prise de conscience*) as is proved by analysands who go into analysis knowing in advance that, as they sometimes formulate it, they have to undergo symbolic castration. With this term, they find a place for what is the least of their disappointments, when they are not hiding from them through resignation or evasion. Thus they "know," but this is not true. In order for it to be true, the experience of what is said (*des dits*) must secrete the saying (*le dire*), must make it ex-sist. This same splitting between knowledge and truth may also divide the very transmission of psychoanalysis. The latter produces a knowledge—a knowledge about truth—that can be known in advance, repeated, even used in the university; it can sustain whatever infatuation you like. Yet this knowledge about truth is true for the subject only if transferential speech enacts it. It *is* and not only *has been* produced because, between truth and knowledge, there is what could be called a sort of hiding game (*jeu d'éclipse*), in which truth loses its way when it is shown, and is forgotten in knowing it. Thus it is necessary to continue the work of the analysand in whatever form it takes. The experience of the treatment is irreplaceable but this does not imply that it is similar to religious initiations, as some people fear. They can be distinguished if, from all the things that are said (*dits*)—the meaning of which runs away and gets lost—there emerges a saying (*dire*) with which what conditions the meaning can be written. The choice between science and religion may not be vital.

I will come back to sexuation: Does the subject who is divided from speech have a sex, or is the difference between the sexes only a matter of either the living real or the ego? The ego itself is very much a synthetic function, but it is an imaginary synthesis. It is certain that it is involved in the question of sex. Lacan even says that it is dominant there, but he adds,

> it is enough for the business of the ego, like the business of the phallus, to be articulated in language for it to become the subject's business and no longer to have the imaginary as its only motive force.

The question can thus be reformulated: Inasmuch as sex would be the subject's business, what is it saying (*dire*) in analysis if the saying is what supports existence? According to Lacan, Freud's saying is a statement that he never formulated, and that Lacan himself "restores": there is no sexual relation. Such is the formula that can be inferred from everything that is said (*tous les dits*) about the unconscious that Freud discovered. Yet what founds this inference?

It is not simply that analysands say, "It isn't working out," since such an observation does not exclude the possibility that someday it will work out; the hope that it will end up working out is, in fact, the hope that leads many people into analysis.

"There is no sexual relation" implies that people are waiting for this relation; we are not astonished enough about this, for it is already an old song, and it very conveniently allows each of us to shelter there all our experiences of solitude, our failures, and even our lapses. This brings us back to the problem of negation, which, if we follow Freud, supposes a previous *Bejahung*. In order for it to be expected, there must be two; difference must have been installed in the unconscious.

Now, what we see is that difference itself is a question. Men's and women's speech is certainly different in style, tone, content. We speak as a man or a woman, and we speak about difference because there are signifiers. We do not, however, know what difference is. Freud had already insisted on the fact that there was no representation of the masculine/feminine distinction in the unconscious. What we certainly see functioning is either the refusal to be a man or a woman or, more frequently, the aspiration to be a real man or a woman. There is no doubt, however, that what is aimed at in these cases, beyond what is imagined about men and women, is always only the phallus, in terms of having or being it. Thus we speak about men and women without being able to make any judgment of attribution about them.

How, then, does this difference impose itself?

We say that they are different because of the little anatomical difference. Yet when we say that they are different, we are not only designating a difference in the form of the body, we are also implying that they are different as subjects. We can imply this because the phallus is already a signifier that differentiates them. To grasp this, one only has to compare it with other anatomical differences: for example, having blue or brown eyes. A difference in being cannot be concluded from this difference in having. It is true that this is what racism, particularly Aryan racism, tries to do: to reproduce, on the basis of an anatomical trait, a difference as radical as that between the sexes. Such racists raise another anatomical trait—the Aryan or Mediterranean type—to the function of a signifier, a signifier in relation to which symbolic places could be apportioned.

It is thus because there is already the phallic signifier that we say men and women are different and because we call them different, they are going to relate differently to the question of difference.

I am insisting on this in order to make you perceive Lacan's effort at formulating a difference that is not a matter of the judgment of attribution, that is, does not operate according to the following form: men are this and women are that. This is the form in which all the ideologies on the question are deployed, and it always supposes, behind the attribution, the reference to a substance.

How then, on the basis of this single term, the phallus, do we obtain the apportionment of individuals into two superimposable halves—the "sex ratio"—an apportionment that "does not become mixed up in their 'coïteration'"?

The distinction between being and having the phallus, which, in "The Signification of the Phallus," Lacan used to approach the division of the sexes, can be clarified by the use of propositional functions.

On this subject, I only have a few remarks.

When one writes $\forall x.\Phi x.$ (for every x, phi of x), the argument x, before being related to the function, is, as Lacan says, totally undetermined. What allows it to be determined, and thus to be differentiated, is the modality inscribed in the quantifier $\forall$. Therefore, when one says, as Lacan does, that there is a universal for man, one can write "all men." Man is completely in the phallic function and what must be noted is that it is not because he is man that he is in the phallic function; on the contrary, it is because such-and-such an undetermined x is placed completely in the phallic function that he can be called man. It is thus a conditional imputation. The signifier "man" will be imputed to every x that is completely situated in the phallic function; this leaves entirely open the question of knowing whether even one of them really exists.

Likewise, when one writes $\overline{\forall} x.\Phi x.$, there is no universal of woman, woman does not exist, women are not wholly in the phallic function, it is not because they are women that they are "not whole," but if they are lined up on the side of the "not whole," then they can be called women.

There is no essence of masculine and feminine and consequently there is no obligation, since anatomy is not destiny. Each of us is free, Lacan says, to line him/herself up on one side or the other; there is a choice for both sexes. If such is the case, it is meaningless to ask why discourse imputes to women the choice of lining themselves up on the side of the "not at all" (*pas du tout*), a choice that makes them radically Other. We could indeed object that it is not because they are women that they have to situate themselves there, but only because they situate themselves there that they are called women.

It must, however, be remarked that we are not free to be indifferent to anatomy, for the signifier is linked to anatomy. An organ of the body makes manifest what the phallic signifier will represent, and because of this, individuals are called boys or girls before they take any position as subject. If there is a choice, it is one about which, at the very least, we have been given some strong advice. We could not understand in any other way the fact that the two halves of humanity can roughly be superimposed on each other as a sex ratio, so that the reproduction of the species is continuing. This, indeed, was what had already astonished Freud, in a note to the *Three Essays on the Theory of Sexuality*, where he remarks that if there are only, as he has established, partial drives, it must then be explained how heterosexuality remains so general. It is certain, in any case, that since the signifiers "man" and "woman" are not unrelated to anatomy, the subject is going to be represented *a priori* by one or the other of these signifiers, and that s/he cannot choose not to confront them. The question therefore remains with us.

The "all" and this "not at all" represent two possibilities for the speaking subject, two sides of structure. In "L'étourdit," Lacan asks what $\forall x.\Phi x$ means. It means that every subject as such is inscribed in the phallic function, and this is why he can also say that if women are not wholly (*pas toutes*) in the phallic function, they are "*not* not there at all."[2]

To define this Φx. and the phallic jouissance that it supports, I will use, among all possible expressions, the following one: the phallic function is the castration function that is due to *lalangue*. Because the jouissance of the body is organized by *lalangue*, it becomes something that is "outside the body," anomalous and identical with the jouissance operating in the symptom. The signifier is the cause of jouissance, but it is also what makes it partial and irremediably exterior. The phallic function therefore designates the way in which the body and the subject are caught in *lalangue*.

What can be said about the not whole? If the phallic function is as we have just stated and if the subject is as Lacan has described it— that which is supposed in relation to the signifier, in the space between two signifiers—it immediately seems paradoxical to speak of a subject who would not be completely in the phallic function. Lacan relates it

---

2. Lacan, *Encore*, p. 72.

explicitly to the S($\bar{A}$), which I mentioned above. This is because there is a gap in the Other as place of speech and this place always remains other, which can be formulated by saying that there is no Other of the Other, or no absolute knowledge is possible. Discourse cannot embrace something that would be a totality of knowledge. In other words, in the Other, there is a hole. What is designated here is an internal limit to the symbolic order.

To say that a being comes to represent this limit is to say that nothing can be said about her, or that one can "say everything" (*tout dire*), in the sense of being able to say anything at all, but nothing that would found a universal definition. The oblique line that comes to bar the Woman who "does not exist" would thus be homologous to the one that bars the Other (as well as the subject). However, as undefined as she may be in the field of the signifier, this being is not completely indeterminate since the speaking subject is not incorporeal, for there is a real body. It must therefore be emphasized that this internal limit to the symbolic, which finds its signifier in the S($\bar{A}$), is not to be confused with another one, which it covers over: the limit that separates the real and the symbolic. What, indeed, "escapes from discourse" if not, by definition, the real outside the symbolic, the real that, when it comes to sex, can only be represented by the body?

There are thus two aspects of the absolute Other: the Other which, as the place of the signifier, is barred, is always Other, and the real, inasmuch as it is absolutely other than the symbolic, which ex-sists to it. This double aspect seems implicitly to be present when Lacan speaks in "La troisième" of the jouissance of the Other, the jouissance that he calls impossible, and that is as much "outside language, outside the symbolic" as phallic jouissance is "outside the body." The Other designates, first of all, the substance of the other body, and as body, it can only be hugged or destroyed, or a piece of it can be caught (*ou en attraper un morceau*). On the other hand, the partner's real body symbolizes the Other as the impregnable place of the signifier.

To say that women are "not whole" is therefore to say that the signifier "woman" connotes what escapes discourse and makes present to us whatever is beyond what can be reached by speech. This beyond is certainly due to the symbolic structure and the lack that is inherent in it, but it would remain totally indeterminate if there were no real—here, that of the body—outside the symbolic. For this reason, the disputes about the sex of the angels deserved to be called Byzantine. To claim to be a woman is thus to give body to an aspect of structure: to be, "by relation with what can be said (se dire) of the unconscious, radically Other." The opacity of the real of the body (of the real by which a body enjoys itself [se jouit] and which is the most foreign to the symbolic as such) comes here at the place of the gap in the symbolic.

Why is it the feminine body that is called, by preference, to take this place and what does this imply for subjects?

Perhaps we should go back to the thing—the aspect of the real that remains foreign, outside the symbolic—the thing encountered, first of all, by every subject as the maternal thing. This is a bad encounter if it is an encounter at all, since it is that of the wall that cuts the speakingbeing from the real. Yet the mother, here, has a double aspect: she is both body and speech, the mystery of the speaking body, to repeat an expression that Lacan applies to the unconscious. The relation with the mother, indeed, is a double one.

On the one hand, it must be said that there is no jouissance of the body of the mother. There is certainly sonorous, olfactory, and tactile contact, but this body remains other, foreign, withdrawn into its internal opacity, which the specular image envelops. The child's sadism seems to me to have no other meaning than that of designating the encounter with this first limit: one can try to cut, to gobble up, to smash the other body, but it remains other. This is what the child's real and imaginary aggressions stumble up against, before the interdiction carried by discourse comes and puts an end to them. The inability to catch the maternal thing, the impossibility of incest with the thing, means that the subject can do no better than obtain pieces of it, bits of objects—breast, voice, gaze, and so on. The child sets up the partial drives, if, however, the Other allows him/her to do so.

Yet the mother also speaks. I will leave aside the question of how the child can discover that there is speech, how speech is separated from noise. The mother speaks, and in speaking, she provides the signifiers that organize the drives in the body. She sets up, with the dimension of the demand, those of desire and the phallic signifier: the dimensions of the very enigma of the Other. What must be emphasized, however, is that this enigma of her desire as articulated, at the horizon of which the S($\overline{A}$) emerges, intensifies the enigma of the real of her body. Here again, we find the same superimposition as the one that concerns the "not whole." It is essential to note that I am not saying that the real in itself is enigmatic. It is simply there, devoid of interest, beyond reality, which itself is constructed. The enigma comes from the symbolic. The real constitutes an enigma for the speakingbeing because the symbolic separates him/her from it. It remains therefore only as a limit, which can be imaginarized in the form of the container.

Can it thus be said that the maternal thing is the place of all the metaphors, that it is what is aimed at by all the metaphors? It is perhaps not by chance that each time that women try to say something about themselves, they succeed in doing so only by making sparkling metaphors. There is indeed, as Michèle Montrelay says, an imaginary that she calls feminine; perhaps it would be better to say that it is an imaginary of the feminine, rooted in the imaginary of the maternal, which aims at making the real itself pass into the signifier. This would be the case because the mother is the first Other, the one in relation to whom the child apprehends the gap of the symbolic and with the latter, the real as what is beyond and impregnable, which the feminine body remains for every subject. Whether one is a man or a woman, the feminine body is "heteros."

An objection could arise here concerning the passage from the maternal to the feminine. When the subject, as *infans*, encounters the maternal thing, it can only classify the mother as being on the women's side after it has recognized the difference between the sexes. Previously, primordially, for both sexes, the phallus is attributed to the mother, and moreover, as we know only too well, maternity can function in part for a woman as a recovery of the imaginary phallus of which she has been deprived. It is therefore only retroactively, after the recognition of sexual difference—that is, of the mother's castration—that the relation to such difference can be connected with woman. Perhaps this distinction should be articulated more precisely, but it must be emphasized that it is present implicitly as soon the enigma of the mother is evoked, since this enigma is only brought to light by the metonymic presence of desire in speech.

How does this relation to the maternal thing, which is identical in the beginning for the boy and the girl, come to be situated differently for them? I will not examine all aspects of this question here. I will only consider two traits.

The first lies in the fact that a woman is related to this other place by her own body, and not only because discourse, and then her partner, put her there. To say that a woman is related to it by her own body is not to misuse the call to the body. Lacan has denounced this abuse in relation to women who, in the analytic movement, "called from the unconscious to the voice of the body, as if precisely, it were not from the unconscious that the body took on its voice." Let us not doubt, but let us also not forget that, as the cry makes the silence heard, the voice of the body brings about the appearance of whatever, from the body, from the real body, does not pass into the voice. Now, it is precisely this "real from which a body enjoys itself (*se jouit*)" which, for a woman, comes in the opaque place of the maternal thing. This is not only true of sexual jouissance but of everything that is added to it, particularly during gestation and childbirth. In these cases, it has been said, a woman is always outstripped by the real. (Outstripped implies no pathos.) No anatomical knowledge (*connaissance*) applies; there is no painless childbirth that succeeds in reducing what is ineffable in the incommensurable encounter. This encounter, moreover, is not reserved to women. A man can be confronted there too, in illness, for example, or even when performing in a sport, beyond the rivalry included in the latter. Quite simply, however, because of the fact that women give birth, it is more difficult for them than for men to be unaware of this real. When Michèle Montrelay argues that in childbirth, a woman encounters the real mother, wouldn't it be more correct to say that she encounters what the mother encountered: the inexpressible real of the body getting jouissance? Between revelation and perplexity, the experience of the inexpressible comes to fill in the mystery of the thing, oscillating, according to the case, between the attitudes "so *that was it*" and "*was that it*?" From here, there appears one of the truthful sides of the hysteric's masquerade; by its artifices, showing the semblance as a semblance, she designates what is beyond it: the point at which every discourse fails.

A second difference comes from the relation that a mother has with her child according to its sex: she gets jouissance differently from a daughter than from a son.

That the child plays the part of an "erotic thing" for a mother is what Freud located precisely from the beginning. Yet the child is evoked here as a signifier, caught in the "equation" of the little separable objects. This is the most obvious and the most general aspect of the mother's feeling, but it does nothing other than emphasize how much the child is placed in a woman's relation to the phallic function. I think that there is more, however, and that it is not emphasized often enough. Here, again, the signifier is incarnated, takes on a body, is knotted to the real, and because of this, the child—who is certainly the most integrated into the economy of the signifier—also makes present what most escapes this economy: the incommensurable real. S/he represents it all the more since s/he is a being who is still marked only to a minimal degree by the signifier and is quite close to "the organic night"[3]; the child is still reduced to the mystery of the life of the body, between cry and sleep. In this, s/he can be,[4] for a mother, for a period of time, the persisting encounter with what concerns her most particularly as a woman: beyond the symbolic and the limits of all knowledge (*tout savoir*). In this case, the child, as a bit of the real, comes to symbolize for her mother the S(Å) itself. Precisely in this sense, s/he participates in her/his own division; for the mother, s/he is the Other that woman is for every subject. Perhaps it is also from the child's status as Other that the mother gets jouissance.

In this respect, the situation is not equivalent for the boy and the girl. For the latter, there is an effect of intensification. To the extent that anatomy and the signifier, which is grafted onto it, place her on the feminine side, she becomes the external place, for the mother, of her own otherness (*autreté*) as a woman. Recent texts insist, once again and quite correctly, on what is interminable in the narcissistic struggle with the mother, on how one gets bogged down in an imaginary—or real—duel whose maddening effects (*effets d'égarement*) are obvious. Yet the identity of specular images would not be enough to account for this duel, which, indeed, also occurs in the father/son relation; it could not account for it if the feminine did not represent the Other, perhaps for reasons that I have tried to say. Here again, therefore, the imaginary is

---

3. The expression is Michèle Montrelay's.
4. S/he can be, but is not necessarily this. What conditions this possibility should be examined.

sustained by the symbolic, and, indeed, is sustained very precisely by the fact that the Other is always other and that thus, nothing can be said about it. Nothing can be said, except what Hadewijch of Antwerp says about God: everything that he is not, for he is beyond everything that can pass into language.

For women, to whom discourse imputes the task of representing this limit, there remains then, in the relation to the other, what I will call the fundamental "we" of the communication between women: the "we" of effusions and affinities, of the confided maternal secret that always calls for losing some phallic hope, which is what would distance the daughter from the intimacy of their silent jouissance and which would leave the mother to her solitude. Yet this is also the reverse side of the situation of being trapped and stuck in relation to the maternal figure; it is the enthusiastic "we," the "we" of the confidence of being carried by what, for lack of another word, we call life. In other words, it is what carries the discourses along. Perhaps it is this faith that, in Agnès Varda's film *One Sings, the Other Doesn't*, makes all the women who have just had abortions sing together.

I come now to the question of this specific effect that is the "other jouissance." First of all, is there another? On what conditions can we put it forward?

There is phallic, partial jouissance, which arouses the protest, "That's not it," and which secretes the mirage of what would be it: the absolute jouissance that could also be attributed to the primal father, because this enjoyment has not encountered castration. Yet the other jouissance, if we follow Lacan, is distinguished from the latter:

> "That isn't it": this is the cry by which the jouissance that is obtained is distinguished from what has been expected. . . . Structure . . . has marked how far it is missing, the one that would be in question if that were it; it does not only suppose the one that would be it, it supports another of them.

It is this other that Lacan superimposes on the not whole. We see, he says, "the logical power [*puissance*] of the 'not whole' lives in the recess of the jouissance that femininity conceals."

Now, it is attested well enough that the two sexes deploy jouissance differently in their bodies, but that does not imply that woman's is other. For us to be authorized to say that it is other, it must be determined, produced differently by the being of *significance*. This is what Lacan puts forward. He not only says that the S(Ⱥ) symbolizes the opacity of feminine jouissance, but also adds that women, thereby, have more of a relation with the S(Ⱥ), and what's more, that they get their jouissance from it.

Does this postulate that jouissance is only produced by the being of *significance*, that it is always knotted to the symbolic? It is certain that the being of *significance* organizes jouissance in analytic experience, but this does not prove that it organizes everything. After all, in the case of animals, for example, we do not rule out the idea that the real of the living body can be enjoyed (*se jouir*) alone, without the signifier. It also does not prove that, where it is *lalangue* that organizes jouissance, all the differences in jouissance can be imputed to it. To hypothesize, for example, that some of these differences derive only from the real of the sexed living being would be to understand that none of them pass into knowledge and that, as Lacan remarks, women cannot say anything about them. To conclude that feminine jouissance is different, that women as subjects have more of a relation with the S(Ⱥ) is not sufficient to prove that they get off on it.

Lacan puts this idea forward, however, and finds support for this in the mystics. Indeed, in them, there is very much the idea of an other jouissance, from which one can—without any guarantee—try to throw light on feminine jouissance. These mystics point to a jouissance that would be produced by evoking what is beyond the Word, by evoking a God who would not be God the Father. God the Father says no to the phallic function and incarnates the paradox of producing the Word without being subject to it, without being caught up in it. On the other hand, the identity of the mystics' God would be beyond any differentiation by the signifier; in the jouissance of the mystics, presence and absence would merge together and the opacity of the body that is getting jouissance would come to fill in the rift in the system of signifiers.

A possible homology with what happens in the partial drives presents itself here. For the latter, Lacan, seeking to articulate a relation between the registers of the signifier and of jouissance, has emphasized the topological unity of "the gaps that the arrangement of libidinal investments by signifiers establishes in the subject" and of the apparatus of the body inasmuch as there are orifices. The erotogenic zone is thus defined by the superimposition of these two gaps, which a single object comes to close up. One could mention an analogous, although different superimposition here, one that would define the very contrary of a zone. This would be the night of the body, where our perception of sensations is no longer fixed on an edge, but exceeds any localization, thus placing any support by the image or the signifier outside the circuit; this would be the body as what cannot be delimited, which would come to be superimposed on the gap of the Other. Thus, without ruling out the possibility that differences may lie in the real of the sexed body, one could speak of the jouissance of the S(A) in which what cannot be delimited in the body would come to represent, to symbolize the very division of the subject. We would then have a basis for saying that the other voluptuousness (*volupté*), beyond any object, is also the product of *signifiance*.

It can be conceived then that such a jouissance can be mobilized in analysis. But if it is called feminine, shouldn't it then be said that analysis is capable of feminizing analysands, and not only women, because the logic of the not-whole is a part of the being of *signifiance*? This would not be to refer, in the case of men, to some sort of homosexuality, at least not to that of Schreber, who aims at being the wife of God-the-Father; it would be, instead, to evoke the relation to what Lacan names the other face of God, which is supported by feminine jouissance; it is not, therefore, on the slope of the Name-of-the-Father, but rather on that of the absence of the Name.

What, then, of the question that has remained unanswered: Is there a saying (*dire*) of the difference between the sexes in analysis? I will leave this question in reserve. There is something of the saying that says (*dit*) that there is something of the Other, whether of solitude or division, and there are also encounters—and thus a contingency—of which it remains to us to clarify what is specific in them to each sex. If for men, they are presented as those of the women who "count" for them, can women be said to count in the same way?

Index

abnegation